IRISH TRADITIONAL FOOD

Born in London of Irish parents, Theodora FitzGibbon is currently living near Dublin with her husband George Morrison, the film maker and photographic archivist. She has been cookery editor of *Image* magazine and the *Irish Times* and has contributed to many other periodicals including *Homes and Gardens, Vogue* and *Harper's Bazaar*. Her novel, *Flight of the Kingfisher*, was made into a successful BBC TV play. Theodora FitzGibbon has written over twenty-five books, three of which were awarded bronze medals at the Frankfurt International Food Fair and one of which won a special Glenfiddich award.

Publishers' Note

Sadly Theodora Fitzgibbon died after this edition had gone to press.

D1340833

Also by Theodora FitzGibbon

Cosmopolitan Cookery
Weekend Cookery
The High Protein Diet & Cookery Book (with Dr Michael Hemans)
Country House Cooking
The Young Cook's Book
Game Cooking
The Art of British Cooking
Eat Well and Live Longer (with Dr Robert Wilson)
A Taste of Ireland
A Taste of Scotland
A Taste of Wales
A Taste of England: The West Country
A Taste of London
A Taste of Paris
A Taste of Rome
A Taste of the Sea
Theodora FitzGibbon's Cookery Book
The Food of the Western World
Making the Most of It
Crockery Pot Cooking
A Taste of Yorkshire
A Taste of the Lake District
Traditional Scottish Cookery
The Pleasures of the Table (Anthology)
Traditional West Country Cookery
Savouries

Fiction
Flight of the Kingfisher

Autobiography
With Love

Irish Traditional Food

Theodora FitzGibbon

GILL AND MACMILLAN

Published in Ireland by
Gill and Macmillan Ltd
Goldenbridge
Dublin 8
with associated companies throughout the world
© Theodora FitzGibbon 1983, 1991
0 7171 1867 3
First published in hardback 1983
First published in paperback 1991
Print origination by
Parker Typesetting Service, Leicester
Printed by
The Guernsey Press Co. Ltd, Guernsey

A catalogue record is available for this book
from the British Library.

3   5   7   6   4

to my friends
Éilís and Tarlach O'hUid
with grateful thanks and affection

contents

acknowledgements

Many friends have helped me considerably in my quest for Irish food. I wish to thank particularly: Desmond, Knight of Glin, who lent me precious old books and papers from his collection; Mrs Cathleen Healy for her most generous gift of the handwritten recipe book of Selina Newcomen, dated 1717; Dr A. T. Lucas for giving me access to his paper 'Irish Food before the Potato'; Mrs Alice Beary for the loan of eighteenth-century manuscripts; Miss Aileen Hamilton for the loan of many out-of-print books; to Ciaran MacMathuna for imparting some of his valuable knowledge; and to all the people who talked to me about their memories of food in the past; and last but by no means least Tarlach O'hUid who gave me a lot of his time and was responsible for the Irish translations.

There is no love sincerer than the love of food.

George Bernard Shaw, 1856–1950

Cookery is an art comparable with literature, painting or sculpture, because it is the most important way of nourishing the sacred body, making it healthy and useful and a true glory to God. When I think of (during seventy-four years) what my feet have done, my hands, how my heart worked and how all my other organs helped to give my whole body fire and functions I'm amazed.

Sean O'Casey, 1880–1964

introduction

The food of a country is part of that country's history and culture, and nowhere is this more true than in Ireland. The two are as interwoven as some of our Celtic designs, although there are large breaks in the pattern. The information about our food is scattered and sometimes conflicting, almost as much a paradox as Ireland herself. Throughout my fifteen years' research I have read what literature is available and also talked to elderly people whose memories were long and informative. Writing this book has not been unlike piecing together an elaborate jigsaw puzzle, but I am happy to say that, despite periods of great economic depression and starvation for many, an Irish food pattern does emerge.

Some of our present day food habits started in prehistory, with the building of the *fulachta fiadha*, pits with an arc-shaped hearth at each end. The pit was filled with water and heated stones were put in which brought the water to boiling point in just over half an hour. The arc-shaped hearths were used for heating the stones and a constant supply was kept going. Large joints of meat were wrapped either in straw or hide, tied with a straw rope, and lowered into these pits. From experiments carried out in 1952 by Professor M. J. O'Kelly and his colleagues (also others later) at one of the many ancient cooking sites discovered at Ballyvourney, Co. Cork, which they reconstructed, it was found that a ten-pound leg of mutton cooked in three hours and forty minutes, which is twenty minutes to the pound and twenty minutes over, just the time we would use today! A nearby pit, stone-lined, was thought to have been used as an oven, and a roasting experiment was carried out with the same results. This is obviously the 'roasting and the boiling', a double operation referred to in early poems; and it is still carried on, probably only among the Irish. It happens at Christmas with the roasted bird and the boiled ham, and also in country districts where it is traditional to serve a roasted meat and a boiled one at the same meal. The Brehon Laws laid down certain rules about food and hospitality and in the latter case we would wish that they were still in operation.

Perhaps the most disastrous ethnographical development in Ireland was the increased reliance on the potato; for where the potato blight destroyed the crops in the nineteenth century the poor had nothing to fall back on, certainly not enough corn or oats, which had been the mainstay of many before that. It is interesting to note that potatoes were not really a general food until the late eighteenth and early nineteenth centuries; before that they had been used mainly for pig-feeding.

Deprivation and hunger for one reason or another were common, but it must be remembered that this state was not peculiar to Ireland. In the sixteenth and seventeenth centuries starvation and persecution were rife all over Europe; hence the flight of the Huguenots and the Palatines to England and Ireland, and of the Quakers from England. The gap between the rich and the poor in England is constantly and vividly portrayed by Hogarth and Dickens. The Hundred Years War and the Thirty Years War were not just names.

Happily these tragic days are behind us, we hope, and Ireland today with her fine cattle and sheep, excellent and varied fish and shellfish and good dairy products can take her place as a first class purveyor of good food. Our cooking has, of course, been influenced by other countries to a certain extent, but I sincerely believe that there is not a country in the world that from the earliest days has not taken the best from her neighbours. I have recorded all the traditional foods in this book, together with dishes from this century. My motive has been to perpetuate tradition, for I do believe that the best food for a country is that which has been continuously tried and tested over the years, which suits the climate and uses the best products of that country. In places like France, which has a superb classical cuisine, you will find that cooking has changed very little over the centuries, and it is for this reason that the cuisine lives. Let us enjoy our heritage and keep it alive.

'Nua gacha bid agus sean gacha dighe.'

'Food should be as fresh and freshly cooked as possible. While drink should be well matured.'

Old Irish saying.

Theodora FitzGibbon, 1982
Deilginis
Baile Átha Cliath

chapter one

SOUPS – *ANRAITHÍ*

Soup, or pottage, has been a staple in the diet of the Irish, English, Scottish and Welsh peoples for many centuries, and is still a popular food. Irish people will eat soup at every main meal both winter and summer. Andrew Boorde wrote in *A Compendous Regyment or a Dyetary of Health* in 1542: 'Pottage is made of the liquor in which flesh is sodden (boiled) with putting-to chopped herbs, and oatmeal and salt.' The pottage was often very thick, much like a savoury porridge. The word comes from the Latin *porrus*, for leek, and the leek figures prominently. It is one of the most important pot-herbs and has been used in all Celtic countries from earliest times.

In prehistory soft clay was moulded into bowls and round-bottomed pots for cooking the pottage but during the Bronze Age, in about the eighth or seventh century BC, the Celts, who had been in contact with Greek and Roman influence, introduced into Ireland vessels of riveted bronze copied from the Greeks.

All kinds of things were put into early pottages: wild herbs, leaves, seeds, nuts and berries, whatever was available in cereals, and small pieces of meat, fish, shellfish, birds or game. Settlements near the coast added seaweeds such as dulse, sloke or laver, or carrageen as well. According to the *Hymn of Columba* the monks of the early church gathered dulse and other seaweeds for their food. Plants which we now call weeds such as wild cabbage, charlock (*Sinapis arvensis*), white goosefoot and knotgrass (*Polygonum*) were used as well as nettles, sorrel, mallows, docks, wild garlic, wild leeks and, in the winter, wild celery, wild carrots, parsnips and turnips, small and tough though the wild varieties might be. In fact the earliest soups or pottages were very like what we call 'farmhouse' soups today – a mixture of what is to hand.

Cereal growing was practised in Ireland from Neolithic times and pulses were grown in the Iron Age, one of the first being the Celtic bean, a very small variety about the size of a pea. Real peas came with the Romans and were an important addition, for they could be dried for the winter as well as being eaten fresh. So as more foods reached this island, they were used in many ways, not least in soups. Therefore, in the words of an old Gaelic adage: '*Lean go dlúth le clú do shinsear*', which translated loosely means 'Adhere closely to the honoured ways of your forefathers'.

Croûtons are a good accompaniment for various soups, particularly the carrot soup, fish soup and mushroom soup found here. To make them, fry two or three slices of crustless white bread in oil until golden on both sides, then cut into small squares. Dust them with salt or garlic salt if liked.

Stocks

The better the stock the better the soup. The tradition of first cracking the bones to get the marrow out of them into the stock is an ancient one, for smashed pig and cattle bones have been unearthed on many an archaeological site in Ireland that dates from very early times.

White stock – *Stoc geal*

This is extremely simple to make from any poultry carcass or meat bones such as chine of pork or veal bones. If the bones are first cracked (a nutcracker will do) then the marrow will go more quickly into the broth. Add a cup of medium-sized carrots (if left whole they will not cloud the soup,) a medium-sized onion stuck with a few cloves, and a little celery or a leaf or two of lovage if available. Add pepper and salt and cover with water, about 2½ litres (4½ pints) for about 1 kg (2¼ lb) bones or a chicken carcass. It is better to use less water rather than more, for later on you can always add more whereas if it is swamped to start with the stock will be too weak and little can be done about it. If making it for a cold consommé you can add a couple of chicken stock cubes, but then be careful about adding extra salt. Bring to the boil and take off any scum, then simmer gently for 1–1½ hours. Alternatively, pressure cooking will cut the time to about half an hour. This does result in a cloudy stock, but it will jell very well.

Take from the heat and add 1 cupful of ice-cold water to bring the fat to the surface; remove it completely. Strain through a fine strainer, and pour into tall deep containers and chill quickly.

This will make about 2 litres (3½ pints) which can be frozen if wanted for future use.

Brown stock – *Stoc donn*

2 kg (4½ lb) beef and veal bones, broken up
any available scraps of bacon or pork
1–1½ tablespoons beef dripping
2 medium-sized carrots, cut up
2 medium-sized onions, chopped
2 celery stalks, cut up
about 3 sprigs of parsley
sprig of thyme
1 bay leaf
pepper and salt

Put the broken bones in a large baking dish with the pork scraps and rub over with the dripping, then put in a hot oven to brown, stirring them about frequently. Take them out and put the bones in a large saucepan, pouring off excess fat. Brown the vegetables in the remaining fat and add to the stockpot. Add the parsley, thyme, bay leaf, pepper and salt. Cover with 2½ litres (4½ pints) of water and bring to the boil quickly, skimming if necessary. Simmer for about 3½ hours, then strain and cool. Makes about 2 litres (3½ pints).

Fish and stock or *court bouillon* – *Stoc éisc*

Do not use the fattier fish such as salmon or mackerel for this stock or it becomes too oily with a rather strong, unpleasant taste. The head of a salmon can be added if the *court bouillon* is meant for a salmon dish.

2 teaspoons butter
1 onion, blanched and sliced
4 sprigs of parsley
bones, skins and trimmings of about
225 g (8 oz) white fish
juice 1 lemon
1 wine glass white wine

Heat the butter in a saucepan, add the onion, parsley, and the fish bones and trimmings. Add the lemon juice, cover and set over low heat. After the essence of the fish has been extracted, add the wine, and about 750 ml (1½ pints) of water. Bring to the boil, and simmer for 20–25 minutes. Let it cool naturally before straining. Makes about 600 ml (1 pint).

Shellfish stock – *Éisc shliogacha*

The shells of lobster, crab, prawns and shrimp should be kept for stock. Make it as the fish stock above, straining when cool. If there are any very small amounts of shellfish leftovers, first make the stock with the shells then add the leftovers with about 1 tablespoon of rice to the strained stock and boil for about 12 minutes until the rice is cooked, then sieve or liquidize. This will make quite an acceptable soup after seasoning, particularly with the addition of a little more fish and a trickle of cream.

Soups

My friend Eilis O'hUid tells me the following story which took place about fifty years ago in Belfast. Pig's head, mostly the cheek and the tongue, was used to make a most filling soup for the poorer people. This soup was cooked with root vegetables and large dumplings. Three hungry boys of the house came home when it was simmering on the stove while their mother was out at the local shop. Unable to resist the delicious smell, they each hooked out a large dumpling and were horrified when their mother came in. The eldest boy with great forethought quickly said: 'Oh, Mammy, I'm glad you're home, the pig's head is chasing all the dumplings round the pot and there's only three left!'

In the early days the fat on top of the soups formed into tiny globules which glistened on the top. It must have prompted the following riddle:

'*Siúd sa chlúid é agus dhá chéad súil air.*'
Answer: '*Anraith.*'

'There it is in the hob [on the fire] with two hundred eyes.'
Answer: 'Soup.'

Almond and watercress soup –
Anraith almóinní agus biolair

(Adapted from a handwritten manuscript book, 1735.)

Almonds were immensely popular in richer homes in eighteenth-century Ireland. They were not only used for cakes and puddings, but also with meats, fish, vegetables and in soups.

Watercress, *biolair* in Irish, is frequently mentioned in early manuscripts and books. In *Eriu*, Volume 3 (1907 edition) it is remarked on as fare for ascetics: 'It is cress which is pure food for sages.' In 1726, Moffet in *Hudibras* enumerates watercress among the 'curious salads' eaten by the Irish. It still grows all over Ireland, in clear unpolluted water, especially in the West.

300 ml (½ pint) milk	2 tablespoons butter
300 ml (½ pint) cream	2 tablespoons flour
rind of 1 lemon	600 ml (1 pint) chicken stock
1 celery heart, finely chopped *or* 1	75 g (3 oz) ground almonds
teaspoon lovage, chopped	salt and freshly ground white
1 cup watercress, finely chopped	pepper

Scald the milk and the cream with the lemon rind, left as whole as possible, and the celery or lovage. Let it simmer gently for 5–7 minutes, then take from the heat and leave covered to infuse for about half an hour.

Meanwhile, heat the butter, stir in the flour and let it cook for two minutes, then gradually add the stock, stirring well, and cook for 5 minutes, stirring all the time until it is smooth and thick. Add the milk and cream mixture and the ground almonds, season to taste and mix very well over very low heat. Take out the lemon rind, and add the chopped watercress, if preferred this soup can be liquidized at this point. Add salt and pepper to taste, and serve hot or chilled. Serves 4.

Bacon broth – *Anraith bagúin*

The pig was probably the first domesticated animal in Ireland. This soup is very like the French *pot-au-feu* in that the soup was often drunk first and then the meat served as a second course with the vegetables. Other meats or game such as mutton, beef, lamb or rabbit can also be used, either in place of the bacon or with it. A mixture of rabbit and bacon is very good. It can also be made with stock from boiled bacon, or with a meaty ham bone rather than with the bacon, in which case salt may need to be added, to taste.

900 g (2 lb) shoulder or collar bacon, soaked overnight
2 tablespoons pearl barley
2 tablespoons lentils
2 medium-sized onions, sliced
4–6 medium-sized carrots, sliced
2 medium-sized parsnips, sliced
½ medium-sized swede, sliced
pepper
1 sprig thyme
1 bay leaf
1 sprig parsley
450 g (1 lb) potatoes, peeled and sliced
1 small cabbage, quartered
1 leek, chopped
2 tablespoons parsley, chopped

Drain the soaked bacon and put into a large saucepan with water to cover. Bring to the boil and take off any scum, then add the pearl barley and the lentils. Bring to the boil and simmer for 15 minutes. Add the onions, carrots, parsnips, swede, pepper, thyme, bay leaf and parsley. Bring to the boil, lower heat and simmer gently for a further 15 minutes. Add the potatoes and the cabbage, and bring again to the boil. Simmer until they are tender, but not mushy, perhaps another 15 minutes. By this time the barley and lentils should be cooked and also the piece of bacon; if not, cook a little longer. Finally add the chopped leek and the chopped parsley and cook for about 5 minutes more or until the leek is just tender.

Remove the bacon and take off the skin. If eating with the soup then cut into either small cubes or thin slices, put back into the pot and serve a little in each soup plate. If the soup is to be eaten first, slice the meat on a serving dish, garnish (perhaps with some freshly cooked vegetables) and keep warm while the soup is served.

This makes a very substantial soup-stew, delicious on a cold day. Serves 4–6.

Beef soup with forcemeat balls – *Anraith mairteola le domplagáin*

In the last century this was known as 'mock hare soup'. The word forcemeat comes from the French *farcer* which means to stuff. Today we would call these balls dumplings.

This is substantial enough for a main course.

3 tablespoons oil or dripping	¼ teaspoon marjoram
1 large onion, sliced	4 whole peppercorns
450g (1 lb) beef, cubed	3 whole cloves
1 tablespoon flour	1 litre (1¾ pints) beef stock
pinch of nutmeg	1 bay leaf
1 large carrot, diced	2 teaspoons Worcestershire sauce

For the forcemeat balls

4 rounded tablespoons breadcrumbs	1 teaspoon grated lemon rind
4 level teaspoons suet, or margarine	salt
1 teaspoon mixed herbs, chopped	cayenne pepper
pinch of grated nutmeg	1 beaten egg

Heat the oil or dripping and lightly fry the onion until soft but not coloured. Trim the meat and cut into quite small cubes, then add to the pan, pushing the onion aside. Brown quickly, and remove the meat and onion to a large saucepan. Add the flour to the pan juices and let it brown for a minute, then put in the nutmeg and the stock, mixing well. Bring to the boil and add the Worcestershire sauce, marjoram, peppercorns, cloves and bay leaf, then the vegetables. Bring to the boil, then simmer for about 1½ hours until the meat is tender.

Meanwhile, make the forcemeat balls by putting all the dry ingredients into a basin and mixing to a stiff paste with the egg, adding a very little water if needed, to make a firm but pliable dough. Shape into small balls (you should have about 8). Lightly roll them in flour and poach them in the soup (strained, or liquidized, or not) for about 10 minutes and serve with the soup. Serves 4–6.

Brotchán roy – *Brachán rua*

This is a traditional leek and oatmeal soup, also known as *brotchán foltchep*, the latter word is the old Irish for leek. Leeks have been mentioned in literature since earliest times, particularly in connection with Lent:

Now leeks are in season, for pottage full good,
and spareth the milchcow and purgeth the blood:
These having with peason, for pottage for Lent,
thou sparest both oatmeal and bread to be spent.

When 'fifty bishops of the Britons' came to visit St Moedoc of Ferns during Lent, the dinner served to them included 'fifty cakes and leeks and whey-water'. And in the *Vision of MacConlinne* there is mention of 'a forest of tall real leeks'.

6 large leeks
1 heaped teaspoon butter
1¼ litres (2¼ pints) milk and stock
  mixed
cream (optional)

4 rounded tablespoons flake
  oatmeal
salt and pepper
pinch of mace
2 tablespoons parsley, chopped

First wash the leeks well, and to ensure that all grit is loosened trim the green ends and cut a cross on them, then stand them green-end-downwards in a deep jug of cold water for a time. When they are clean and trimmed, cut into chunks about 2.5 cm (1 inch) long, both the green and white parts. Heat the butter with milk-stock mixture, bring to the boil and add the oatmeal, stirring well. Boil up, then lower heat and simmer for about 20 minutes. Add the leeks and the seasonings. Bring again to boiling point, then lower heat and simmer until the oatmeal is cooked, about 15 minutes. At this point the soup is ready, or it can be liquidized: serve hot. Just before serving stir in the parsley and a little cream can be added to each portion if liked. Serves 6–8.

Carrot soup – *Anraith meacan dearg*

Carrots and other root vegetables have been eaten since prehistoric times in Ireland. Carrots were part of St Ciaran of Saigher's evening dinner. *Meacan do murrathaig* was eaten as a relish.

In the winter carrots not only give added sweetness to meals but stand up to long boiling with meat.

'*Is e mil fe'n talmh*
A th'anns a' churran gheamhraidh,
E'adar Latha an Naoimh Aindreadh agus An Nollaig.'

'Honey underground
is the winter carrot
Between St Andrew's Day and Christmas.'

6 large carrots
1 leek, or 1 medium-sized onion
1 clove garlic, or a few wild garlic
  leaves
1 heaped tablespoon butter

1 litre (1¾ pints) chicken stock
pinch of ground mace, or nutmeg
salt and pepper
150 ml (¼ pint) cream
croutons of fried bread

Scrape the carrots and cut them into small pieces. Peel and chop the leek or onion and the garlic. Heat the butter and just soften the vegetables in it. On no account let them brown. Add the stock and the mace or nutmeg. Bring to the boil, then return to a simmer and cook gently for about 1 hour or until the vegetables are tender. Taste for seasonings. Sieve or liquidize, and return to the heat. Add the cream and heat, but do not let it boil. Serve with *croûtons*. Serves 4.

Celery soup – *Anraith soilire*

Wild celery was originally used for pottages in Ireland, but after it was cultivated it became most popular not only for soups and sauces but also as a vegetable. The soil in Ireland is extremely good for the growing of celery and a great deal of it is canned for both home consumption and export.

1 large head celery
1 large potato
2 medium-sized onions
1 large clove garlic
2 level tablespoons butter
1 level tablespoon cornflour
1½ litres (2½ pints) chicken stock

1 small blade mace
pinch of nutmeg
salt and pepper
225 ml (⅓ pint) cream
chopped parsley or chives for
    garnish (optional)

Wash and trim the celery, leaving on a few of the younger leaves, then chop it fairly finely. Prepare the other vegetables and the garlic and chop them. Heat the butter until foaming, then gently sweat the vegetables and garlic until they are soft but not coloured.

Cream the cornflour with about 2 tablespoons of the stock and reserve. Heat the rest of the stock, adding the mace, and nutmeg. Bring to the boil, then reduce to a simmer, cover and cook for about half an hour. Add salt and pepper to taste, and when the vegetables are well cooked, add the creamed cornflour and stir until the soup returns to the boil and thickens slightly.

Sieve or liquidize, and return to the saucepan, then either add the cream and bring to just below boiling point, or add cream to each soup plate; serve if liked with a little chopped parsley or chives added as a garnish. Serves 6.

Chicken farmhouse soup – *Anraith tiubh puiléid*

This soup was often made in the days when boiling fowls were easy to get and were full of flavour. It can be a hearty meal or equally well be served as a fine-flavoured soup for a dinner party.

1 boiling fowl about 1½ kg (3¼ lb)
    cut into joints or equivalent
    chicken portions
salt
bouquet garni of parsley, thyme,
    tarragon
1 medium-sized onion, sliced
1 medium-sized carrot, sliced
1 small blade mace

small pinch mixed spice
2 stalks celery, chopped
1 bay leaf
100 g (4 oz) bacon or ham, coarsely
    chopped
50 g (2 oz) oatmeal *or* 2 large egg
    yolks beaten with 3 tablespoons
    cream
pepper

Wipe the chicken over and remove any lumps of fat from its inside. Rub with salt and put the bouquet garni inside. Put into a large saucepan with about 2¼ litres (4 pints) water. Bring to the boil, then simmer for half an hour after skimming off any scum. Add the onion, carrots, mace, mixed spice, celery, bay leaf, bacon or ham. Bring back to the boil, lower the heat and simmer for about 2 hours or until the chicken is tender. If including the oatmeal add it after 1 hour and stir well. Take out the chicken portions and bone and skin and chop them into neat pieces. If not including oatmeal strain the soup before returning the chicken pieces to it and add the beaten egg/cream mixture. Otherwise simply return the chicken pieces to the soup. Heat almost to boiling point, adding pepper and salt to taste. Serve in large soup plates with a good portion of chicken in each. Serves at least 6.

Cleare soupe – *Anraith glé*

This recipe comes from a manuscript book written by Sara Power in 1746. I give it in its original form. In some places this clear soup was, and still is, traditionally served as the first course to the Christmas dinner.

> Put a knuckle of veal, a pound of lean beefe and a pound of the lean of a gammon of bacon all sliced, into a stewpan, with two or three scraped carrets, two onions, two turnips, two heads of sollory sliced, and two quarts of liquid. Stew the meat until quite tender, then strain through muslin. To clere it put in two whites of the eggs and see that it is whipt well till it boyles, leave it then to a gentle fire for half an hour, taking care not to break the crust. Wring out your muslin in clear water and strain thru it holding back the crust. Beat it up, add to it your seasonings and a good glass of brandy or whiskey.

Sara Power adds: '. . . when thus prepared it will serve either for soupe or for a good brown gravey.'
I would say that it certainly should!

Sollory is celery. I would be inclined to omit the turnips as they can give a very strong flavour, and I would add some parsley, a bay leaf, a little thyme and a sprig of tarragon. In the event of not being able to get a knuckle of veal, I would use one split pig's foot, and it should all simmer very gently for 5 or 6 hours with occasional skimming if any scum appears. It is delicious served with cheese biscuits. It can be served hot or cold, and if the latter it will be a soft jelly. Serves 10–12.

Cockle soup – *Anraith ruacan*

> 'Cockles and mussels alive, alive oh!'

These members of the Cardium family are first cousins of clams and are very numerous on shores particularly in the west of Ireland. In Kerry they are known as 'carpetshell' and 'kirkeen' and are easy to distinguish as they have a smooth surface with a slight ridge running vertically over the shell. Many are exported nowadays to Europe.
In the old days when white flour was not only a luxury but also a

rarity, this soup would have been thickened with a handful of wheaten flour or oatmeal, either of which would give a lovely nutty flavour.

about 50 cockles	1 cup celery, chopped
2 heaped tablespoons butter	2 tablespoons parsley, chopped
2 heaped tablespoons flour	salt and pepper
600 ml (1 pint) creamy milk	150 ml (¼ pint) cream

Scrub and wash the cockles very well and discard any that are open. Put into a large saucepan with enough salted water (preferably using sea salt) to barely cover. Bring to the boil, shaking the pan occasionally. Cook until the shells are open, then remove at once, and let cool until you can handle them. Take the cockles from their shells and strain the liquid. Heat the butter and when foaming add the flour and cook for 1 minute, then gradually add the strained cockle juice and the milk, stirring until smoothly blended. Add the chopped celery and cook for 5 minutes, then add the chopped parsley and taste for seasoning. Bring to the boil for a few minutes. Finally put back the cockles and heat gently. Add the cream either to the saucepan or to the individual soup bowls. Serves 4–6.

Fish soup – *Anraith éisc*

This soup can be made with fresh fish, or in stormy weather it is equally good, but completely different in flavour, if made with smoked haddock or smoked cod.

4 medium-sized fillets of fresh or smoked haddock or cod or other white fish about 700 g (1 ½ lb)	cut up
	2 tablespoons parsley, chopped
	1 wine glass white wine or cider
1 litre (1¾ pints) milk	2 heaped tablespoons butter
salt	1 heaped tablespoon flour
2 medium-sized carrots, sliced	pinch of nutmeg
2 stalks celery, chopped	150 ml (¼ pint) cream
1 medium-sized onion, sliced	pepper
1 large leek, thoroughly cleaned and	cayenne pepper

Cut up one of the fish fillets, put in a saucepan with the milk and a little salt and bring to the boil. Add the four vegetables and 2 teaspoons of the chopped parsley. Bring to the boil, cover and simmer for half an hour; strain. Meanwhile, poach the remaining fillets gently in the wine or cider in a shallow pan covered with buttered paper or foil, until the liquid reduces. When cooked, either press the fillets through a sieve or liquidize. Then add half the butter and beat well to make a smooth purée. Strain the poaching liquid.

Heat the remaining butter and when foaming stir in the flour and let it cook for 1 minute, stirring constantly, then add the poaching liquid and stir until it boils. Whisk in the fish purée, taste for seasoning, and add the rest of the chopped parsley and the nutmeg.

Finally fold in the cream and bring to just below boiling point. Sprinkle with cayenne pepper and serve. Fried bread *croûtons* may be served separately as an accompaniment. Serves about 6.

Irish farmhouse soup (mutton broth) — *Brat caoireola*

From about 1846 rice was used a lot in Irish cooking. This type of soup, made with the cheaper cuts of meat, vegetables and a cereal, exists in country kitchens all over the western world. Rather than mutton, this one can be made with stewing beef, a little ham or bacon or simply some meaty bones, and whatever vegetables are available.

700 g (1½ lb) neck of mutton, or equivalent meat and bone
1 tablespoon dried split peas, soaked or 100 g (4 oz) fresh peas
2 tablespoons pearl barley or rice
salt
1 large onion, chopped

3 medium-sized carrots, cut up
1 or 2 celery stalks
1 large leek, thoroughly cleaned and cut up
1 or 2 turnips, thinly sliced
parsley, chopped

Bone the meat and trim it of fat and gristle. Cut into small pieces. Put the bones on to cook in enough water to cover; let them simmer gently while you prepare the vegetables. Strain the bones, reserving the stock. Put the meat into a large saucepan with the peas (if using dried ones) and the pearl barley (if using). Add about 2¼ litres (4 pints) of the bone stock made up with water. Add salt, bring to the boil, then simmer, skimming if necessary. Cover and cook for about half an hour, add all the cut-up vegetables and continue simmering for another half an hour. Add the fresh peas and rice (if using) and cook for another 10–15 minutes. Serve with a lot of chopped parsley. Serves 8–10.

Kidney soup — *Anraith duán*

This soup is very good with a little sherry added before serving. It is best to use ox kidney, but pig's kidneys also make a succulent soup.

1 beef kidney, about 700 g (1½ lb)
2 tablespoons bacon dripping or oil
2 tablespoons flour
2 litres (3½ pints) beef stock
1 teaspoon sugar
salt and pepper
bouquet garni of parsley, thyme and bay leaf

spice bag of 10 black peppercorns, small blade of mace, pinch of celery seed
squeeze of lemon
thinly sliced cooked carrot for garnish (optional)
1 wine glass sherry (optional)

Skin the kidney, cut down the middle and remove the fatty core and discard, then cut into small pieces. Heat the fat and brown the kidney in it quickly. Pour off any excess fat, then stir in the flour turning the kidney pieces in it. Cook for 1 minute, then add the stock, sugar, bouquet garni and the spices tied in a piece of muslin or nylon. Bring to the boil, then cover and simmer gently for about 3 hours. This can be done on top of the stove, or in a slow oven or electric slow-cooker.

Cool the soup, then refrigerate. When it is quite cold take off any fat from the top, then remove the bouquet garni and spice bags. Taste for seasoning, add the lemon juice and salt and pepper if needed. If the pieces of kidney are not liked, strain the soup or it can be liquidized. Personally I like it with the kidney pieces in it and a few freshly cooked thin slices of carrot for garnish. Add the sherry if liked, and bring to just under boiling point before serving with thin slices of dry toast or cheese biscuits. Serves about 8.

Mushroom soup – *Anraith beacán*

Mushrooms are plentiful in some Irish country districts where a large number of horses or cattle are kept. Field mushrooms (or 'horse mushrooms') are large and have a very good taste, but there is also a large cultivated mushroom industry in Ireland and these are in season all the year round. In all old manuscript books they are spelt 'musharooms' and it is this word that is still cried out by the sellers in Dublin's Moore Street market.

This is a quick method of making a delicious mushroom soup.

450 g (1 lb) fresh mushrooms
1 medium-sized onion, finely
   chopped
2 heaped tablespoons butter
2 tablespoons butter
2 tablespoons oil
2 heaped tablespoons flour

parsley, chopped
1 litre (1¾ pints) creamy milk
salt and freshly ground white
   pepper
300 ml (½ pint) double cream
croûtons or crisp bacon for garnish

Wipe the mushrooms over with a damp cloth and slice them finely. Put the creamy milk over low heat. Heat the butter and oil and when foaming add the onion; let it just soften, then push to one side. Add the mushrooms and let them soften. On no account let them brown or crisp up. Sprinkle the flour over, turn well and let it brown for 1 minute. Then add the hot milk, stir, and let it come to the boil, then lower heat and simmer, stirring for 5–7 minutes. Taste for seasoning and add the parsley and half the cream. Whip the other half and serve the soup with a blob of whipped cream on each portion, and with crumbled bacon scattered on top of the cream. *Croûtons* can be served, separately, as well, if liked.

Nettle soup – *Anraith neantóg*

This soup is a great favourite in the spring when the nettles are young. Nettles are full of minerals and vitamins which purify the blood. In the country nettle tea was drunk, made by pouring boiling water over chopped nettles, then boiling for about 15 minutes, straining it and adding milk and sugar. This was often given to children who had measles. It is said to have been a favourite of St Columcille.

Nettle soup is still served in some hotels in Ireland; this recipe is from Declan Ryan, chef-proprietor of the much-starred Arbutus Hotel, Cork. Cut the nettles with scissors and wearing gloves. Do not gather them after the end of May as they will be too tough, or from sprayed verges.

100 g (4 oz) butter
1 large leek or 2 medium-sized leeks
4 cups nettle tops, chopped
450 g (1 lb) potatoes, sliced

1 litre (1¾ pints) chicken stock
salt and freshly ground pepper
150 ml (¼ pint) cream

Heat the butter until foaming. Add the chopped leek and the nettle tops and cook until they look glossy. Stir in the potatoes then add the stock. Simmer gently for 30–35 minutes. Sieve or liquidize the soup, return to the heat, season to taste, and add the cream. Serve hot. Serves 6.

Oat soup with cream – *Anraith coirce le hUachtar*

This is a very subtle soup; it tastes quite unlike its simple ingredients.

1 heaped tablespoon butter
1 large onion, finely chopped
2 rounded tablespoons oatmeal (the larger flakes)
1 bay leaf
pinch of ground nutmeg or mace

1 teaspoon sugar
750 ml (1½ pints) chicken stock
300 ml (½ pint) cream, or half milk and half cream
chopped parsley and a dash of cayenne pepper for garnish

Heat the butter until foaming. Add the chopped onion and cook until soft but not coloured. Add the oatmeal, bay leaf, nutmeg or mace, sugar and salt and pepper; cook for a few minutes, stirring. Gradually add the stock, bring to the boil, lower heat and simmer, covered, for about half an hour. Then either sieve or liquidize, and return to the pan. Add the cream or cream and milk and reheat to just under boiling point. Garnish with chopped parsley and a very little cayenne pepper. Serves 4.

Onion soup – *Anraith oinniún*

When I was a child in the counties of Clare and Tipperary there were two cure-alls for everything, even broken ribs – white onion soup and hot whiskey ! I still love this creamy comforting soup, so completely different from the brown onion soup of the French.

2 heaped tablespoons butter
450 g (1 lb) onions, thinly sliced
2 cloves
2 heaped tablespoons flour
pinch of powdered mace or nutmeg
1 bay leaf

1 litre (1¾ pints) chicken or pork stock
300 ml (½ pint) milk
salt and pepper
150 ml (¼ pint) cream, or 1–3 tablespoons grated cheese

Heat the butter and when foaming add the onions and the cloves, let the onions soften but not colour at all. Sprinkle over the flour, mix well and cook, stirring, for about 1 minute, then add the mace or nutmeg, the bay leaf and the stock. Stir all the time until it boils and see that it is smooth. Simmer until the onions are cooked, then gradually add the milk, stirring, and when that boils lift out the cloves and bay leaf.

It can now be liquidized or served as it is with the cream added, or a scattering of grated cheese. Serves 4–6.

Parsnip soup – *Anraith meacan bán*

Parsnips, not the plump cultivated ones of today, but parsnips of some kind, have been eaten since earliest times, and it has often been made the basis for sweet dishes combined with wild fruits. Parsnips are included in many vegetable soups and, before potatoes were generally grown, they were traditionally served with roast beef. They were also used medicinally for stomach disorders and, believe it or not, toothache.

This is not the traditional soup from earlier times, but one flavoured with curry spices that has become rightly popular during this century.

1 heaped tablespoon butter
900 g (2 lb) parsnips, thinly sliced
1 medium-sized onion, chopped
2 teaspoons curry powder or 1 teaspoon curry paste
1 teaspoon ground cumin
1 teaspoon ground coriander
½ teaspoon ground cardamon

1 large clove garlic, crushed
1¼ litres (2¼ pints) beef or chicken stock
150 ml (¼ pint) cream
salt and pepper
chopped chives or parsley for garnish

Heat the butter and when foaming add the parsnips and onion. Soften them but do not let them colour. Add the curry powder or paste, the spices and the garlic, cook for about 2 minutes, stirring well. Pour in the stock slowly, stirring until it is all well mixed. Cover and simmer gently for about half an hour or until the parsnip is quite soft. Taste for seasoning. Sieve or liquidize and if it seems too thick dilute it with a little stock or water. Add the cream and reheat but do not let it boil. Serve garnished with chopped chives or parsley. Serves 6.

It is also excellent made with half parsnips and half apples.

Pea soup – *Anraith pise*

An enchanting recipe from Sara Power's manuscript book, 1746, is for 'Pease Soop':

> Boyl 2 quarts of pease, in six quarts of water till tender then take out some of the clear liquor, and strain the pease clean from the hasks, then put in your pease, and liquor together, and boyl them well, take what butter you think fit, and boyl it up in a pan, then put in some onions cut Small, some Sorrell, Sollory, and Spinage cut them pritty large and let them boyl for a quarter of an hour in the butter. Take some flower and bland it and mix it with a little of the liquor, or in the butter which you will then mix all with your soop, and put in salt, pepper, cloves and other spices as you please, with some sweet cream mix'd with all. Then take french rouls and crisp them before please, and lay them in the middle of the dish, and power in your soop and serve it hot, with a little lemon peel grated round the brim of the Dish.

I would say that generally peas are the most popular vegetable in Ireland: fresh, frozen and dried. The large whole dried peas are usually the variety called 'marrowfat' and maybe it was the name which attracted a lot of hungry people. They are large and mealy and need an overnight's soaking before they can be cooked, although nowadays they are processed and 2 hours' soaking is often enough. They are still much used especially with corned pork or beef, and when mashed are known as 'mushy' peas. They make a good winter soup, as do also the split version of the dried peas which come in both a green and yellow colour. I have found no difference in the taste but perhaps the green looks more appetizing. The perfect stock to use with dried peas is that left from boiling bacon or ham or, if it is not too salty, corned beef or pork.

4 streaky rashers bacon, or a hambone
1 tablespoon bacon fat or oil
1 large onion, chopped
450 g (1 lb) dried, split peas soaked for at least 3 hours or whole ones soaked overnight
2 teaspoons Worcestershire sauce
salt and pepper
milk or cream (optional)
chopped parsley for garnish
1 sprig thyme
1 sprig mint
2½ litres (4½ pints) stock

De-rind the bacon and cut into dice, and put into a large saucepan with the bacon fat or oil. Soften, then add the chopped onion and soften that. Add the soaked peas, bay leaf, thyme, mint, and stock. Bring to the boil, cover and simmer for about 2 hours or until the peas are a purée. Add the Worcestershire sauce and taste for seasonings. Lift out the herbs and stir the soup well. If too thick add some milk or cream and bring back nearly to boiling point. Garnish with chopped parsley and if liked some crumbled bacon. Serves 6–8.

Fresh Pea soup – *Anraith pise glaise*

Frozen peas can also be used for this.

350 g (12 oz) peas, freshly shelled
2 rounded tablespoons butter
1 medium-sized onion, chopped
1 head iceberg or cos lettuce, chopped
1 sprig of mint, chopped
1 sprig of parsley, chopped
2–3 rashers streaky bacon
1½ litres (2½ pints) ham stock
salt and pepper
sugar
chopped parsley for garnish

If using fresh peas, save the pods, wash them and put them to boil in the ham stock while preparing the soup. Heat the butter in a large saucepan and soften the onion in it, then add the lettuce, mint and parsley. De-rind and chop the bacon. Fry it for about 2 minutes, turning it from time to time; add to the saucepan with the peas, salt, pepper and a small amount of sugar. Strain the stock and add. Bring to the boil, stirring, then simmer for about half an hour or until the peas are quite soft. Sieve or liquidize, taste for seasonings and add a little milk or cream if needed (but not too much as the fresh flavour must be preserved). Garnish with chopped parsley or mint. Serves about 6.

Potato soup – *Anraith prátaí*

This is an excellent soup, and most useful, for it is the basis for many good soups, each created simply by the addition of a different ingredient: use leeks instead of onion and it becomes a kind of vichyssoise, good either hot or cold; with chopped watercress and/or parsley or finely chopped lovage, added when liquidizing it becomes watercress or lovage soup; while chopped prawns, lobster or crab, or chunks of any cooked smoked fish, will also make a different and most pleasing soup of it.

2 heaped tablespoons butter
900 g (2 lb) potatoes, sliced
2 medium-sized onions, sliced
salt and pepper
1½ litres (2½ pints) half milk and half stock
1 cup single cream
chopped chives or parsley for garnish
6 rashers streaky bacon, crisply fried and crumbled

Heat the butter in a large saucepan and soften the potatoes and onions in it. Season to taste, then pour milk and stock in and stir. Bring to the boil, cover and simmer for about an hour.

Sieve or liquidize, and taste for seasoning. Add the cream and reheat but do not let boil. Serve garnished with chopped chives or parsley and crumbled bacon. Serves 6–8.

Shrimp bisque – *Bísc ribí róibéis*

This is a grander version of the ordinary shellfish soup based on similar soups served in eighteenth-century France. The small shrimp

(*Crangon crangon*) was originally used, but the larger prawn or Dublin Bay prawn (*Nephrops norvegicus*) can also be used if chopped smaller. Frozen shrimp or prawns can also be used for this.

350 g (12 oz) shrimps or prawns
2 tablespoons butter
2 stalks celery, finely chopped
100 g (4 oz) mushrooms, sliced
1 rounded tablespoon flour
300 ml (½ pint) milk
300 ml (½ pint) cream

salt and pepper
4–5 tablespoons dry sherry or dry white wine
2 egg yolks beaten with a spoonful of cream (optional)
cayenne pepper

Shell the shrimps or prawns and put the shells in a saucepan with 600 ml (1 pint) water. Simmer for about half an hour, then strain the stock.

Melt the butter in a saucepan and when foaming put in the celery; when that is just becoming opaque add the mushrooms and soften them. Add the flour, mix well and cook for 1 minute, stirring. Add the stock (or water), bring to the boil and simmer for about 15 minutes. Either sieve or liquidize, then put into a clean pan. Add the shrimps or prawns and the milk and cream, and season to taste. Bring to the boil and simmer for 5 minutes. Add the sherry or wine and reheat. If a richer soup is liked the yolks of 2 eggs beaten with a spoonful of cream may be added gradually; do not let it boil after this addition. Garnish with a little cayenne pepper. Serves 4.

Sorrel soup – *Anraith samhaidh*

The cresses on the water and the sorrels are at hand,
And the Cuckoo's calling daily his note of music bland . . .
                    From the Irish of Sir Samuel Ferguson.

This family recipe can be made with spinach in place of sorrel, or a mixture of the two.

450 g (1 lb) sorrel
75 g (3 oz) butter
1 large onion, chopped
2 heaped tablespoons flour
2½ litres (4½ pints) stock

2 tablespoons breadcrumbs
salt and pepper
2 egg yolks
150 ml (¼ pint) cream

Wash the sorrel well and chop it up. Heat the butter in a saucepan and just soften the sorrel and onion in it. Shake the flour over the vegetables and mix well. Let it cook for about 1 minute. Meanwhile bring the stock to the boil, then add to the pan. Add the breadcrumbs, season to taste, and bring to the boil, then simmer for about 1 hour covered. (It can be liquidized at this point but it needn't be.) Beat the egg yolks with the cream and add a little of the hot soup to the mixture stirring well, then gradually add to the soup pot, stirring well, over the heat but being careful not to let it boil. Serves 8.

Spring soup – *Anraith Earraigh*

Almost any young green stuff can be used in this fresh soup: nettles, watercress, sorrel, hawthorn buds, even a few sticks of pink rhubarb (but never the leaves) will be quite delicious and blend in well. In spring it is a great change after all the root vegetables and dried pulse soups. It is a particularly pleasant lunch dish served with a poached egg floating in it, sprinkled with cheese.

large lettuce
mixed bunch of watercress, sorrel, nettles, etc. if available
10 spring onions
50 g (2 oz) butter
600 ml (1 pint) stock
600 ml (1 pint) milk

1 tablespoon cornflour dissolved in 2 tablespoons milk
salt and pepper
pinch of nutmeg
1 teaspoon sugar
4 thin slices bread

Wash the greens very well, and peel the onions. Then chop them all up. Heat the butter in a saucepan and soften the vegetables in it for about 5 minutes turning the pieces over well. Add the stock and the milk. Bring to the boil and simmer gently for about 10 minutes. Add the cornflour mixture and stir until it boils, then let it simmer for about another 10 minutes, giving it a stir from time to time. Season with the salt, pepper, nutmeg and sugar. Cut the bread into thin strips and either dry until crisp in the oven or toast slowly. Put the toast strips into the soup tureen liberally scattered with chopped parsley or chives and pour the hot soup over them, (or put a few toast strips into each soup dish before filling it with soup). Serves 4.

Tomato soup – *Anraith trátaí*

This has been a popular soup in Ireland since about the turn of the century when tomatoes first arrived here. This recipe from Mrs Barbara Mulgrew of Castle Dargan, Collooney, Co. Sligo was a first prizewinner in the *Irish Times* Menu competition in 1979.

1 heaped tablespoon butter
1 stalk celery, chopped
bouquet garni of parsley, thyme, basil and bay leaf
1 medium-sized onion, sliced
1 carrot, sliced
1 rasher bacon, chopped

2 tablespoons flour
700 g (1½ lb) tomatoes, skinned
1 litre (1¾ pints) stock
salt and pepper
pinch of sugar
sqeeze of lemon
chopped parsley for garnish

Melt the butter and cook the celery, onion, carrot and bacon for 5 minutes. Sprinkle flour over, stir well, then add the bouquet garni, tomatoes, stock, salt and pepper. Bring to the boil, then simmer gently for 30 minutes. Sieve or liquidize, return to the pan, add the sugar and lemon juice before serving, with chopped parsley and with fried *croûtons* if liked. Serves 4–6.

chapter two

First courses and egg dishes – Céad chúrsaí agus miasa uibheacha

Traditionally there are very few cooked first courses served in Ireland; in most homes soup takes precedence.

The practice of serving a single dish for a course came about quite late, possibly early in this century. Previously the courses, or 'removes' as they were called, consisted of a selection of different dishes from which you chose whatever appealed to you, rather like a very elaborate buffet today. I remember elder members of old Irish families continuing this practice into the 1940s.

An Irish menu for three courses in the eighteenth century was as follows:

First course: Soup, fish, beefsteaks, rabbits or chickens with onions, fillets of veal, cherries, and Dutch cheese.

Second course: Turkey, fricassée of eggs, grilled salmon, quails, musharooms, leveret, crab, and cheese cakes.

Third course: Gooseberries, strawberries, raspberries, currants, melons with cream, almond cream and orange butter, jellies, pastries, and sweetmeats.

Large numbers of guests were invited and the atmosphere was informal compared to that in England and Europe.

Mrs Delany of Delville, Glasnevin, friend of Dean Swift, and a well

31

known eighteenth-century Irish hostess, wrote of one of her parties, the table amongst other things being laden with: 'Plates of all sorts of cold meat, neatly cut, and sweetmeats wet and dry, with chocolate, sago, and salvers of all sorts of wine . . .'

This kind of service did not always appeal to the more conservative French and le Chevalier de la Tornaye remarked after a party in 1796 that: 'the handsome well-dressed ladies were so closely packed that they could hardly stir and had to speak through their fans!'

In 1897, Sir Herbert Maxwell, Bt wrote: '. . . the whole is crammed on the table at once without any regard to order or consistency . . .'

Other notables were kinder: Mrs Sarah Siddons who stayed at Shane's Castle, Co. Meath, in the 1780s recalled 'the table served with a profusion and elegance' to which she had never seen anything comparable. She also noted the immense flagons of claret.

Meal times too were different from today. Country people rose very early and breakfasted on porridge, bread and butter, and dined between noon and two o'clock, with a high tea or supper at night. The richer town and country people had a late breakfast and dined at about four o'clock and ate a supper at night.

First courses

'Potting' was one of the essential methods of preserving fish, poultry or meat other than by salting or smoking. The spices with which they were flavoured, and the butter they were covered and sealed with, preserved them for many months, so people could have pleasing and fresh-tasting food in mid-winter, as a change from the salt fish and smoked and salt meats generally available. Cheese was also potted.

As these potted foods could be made in bulk like sweet or pickled preserves, they were useful not only for home consumption but also to be taken out by farm workers or for shooting parties, picnics, long journeys by coach or post-chaise and, perhaps most important of all, sea voyages on which the food was often very restricted.

Potted foods of all kinds were served at all hours, including breakfast, not only in large houses but also at coaching inns.

> The traveller dines on potted meats;
> On potted meats and princely wines,
> Not wisely but too well he dines.
> Robert Louis Stevenson

Potted beef – *Mairteoil potáin*

This is exellent for a first course or it can be the main dish for a light meal, served with a salad. This recipe will make two 450 g (1 lb) dishes.

10 rashers of bacon (optional)
900 g (2 lb) lean raw beef, minced twice
175 g (6 oz) streaky pork or bacon
½ teaspoon salt
½ teaspoon black pepper
pinch of ground mace
pinch of ground nutmeg
pinch of ground ginger
175 g (6 oz) butter
150 ml (¼ pint) red wine or strong consommé
2 bay leaves
275 g (10 oz) clarified butter

If you plan to keep the dish before eating (up to 3 weeks in the refrigerator), line the casseroles or terrines, which should be lightly buttered first, with 8 bacon rashers that have been stretched with a knife.

Mix together the beef, pork or bacon, salt, pepper, mace, nutmeg, ginger and most of the butter, either in a blender or by hand, to a soft smooth paste. Gradually add the wine or consommé and about 2 tablespoons of water. Press the mixture down well in the buttered or bacon-lined dishes, taking care not to leave air pockets, then dot the top with the rest of the butter. Lay a bacon rasher on top of each, and a bay leaf. Cover tightly with foil and a lid. Stand in a container with water half-way up the side, and bake for 2–3 hours (replacing water if needed) at 150°C, 300°F, Mark 2–3. Pour off liquid and cool, then when cold pour clarified butter over the top to a depth of about ½ cm (¼ inch).

Note: small amounts can be made in the same way using cold cooked meats, etc. but in that case do not drain off the liquid when cooked.

Potted chicken and ham – *Sicín is liamhás potáin* (Rabbit can also be used)

1 lightly boiled chicken, about 1½ kg (3¼ lb)
450 g (1 lb) cooked ham or bacon
2 tablespoons butter
1 shallot or small onion, chopped
pinch ground cloves
pinch ground allspice
300 ml (½ pint) chicken stock
10–12 rashers streaky bacon
salt and pepper
225 g (8 oz) clarified butter

Take all the meat from the chicken, then bone and skin it. Trim the ham of fat, bone and chop it up. Then mince the two until fairly fine. Season with salt, pepper and the spices, and the finely chopped shallot or onion, then stir in the stock, or liquidize all these ingredients.

Well butter a deep casserole or dish and stretch the bacon rashers with a knife, then line the dish with them, keeping back some for the top. Pour in the meat mixture and level off. Dot the top with butter. Lay the rest of the rashers on top. Cover with foil and a lid. Stand the casserole in a container with hot water half-way up the side. Bake at 180°C, 350°F, for about 1½–2 hours. When ready run round the edges with a knife and leave to get cold. When cold press down with a spoon, pour the clarified butter over the top, and keep in a cold place until needed. Serves 8–10.

Potted crab – *Portán potáin*

This will keep for about a week but once the butter cover has been opened up it should all be eaten.

450g (1 lb) crabmeat	¼ teaspoon ground mace
juice of 1 lemon	salt and pepper
100g (4oz) butter	150g (5oz) clarified butter

Mash the crabmeat finely. Pound it with the lemon juice, butter, mace, salt and pepper. Put into a pot, pressing down well into all the corners, then cover thickly with the clarified butter. Chill until use. Serves 4.

Potted herrings – *Scadáin potáin*

Recipe dating from the 1890s. Serve brown bread and butter with this. A variation is to replace the water with Guinness, and very good this more modern version is too. Mackerel are potted in the same way.

8 fresh herrings, cleaned	1 teaspoon pickling spice
2–3 bay leaves	1 onion, sliced thinly
salt and pepper	vinegar

Clean the herrings and scrape off some of the scales, then take off the heads and tails. Rub with salt all over, then put into an ovenproof dish. Add the bay leaves, pickling spice and the sliced onion. Barely cover the fish with a half-and-half mixture of vinegar and water. Cover with foil or a lid and bake at 160°C, 325°F, Mark 3 for 30–40 minutes. Let it cool in the liquid and serve cold with a little of the tangy liquid. Serves 4.

Potted trout – *Breac potáin*

Adapted from the recipe book of Catherine Hughes of Co. Tipperary, 1755.

8 trout, cleaned	¼ teaspoon ground cloves
about 4 tablespoons wine vinegar	¼ teaspoon ground mace
salt and pepper	¼ teaspoon allspice
175g (6oz) butter	175g (6oz) clarified butter
¼ teaspoon ground nutmeg	(optional)

Wash the trout over with the wine vinegar, then slit them down the back and take out the backbones. Salt and pepper them inside and leave for a few hours. Put in each one a pinch of nutmeg, cloves, mace and allspice, then put them head to tail in a well-buttered ovenproof dish and dot with the rest of the butter. Cover and bake for 1 hour at 150°C, 300°F, Mark 2. Cool and cover with the clarified butter if you wish to keep (for up to 3 weeks in the refrigerator).

Cod's roe fritters – *Friochtóga eochraí throisc*

This recipe comes from the turn of the century. Serve these on toast; on French toast (bread soaked in beaten egg and milk, then fried) or with grilled bacon, tomatoes and mushrooms. Dip the roe in batter made of 4 tablespoons flour, 4 tablespoons milk and 2 eggs; or the roe can be mashed and added to the batter, then fried in spoonfuls.

450g (1 lb) cod's roe
2 tablespoons flour
1 beaten egg

2–3 tablespoons bacon fat or oil
wedges of lemon

Wrap the roe in cheesecloth and cook gently, just at the simmer, for about half an hour. Let cool, then take the skin from the roe and cut it in 1 cm (½ inch) slices. Dip the circles of roe first in the flour, then in the beaten egg. Heat in a frying pan the fat or oil and when it is very hot drop in the fritters. Fry on both sides until golden. Garnish with lemon wedges. Serves 4.

Cod's roe ramekins – *Raimicíní eochraí throisc*

Recipe adapted from Anne O'Brien, 1880s.

450g (1 lb) cooked cod's roe
2 cups loosely packed fresh
   breadcrumbs
a pinch of mace
salt and pepper

1 tablespoon parsley, chopped
1 tablespoon lemon juice
2 egg yolks, beaten with 50 ml
   (¼ pint) cream
2 egg-whites, stiffly beaten

Skin the roe and mix with the breadcrumbs, mace and seasonings. Add the parsley, lemon juice and beaten eggs with the cream. Leave for about 10 minutes until the breadcrumbs have absorbed the cream and eggs. Then add the stiffly beaten egg-whites.

Put into either 8 individual greased small dishes or 1 large one and bake in a hot oven 200°C, 400°F, Mark 6 for about 15 minutes for the small ones, or about 30 minutes for the large one, or until they have puffed up and are golden brown. Serve at once. Serves 6–8.

Buttered crab – *Portán le hIm*

This recipe dates from around the turn of the century.

2 anchovy fillets, drained
300 ml (½ pint) dry white wine
¼ teaspoon ground nutmeg or mace
6 tablespoons fresh white
   breadcrumbs

salt
cayenne pepper
2 heaped tablespoons butter
450g (1 lb) crabmeat
toast

Mash the anchovy fillets and combine with the wine, the nutmeg or mace and the breadcrumbs, and season to taste. Bring to the boil and simmer for 5 minutes. Mix the butter and the crabmeat and add to the hot wine mixture. Cook for 4 minutes and serve, either on hot buttered toast or in little pots with toast triangles on the side. Serves 4.

Devilled crab – *Portán gríosctha spíosraithe*

This was a famous dish in Ireland in the eighteenth and nineteenth centuries. Also used as a savoury.

700 g (1½ lb) crabmeat
300 ml (½ pint) whipping cream
1 teaspoon anchovy essence
2 teaspoons mushroom ketchup
2 teaspoons Worcestershire sauce

¼ teaspoon dry mustard
salt and pepper
cayenne pepper
8 green olives, stoned and chopped
1 lemon, cut into wedges

Put the crabmeat in an ovenproof dish. Whip the cream until firm and gradually add all the remaining ingredients, except the lemon wedges, whisking gently to keep the sauce thick. Spread this sauce evenly over the top of the crabs and bake high up in a preheated oven, 200°C, 400°F, Mark 6, for about 15 minutes. Serve with the wedges of lemon. Serves 6.

Fish creams – *Uachtar éisc*

These 'creams' were very popular in the last century.

450 g (1 lb) smoked haddock,
   cooked, boned, skinned
100 g (4 oz) breadcrumbs

salt and pepper
100 g (4 oz) butter
2 eggs, beaten

For the sauce
1 heaped tablespoon butter
2 level tablespoons flour
600 ml (1 pint) milk
100 g (4 oz) mushrooms, sliced

Prepare the fish, then flake it up and mash it lightly. Add the breadcrumbs and season to taste. Melt the butter in the milk and pour over, mixing well, and then add the well-beaten eggs. Pour into either 1 large buttered basin or 4 small ones, cover the top with foil and steam over boiling water for 1 hour if large and half an hour if the small ones. Remove the foil, put a warmed dish over the top, then tip over to unmould. Keep warm.

Meanwhile, make the sauce by melting the butter and stirring in the flour, then cooking for 2 minutes. Gradually add the milk, stirring all the time until it is smooth and creamy. Add the prepared, sliced mushrooms, cook for 5 minutes then taste for seasoning. Pour this sauce over the cream or creams and serve hot. Serves 4–6.

Fried oysters – *Oisrí friochta*

If other shellfish besides oysters are also put into the batter for this dish, it helps cut down the expense. A few mussels or pieces of scallops will go well with the oysters.

about 50 oysters, or mixed fish

Batter
100 g (4 oz) flour
1 tablespoon oil
pinch of salt

1 large egg-white, beaten stiffly
oil for deep frying

Mix the flour, oil and salt together, then gradually add ½ cup of tepid water and mix to a thick, smooth paste, free of lumps. Set aside uncovered for at least half an hour.

Heat the oil for deep-frying. Add the beaten egg-white to the batter mixture and dip each oyster or piece of shellfish in the batter, and then drop into the hot oil. Fry until golden on each side, drain on kitchen paper and serve hot with wedges of lemon. Serves 4–6.

Oyster loaves – *Builíní oisrí*

Take French roul's and cut a little hole on the top as big as half a Crown, then take out all the Crumbs, but don't break the crust of the loafe. Then stew some oysters in their own liquor, a blade of Whole Mace, a little pepper, Salt, Nutmeg, and a little White Wine, skim it very well, and thicken it with a piece of Butter rouled in flower, then fill the roul's with it, and put on the piece again that you cut off, then put the roul's in a mazerine dish and melt the butter and power it into them, then set them in your Oven, and let the Oven be as hot as for an Orange Pudding.

This is from the eighteenth-century recipe book of Cicely D'Arcy, kindly lent to me by Mrs O'Toole of Edenderry. I have also made this with mussels.

Dublin Bay prawns – *Piardóga*

These are certainly an Irish speciality, very similar to the Adriatic scampi. They are actually not a prawn at all, but the Norway lobster (*Nephrops norvegicus*). They are most delicious when freshly caught. The best way to cook them is to steam them, then shell and turn gently in butter with a little salt and lemon juice. They can also be served cold with mayonnaise and lettuce.

Prawn paste – *Taos cloicheán*

This is an old recipe which has been in my family for at least a hundred years. It is excellent for a buffet as well as a first course.

350 g (12 oz) prawns or shrimps, cooked and shelled
350 g (12 oz) butter
450 g (1 lb) filleted haddock or cod

pinch of mace
1 teaspoon anchovy essence
pinch of cayenne pepper
salt

Put the shells to boil with water to cover for half an hour. Strain then simmer the skinned fish in the liquid for 15 minutes, and strain again, leaving only a trace of liquid in the saucepan. Add the mace, anchovy essence and cayenne pepper. Pound to a smooth paste and leave to cool. Add all but 1 tablespoon of the butter and beat until smooth. Then add the prawns or shrimps (chopped up if they are the very large prawn). Heat the mixture for about 2 minutes, then press it into a deep dish. Melt the remaining tablespoon of butter and pour it over the top. Chill and serve, cut into slices, on crisp lettuce. Serves 6–8.

Cured salmon – *Bradán leasaithe*

This is quite delicious, like a most delicate smoked salmon, but unlike smoked salmon it will only keep for about a week. Serve cut in very thin slices with brown bread and butter. Do not attempt to make this with frozen fish; the texture breaks down.

2 fillets from 1 large fresh salmon or salmon trout, with skin
50 g (2 oz) coarse sea salt
2 teaspoons white peppercorns, coarsely crushed

1–2 tablespoons brown sugar
olive oil
fresh dill or fennel
a little whiskey or (better still) poteen

Put the fish, skin side down, in a large dish. Mix together the salt and peppercorns and the sugar and rub the fish surface with about half of the mixture, rubbing in very well. Sprinkle with a little whiskey and leave in a cool place overnight. The next day blot up any moisture from the dish with kitchen roll. Pour the oil over the fish, then add the rest of the salt mixture and the dill. Put one piece of fish on top of the other, cover with foil and set a heavy weight on top. Leave in a cool place for 36–48 hours. Drain the fish, scrape off the dill and hang up the fish in a cool airy place for a few hours to dry it and firm up the flesh. Slice on the slant like smoked salmon. Serves 14–16.

Smoked salmon mousse – *Mús bradáin dheataithe*

This is a modern adaptation of an old recipe. It has the advantage of making a very little smoked salmon go a long way and is made with trimmings, which are sold cheaply at most good fish shops. It is best made in a liquidizer. Boned kippers, smoked mackerel or smoked trout can be used instead of salmon, but then the fish content should be doubled.

1 level tablespoon aspic powder, or ½ level tablespoon gelatine
225 g (8 oz) cottage cheese, or curd cheese

50 g (2 oz) smoked salmon scraps
squeeze of lemon juice
few drops of tabasco, or pinch of cayenne pepper

Put 300 ml (½ pint) of boiling water into the liquidizer, add the aspic powder or gelatine and blend for 30 seconds. Add all the other ingredients and blend for about 1 minute. Taste for seasoning and put at once into a dish or individual dishes and leave in a cool place to set. It will set very quickly, within an hour. Serve on a bed of lettuce. Serves 4–6.

Scallops with mushrooms and bacon – *Camóga le beacáin agus bagún*

This is a delightful first course usually made with the small scallops known as 'queenies' or 'closheens' in the west of Ireland. Large scallops can be used, but should be cut small.

450 g (1 lb) scallops
3 tablespoons olive oil
1 large onion, sliced
50 g (2 oz) button mushrooms, sliced
6 slices streaky bacon, grilled and

diced
juice of 1 lemon
salt and pepper
1 tablespoon chopped chervil or
  parsley

Blanch the scallops in boiling water for 2 minutes. (If using the larger ones, make it 5 minutes.) Cool and dry on a cloth. Heat the oil and quickly fry the onion until soft but not coloured, then add the mushrooms and the scallops. Turn them from time to time. Add the lemon juice, salt, pepper and chervil. Take from the heat and mix in the bacon bits. Serves 4.

Musharoom frigassy

This recipe is from the handwritten manuscript book of 1717 kindly given to me by Cathleen Sealy:

> Take large thick Musharooms, pull the stems and put them into a stew-pan with Butter and Oneon, shred small some sweet Majerum and thyme stript, season with pepper and salt and make a sauce for them with Eggs beaten, with the juice of Oranges and some clarett, the Gravey of a leg of Mutton and Nutmeg. Shake them well, and give them a few tosses in the pan, then put them in a dish rubbed with a shallot, and garnish'd with lemon and Orange.

Surprisingly, this is a delicious dish, adapted only a little. I have served it many times, made in the following way:

100 g (4 oz) butter
8 large field or flat mushrooms,
  stems trimmed and wiped clean
1 small onions, very finely chopped
1 teaspoon fresh marjoram,
  chopped
1 teaspoon fresh thyme, chopped, or
  ¼ teaspoon dried

pepper and salt
½ cup good stock
½ cup red wine
good squeeze lemon or orange juice
pinch of nutmeg
beurre manié of 1 heaped teaspoon
  each butter and flour

Heat the butter until foaming. Add the mushrooms, and scatter the chopped onion in the pan among the mushrooms. Sprinkle over the marjoram and thyme, pepper and salt. Simmer for 5–7 minutes, turning the mushrooms over once but on no account let them brown or crisp up.

Meanwhile, mix the stock, red wine and lemon or orange juice, and add a pinch of nutmeg. Pour this over the mushrooms and bring to the boil, then simmer, gradually adding the *beurre manié*, stirring to thicken slightly. Serves 4.

Mushrooms under a cloche – *Beacáin faoi chlogad*

This dish was a favourite of my father's. The recipe given here comes from the eighteenth century and makes a delicious first course or indeed a light meal if enough mushrooms are used. Individual servings are easier to serve if baked in separate, small, covered ovenproof dishes.

450 g (1 lb) mushrooms, medium-sized
225 g (8 oz) butter
salt and freshly ground pepper
about 4 thick slices of bread

Trim the mushrooms and wipe them over, but leave whole. Lightly butter the individual dishes, or a deep dish and put a crustless slice of bread at the bottom of each of the dishes, or arrange at the bottom of the deep dish. Arrange a pyramid of mushrooms on the top, lavishly spreading each layer with butter, salt and pepper and ending with a dot of butter on top. Cover with the lid and bake in a hot oven 220°C, 425°F, Mark 7, for about half an hour. The bread at the bottom is unbelievably good too. Serves 4.

Egg dishes

From a description of Market Day in Galway from *Irish Holiday* by Dorothy Hartley, 1938:

Donkeys trot in, bulky with panniers full of carragheen and dillisk, and by truck, lorry, bus and cart come eggs, eggs, eggs, hundreds of eggs in big deep baskets made from sally willow.

Eggs have formed a large part of the Irish diet for many hundreds, even thousands, of years, eggs of all kinds, from both wild and domesticated birds generally cooked in the simplest of ways.

Mary Carbery wrote about farm life in County Limerick in the late 1860s:

At nine we had our breakfast: two boiled duck eggs every day for our father, a hen's egg for mother, for us children, stirabout, home-made bread, and butter and milk.

Indeed the old Limerick phrase for speeding an unwanted guest was 'Give him two eggs for the road!'

The most usual method of cooking eggs is either by boiling or frying (often with bacon, or sausages and black pudding for Sunday breakfast).

Rashers of bacon and eggs have long been a favourite of the Irish at all hours of the day. In the 1730s Mary Delany, the celebrated Dublin hostess whose table was highly thought of, writes of her husband, Dr Patrick Delany, Dean of Down: '... the greatest feast to him is a fried egg and bacon'.

Scrambling and poaching follow very closely behind, and in houses with kitchen ranges they were often baked in the oven. Up until the seventeenth and eighteenth centuries eggs were roasted in their shells in the turf or wood ashes (never use coal ash), rather like doing potatoes. To do this they are first pricked with a fine needle, to prevent them exploding.

Poaching eggs has been done since the Middle Ages, and in the seventeenth century it reached a lavishness not known earlier. They were often poached and then; '... laid on butter'd toast and cover'd with a cream of Butter and New Milk'. Poaching sometimes meant cooking them in milk with a knob of butter in it, and that was afterwards thickened with a paste of flour and butter mixed. Or they were poached in gravy or stock with herbs, sorrel, spinach or endives. In fact a lot of the ways were more imaginative than the methods used today. Many of these dishes can be served as first courses.

To dress eggs

Here is an eighteenth-century recipe for eggs, 1736, by Charles Carter, which gives a fair idea of a usual method.

Put Butter or Hogs Lard in a Stew-pan, set it on the Fire, and when it is very hot, break an Egg in it, and let it colour on all sides; poach as many as you would serve in the Dish the same way. Then having the following Sauce: *viz.* a Bit of Butter kneaded in Flour and put into a Stew-pan with a little Gravy, Salt, Pepper and Vinegar, bind the Sauce, put it in the Dish you design serve it in, put the Eggs above it, and serve it hot.

Buttered eggs – *Uibheacha in im*

When eggs are very plentiful they are 'buttered' in Ireland and this preserves them for at least three months. There are a few rules to ensure success in this operation.

(1) Only hen's eggs should be preserved this way.
(2) Use eggs that are at least 24–36 hours old, but not over three days old. They must be cool, the internal temperature as well as the exterior.
(3) The eggs should be clean, if dirty then wipe over with a damp cloth.

(4) Do not use rough or mis-shapen eggs.
(5) The butter or other fat (see below) must be cool, and the place they are stored in should also be cool, but not chilled.
(6) Store pointed end downwards.

Other fats for preserving

As butter is very expensive nowadays, other fats can be used. An excellent method is to use lard mixed with a little borax powder – about 225 g (8 oz) lard to 25 g (1 oz) borax. Work in the borax powder very thoroughly, then rub some of this mixture, or butter in the palm of your hand and gently roll the egg round in it so that all parts of the shell are covered by fat. This excludes the air and keeps the contents fresh.

Convent eggs – *Uibheacha clochair*

This recipe, which I have adapted very slightly for modern use, comes from Soyer's *A Shilling Cookery for the People* of 1859, a book which circulated in many parts of Ireland after Soyer came over to help provide edible food for the famine victims. My copy originally belonged to my aunt in Co. Clare and was much used by her.

4 eggs	300 ml (½ pint) milk
1 medium-sized onion, sliced	½ teaspoon salt
2 tablespoons butter	¼ teaspoon pepper
1 tablespoon flour	

Put the eggs into cold water, bring to the boil and boil for 10 minutes, then put the eggs into cold water. Peel and cut across into six pieces each. Heat the butter and lightly fry the onion in it until soft, but not coloured. Add the flour and mix well, then add the milk, stirring until it forms a nice white sauce; add the salt and pepper. Add the eggs, toss and when they are hot through serve on toast. Grated cheese or chopped herbs can also be added.

Egg cutlets – *Gearrthóga uibhe*

This dish, also known as Ulster eggs (uibheacha Uladh), was a popular one for a meatless day. As a child I remember a small strip of either celery or carrot being put into the narrow end of the cutlet before frying, to represent the bone; we always ate that first!

3 hard-boiled eggs	1 egg, beaten
3 cups cold mashed potatoes	about 1 tablespoon brown flour
1 tablespoon parsley, chopped	(wheatmeal)
1 tablespoon chives, chopped	2 tablespoons breadcrumbs
½ teaspoon ground nutmeg	fat or oil for frying
salt and pepper	

Shell the eggs and mash the whites and yolks separately, then mix together. Combine the potatoes, parsley, chives, nutmeg and salt and pepper. Mix in half the beaten egg, then add just enough wheatmeal flour to make a fairly firm consistency; the amount needed will depend on the flouriness of the potatoes. Taste for seasoning, then shape into cutlets and dip in the remaining egg and then into the breadcrumbs. Fry in hot fat or oil until golden on both sides. Serves 4.

Farmhouse eggs – *Uibheacha theach feirme*

This used to be a favourite dish for supper eaten just after the evening milking time. However, it is elegant enough for a simple lunch or first course served in small individual pots.

Well butter a shallow ovenproof dish and break in the eggs, the number depending on how many people you want to serve; allow 2 eggs per person. If you have any cooked bacon or ham available add some small pieces, finely chopped, scattered around the eggs, or some chopped fresh herbs, or a sprinkling of grated cheese. Then cover each egg yolk with a spoonful of thick cream. Lightly sprinkle with salt and white pepper and bake in a moderate oven, 180°C, 350°F, Mark 4, for 15–20 minutes depending on how well cooked you want the eggs to be.

Eggs Fitzmaurice

This unusual egg dish was often served by a very elderly cousin of mine, who must have been born in the 1870s. She got the recipe from her grandmother, Geraldine Fitzmaurice, who was born in 1831. It makes a most delectable first course.

8 eggs, lightly poached in advance	salt and pepper
2 tablespoons butter	cayenne pepper
2 tablespoons flour	50 g (2 oz) breadcrumbs
1 heaped tablespoon hard grated	lard or oil for deep frying
cheese, preferably parmesan	several fresh sprigs of parsley
300 ml (½ pint) milk	

It is important that the eggs be poached some time before they are needed as they must be quite cold, and drained well. Trim them neatly if they were not cooked in a poacher.

Heat the butter and when foaming add the flour and stir well. Cook for about a minute, then gradually add the milk, stirring all the time until the mixture is thick and smooth. Add the cheese and stir until it melts thoroughly, then add salt, pepper and cayenne. Beat well, then leave for a few moments to cool slightly. Heat the lard or oil for deep frying. Dip the eggs in the sauce and then into the breadcrumbs, and lower into the hot fat. Fry them until golden brown, then put the eggs into a warmed dish and keep warm while you deep-fry the parsley sprigs for about 20 seconds. Garnish the dish with the parsley sprigs. Serves 4.

Frigassy of eggs

Eggs fricasséed were a very popular eighteenth- and nineteenth-century dish. I have adapted this from an eighteenth-century recipe of Sara Power's.

8 eggs
100 g (4 oz) butter
300 ml (½ pint) double cream
squeeze of lemon juice

2 tablespoons chopped parsley
salt and pepper
toast triangles

Boil the eggs for 8–10 minutes, then run them under the cold water tap. Shell the eggs and cut into quarters. Place them in 8 small individual serving dishes or one large one. Heat the butter until foaming in a flat pan and over very low heat let it reduce slightly but not too brown. Add the double cream, stirring all the time with a wooden spoon. Add the lemon juice and keep stirring for about 2 minutes until all has blended thoroughly and the sauce is quite thick. Add the parsley, salt and pepper, stir, and then pour over the eggs. Tuck little triangles of toast into the side of the dish or dishes and serve. Serves 8.

Poached eggs with sorrel – *Samhadh le hUibheacha scrofa nó scallta*

This is another eighteenth-century dish, very fresh-tasting in the spring. Spinach can be used instead of sorrel.

Take a handful of Sorrel to each Person, wash the leaves and take off the stalks; put them in a saucepan with a good piece of Butter and melt over a slow fire: add Salt, pepper and a little cream. Place in a hot Serving dish with a poached egg for each Person on the Top.

Eggs with lettuce – *Uibheacha le leitís mhór*

This old recipe, from *The Lady's Assistant* by Charlotte Mason (Dublin, 1778), is very good for using up lettuce which is inclined to bolt and go to seed. Spinach could be used instead or a mixture of lettuce, sorrel and spinach. I serve this dish with plain boiled rice underneath the lettuce, and some curls of bacon with the eggs on top.

Scald you Cabbage Lettuce, slice them and put them in a pan with a good piece of Butter and season'd with Nutmeg, Salt and Pepper. Stew gently for half an hour and put all thru a sieve. Serve with Eggs fried in Butter on the Top. Garnish with Slices of Sevile orange.

Broad bean or nettle purée with sausages and eggs – *Purée pónairí leathana le hUibheacha is Ispíní*

This is my grandmother's recipe which she used to make when her broad beans had become too old to eat without being skinned. Nettles in place of beans are delicious in spring and very good for you. Gather the nettles before the end of May, wearing gloves, and not from any verge that might have been chemically sprayed.

450 g (1 lb) broad beans, or nettles
2 tablespoons melted butter
salt and pepper
6 eggs, scrambled

8 sausages
4 slices bread
2 tablespoons butter

Cook the broad beans, drain and then sieve them, or put through a vegetable mill so that the skins are left behind. If using nettles, cook and chop the tops. Put into a saucepan with the melted butter and salt and pepper. Mix well and keep warm. Grill the sausages and keep hot. Toast the 4 slices of bread and butter the toast slices. Spoon the broad bean purée over, dividing it among the toast slices; keep warm. Scramble the eggs very lightly, that is take them off while the top is still creamy, and spoon over the bean purée on the toast. Add the grilled sausages, two to a portion. Serves 4.

Irish omelette – *Uibheagán Gaelach*

This I found in a tattered eighteenth-century manuscript with omelette spelt as 'amulet', so maybe it was thought lucky to eat it? It is very good, and filling too.

4–6 eggs, depending on size
1 large cooked potato, mashed well
squeeze of lemon juice
1 tablespoon chopped chives or

scallions
salt and pepper
1 tablespoon butter

Separate the eggs and beat the yolks; add to the mashed potato, mixing thoroughly, then add the lemon juice, chives and salt and pepper. Melt the butter in the omelette pan. Whisk the egg whites until stiff and stir them into the potato mixture. Cook the mixture until golden, then run under a hot grill to finish and to puff it up. Serve at once. Serves 2.

Wicklow pancake – *Pancóg Chill Mhantáin*

This is a traditional Wicklow dish, and although called a 'pancake' it is more like a substantial omelette.

4–6 eggs, depending on size
600 ml (1 pint) milk
100 g (4 oz) fresh breadcrumbs
1 tablespoon parsley, chopped
pinch of chopped thyme

2 tablespoons chopped chives or
    scallions
salt and pepper
2 tablespoons butter

Beat the eggs lightly, then add the milk, breadcrumbs, herbs and seasonings, and mix well. Heat 1 tablespoon of the butter in a pan until foaming, then pour in the mixture and cook over a low flame until it is brown underneath and just set on the top. Put under the grill to finish. Serve cut into wedges with a knob of butter on each portion. Serves 4.

Buttermilk pancakes – *Pancóga bláthach*

These were a country favourite for tea in Ireland.

225 g (½ lb) flour
½ teaspoon salt
½ teaspoon bicarbonate of soda

2 eggs, well beaten
about 1½ cups buttermilk

Sift the dry ingredients, then add the eggs and enough buttermilk to make a fairly thick batter. Fry in spoonfuls on a hot griddle and serve with syrup, honey or jam. Makes about a dozen pancakes. They can also be made with fresh milk.

Oatmeal bacon pancakes – *Pancóga le min choirce*

These pancakes have a nutty flavour and are delicious for breakfast.

100 g (4 oz) flour
25 g (1 oz) oatmeal
about 1 cup milk or buttermilk
salt

1 egg, beaten
8 bacon rashers
mustard

Sift the dry ingredients, then add the egg and enough milk or buttermilk to make a batter like thick cream. Fry the bacon rashers and drain, then make a large pancake, pouring the batter over the entire bottom of the pan. Cook on one side, toss over, spread with a little mustard if liked, then add the bacon and fold over. Make the rest of the batter into pancakes the same way. Makes 4 very large pancakes or 8 smaller ones.

Selina Newcomen of Mosstown, Co. Longford, 1717, gives a very lavish recipe for pancakes which is interesting historically.

> Eight Egg yolks and whites, half a pint of flower blended smooth with a pint of Milk, a naggin of Brandy, a little Nutmeg and Ginger. Two ounces of melted Butter – Salt and Sugar to your taste. Mix them well together very little Butter will answer for frying them.

And underneath is written: Pan Cakes.

> One Doz Eggs to a pint of flower and a quart of Milk makes a great deal more and I find answer as well.

chapter three

FISH AND SHELLFISH –
IASC AGUS IASC SLIOGACH

The fish and shellfish of Ireland are of superb quality and have formed a major part of the diet for thousands of years. The people here in Mesolithic times were, in the main, hunters and fishermen; they relied greatly on fish, shellfish and also marine vegetation such as seaweeds. Molluscs and shellfish have always provided the necessary protein for coastal and island dwellers, and in later times quantities of fish, particularly ling and herring, were dried and salted for use in the winter months. Indeed during the dreadful famine years it was the people in fishing communities who survived best.

Inland waters, too, were well-stocked and the value of fisheries was well known from early times. The ninth-century *Life of St Ciaran of Clonmacnoise* describes the Shannon as a river 'very rich in different varieties of fish'. Giraldus Cambrensis, who was born about AD 1166 of an Anglo-Norman chieftain father and a noble Welsh mother wrote:

This Ireland is also specially remarkable for a great number of beautiful lakes abounding in fish and surpassing in size those of any other countries I have visited. The rivers and lakes also are plentifully stored with the sorts of fish peculiar to these waters, and especially three species, salmon and trout, muddy eels and oily shad.

47

The Shannon abounds in lamprey, a dangerous delicacy indulged in by the wealthy, the lakes of the country contain three species of fish which are found nowhere else. One is a sort of trout called also *salares* which are longer and rounder than trout, and which are white, close-grained and of good flavour. The tymal commonly called the *umber* [possibly the grayling] resembles the former kinds of fish except it is distinguished by a larger head. There are others which very much resemble the sea herring [probably pollan] both in shape and quality and in colour and taste. The first sort is called *glassans*, the second *cates* and third *brits*. These three species make their appearance in summer only and are never seen in winter.

An old list of fish bought from the Claddagh quays lists:

> . . .cods, lings, hawkfish, turbets, plaises, pilchards, a liberal of oyster, scallops, cokles, musles, razure̕s (razor-fish), also plentie of lobsters, crabs and shromps.

Not only fish, but also shellfish must have been taken inland either by curragh or dugout canoes, and many shells of scallops, mussels and cockles were found during excavations at Cahercommaun, which is eight miles from the sea. Salmon has figured in literature and legend since the earliest times, and wonderful descriptions of eating fish occur so many times through the ages that one is convinced of the excellence of Irish fish.

'The pleasant Boyne, the fishy fruitfull Ban . . .' wrote Edmund Spencer in *The Faerie Queene* and Arthur Young in *A Tour of Ireland*, 1776–9, tells us of the plentiful river stocks . . . In conversation with Lord Longford . . .

> His Lordships has seen 500 hundred children fishing at the same time, their being no tenaciousness in the proprietors of the lands about a right to fish; besides perch there is a pike upwards of five foot long, bream, tench, trout of 10 lb, and as red as a salmon, and fine eels; all these are favourable circumstances, and are very conspicuous in the numerous and healthy families among them.

So the fish was not simply reserved for the rich. In Wexford the situation is even better.

'The poor have all barley-bread and pork, herrings, etc. and potatoes. On the coast a considerable fishery of herrings . . . the merchants of Wexford barrel them for the West Indies.' Of Lima-vaddy he writes: 'The poor live on potatoes, milk and oatmeal with many herrings and salmon . . .'

Tomás Ó Crohan who was born on the Great Blasket Island in 1856 wrote in *The Islandman* (Oxford University Press, 1978):

> And the food I got was hens' eggs, lumps of butter and bits of fish, limpets and winkles – a bit of everything going from sea or land . . . we had fish with them [potatoes] – salted scad [horse mackerel] and

that's a very sweet fish. My mother had brought a dish of limpets from the strand with her ... she was roasting the limpets and throwing them to us one by one like a hen with chickens.

Generally speaking, methods of cooking fish in Ireland are not elaborate or unusual; often it is cooked very simply with plenty of good butter and cream.

Sea fish

Baked bass — *Doingean bácaílte*

Bass is a good firm fish, often sold whole, weighing about a kilogram (2 to 3 pounds). Bought this way it is best cooked whole by baking or braising. Larger bass can be filleted or cut into steaks which can be fried or grilled and served with parsley butter.

1 bay leaf
1 sprig parsley
1 bass, about 1 kg (2¼ lb), cleaned and scaled
2 tablespoons butter
1 medium-sized onion, sliced

2 lemons, sliced
1 sprig of fresh fennel, chopped
300 ml (½ pint) cider, or 150 ml (¼ pint) dry white wine
salt and pepper

Put the bay leaf and sprig of parsley inside the fish. Heat half the butter in a frying pan and soften the onion. Transfer to the bottom of an ovenproof dish in which the fish will just fit. Lay the fish on top of the onion. Finely slice one of the lemons and lay the slices along the centre of the fish. Sprinkle the chopped fennel over the top, season well with salt and pepper and pour the cider or wine into the dish. Dot with the remaining butter and cover with a piece of buttered paper and cook in the centre of a moderate oven, 180°C, 350°F, Mark 4, for about half an hour. Serve on a warmed dish with the sauce and onion around the fish and with the other lemon slices as garnish. Serves 4.

Brill with parsley sauce — *Broit le hAnlann peirsile*

Brill is the smallest of the flat fish and therefore it is often sold in steaks which are excellent poached and served with a sauce. These steaks can also be grilled and served with a savoury butter. Small brill, weighing about 1 kg (2¼ lb) can be filleted and fried, grilled, or stuffed and baked.

4 brill steaks or fillets
milk to cover
3 tablespoons parsley, chopped
2 tablespoons butter

2 tablespoons flour
a pinch of ground nutmeg
salt and pepper
1 tablespoon cream

Salt the fish and place it in a deep pan; barely cover with milk and sprinkle with 1 tablespoon of the chopped parsley. Bring gently to the boil, then simmer for about 5 minutes before turning over and cooking the other side for another 5 minutes. Remove carefully from the pan and keep warm. Strain the milk, measure and add water to make 600 ml (1 pint); reserve. Heat the butter, add the flour and mix well. Cook for about a minute, then add the milk stock gradually, stirring all the time, until a smooth sauce is obtained. Add the nutmeg, salt and pepper, mix then stir in the cream and finally add the rest of the chopped parsley. Serves 4.

Baked and stuffed cod – *Trosc bácáilte le búiste*

Cod is at its best in the winter months. It is much used for fish pie or for fish cakes.

4 cod cutlets or fillets
2 tablespoons butter
1 small onion, peeled and chopped
4 rashers streaky bacon, diced
50 g (2 oz) fresh white breadcrumbs
salt and freshly ground pepper

25 g (1 oz) grated cheese
1 tablespoon parsley, chopped
juice and grated rind of ½ lemon
2–3 tablespoons milk
300 ml (½ pint) cider
wedges of lemon for garnish

Butter an ovenproof dish well, then prepare the fish: cut out the cutlets or fillets, if using cutlets take out the centre bones. Heat the rest of the butter and soften the onion in it, then add the chopped bacon and cook for a few minutes. Add all the other ingredients except for the cider and mix well. Let the mixture stand for a while so the crumbs can absorb the liquid. Put a quarter of the stuffing mixture on each fillet or cutlet, if fillets roll them up, if cutlets mound it over the top. Pour the cider into the dish, cover with foil and bake at 180°C, 360°F, Mark 4, for 25–30 minutes, depending on thickness of the fish. Serve with lemon wedges. Serves 4.

Cod with cockles – *Trosc le ruacáin*

This is a traditional Galway dish made with a young codling. It can be made with any white fish. Cockles are also used a great deal in counties Mayo and Donegal. Clams may be used instead, or mussels. If using mussels, chopped fennel should replace the thyme.

24 cockles
1 kg (2¼ lb) codling
4 heaped tablespoons butter
salt and pepper
1 sprig fresh thyme or ½ teaspoon

dried thyme
12 new potatoes, parboiled
5 small onions, parboiled
1 tablespoon parsley, chopped
lemon wedges for garnish

First discard any open cockles, then scrub the closed ones well. Put into a saucepan, barely cover with water and put on to the stove with a lid. When the liquid boils, shake the pan for a minute or two, and then take off the lid. Strain, reserving the juice, and when the cockles are cool enough shell them.

Meanwhile, put the codling into a well-buttered ovenproof dish and season well with salt, pepper and the thyme. Put the partly cooked potatoes and onions around the fish, and pour the cockles and the strained cockle juice over the cod. Melt the rest of the butter and pour over the fish, cover with foil or buttered paper and bake at 200°C, 400°F, Mark 6 for 20–25 minutes.

Scatter the chopped parsley over the fish and serve with lemon. Serves 4.

Cod with egg sauce – *Trosc le hAnlann uibhe*

1 kg (2¼ lb) cod fillets or filleted cod
   steaks
600 ml (1 pint) milk
1 bay leaf
salt and pepper

2 tablespoons butter
2 tablespoons flour
2 hard-boiled eggs, chopped
juice of ½ lemon

Cook the cod fillets gently in the milk with the bay leaf for about 15 minutes. Remove the bay leaf and drain, reserving the milk and carefully remove any skin or bones, then put the cod into an ovenproof dish. Heat the butter and when foaming stir in the flour, cook for 1 minute then add the milk gradually, stirring all the time and adding salt and pepper. Add the chopped hard-boiled eggs and the lemon juice, stir, and simmer for 2 minutes, then pour over the fish. Bake in the upper part of the oven at 200°C, 400°F, Mark 6 for about 20 minutes until the top is golden brown. Serves 4.

Cockle or cockelty pie – *Pióg ruacán*

Scrub the cockles very well, discard any open ones and cook, barely covered with salted water, shaking the pan occasionally until the cockles open, then remove at once and when cool enough to handle, shell them. Put into a pie dish with 1 grated onion, cover with a rich short crust pastry and bake for 30 minutes. This can be served hot or just warm. Serves 4.

Conger eel steaks – *Stéigeanna concair*

They can be grilled or baked in fish stock or cider with herbs. Also excellent in fish soups or pies. Potted like herring it is very succulent. The best sauce for grilled steaks is melted butter with plenty of lemon juice and chopped mint or chives.

Fried sand-eels – *Corr gainimh*

These miniature long, silvery little eels, also called sand-lances, used to be eaten a lot in Ireland, and collecting them was a favourite occupation for older children. They are so-called because they hide themselves in the wet sand at the water's edge where they can easily be dug out. W. H. Maxwell in *Wild Sports of the West*, 1832, describes the process:

> The sand-eels are generally from four to nine inches in length and lie beneath the surface seldom deeper than a foot. The method of taking them is very simple; it is effected by passing a case-knife or sickle with a blunted edge quickly through the sands; and by this means the fish is brought to the surface, and its phosphoric brilliancy betrays it instantly. At the particular times during the summer months when these eels run in upon the estuary quantities sufficient to fill several barrels have been collected during a night. When dressed the fish is reckoned by the peasantry a great delicacy.

The small ones can be treated like whitebait, but the heads should be cut off . They should be floured and salted and fried on both sides in hot oil or clarified butter. Serve with lemon wedges and bread and butter.

Dressed crab – *Portán cóirithe*

Ireland has plenty of crabs, many of which in the West are just tossed aside on the quays or strands. Some are now being processed and frozen, but live crabs are still easy to find and cheap to buy.

Always choose a heavy crab for its size, and if possible a hen-crab which can easily be recognized by a sort of strap at the opening of the heart-shaped body between the main claw pincers when they are in repose.

The easiest and perhaps the most humane way to cook live crabs is to put them in cold sea-water (or heavily salted fresh water), cover tightly (I use my pressure cooker without putting on the pressure knob), bring to the boil, and boil for 10–15 minutes. If you don't have a tight-fitting lid then put a weight on top, for I have known crabs to push the lid off, which was a most distressing sight (and meant I didn't cook them but put them back in the sea). Leave to cool in the cooking water. In this method the fish faint away, as if in too hot a Turkish bath, and this results in less pain for them and more tender flesh for us as there are no death spasms. Lobsters and crawfish should also be cooked like this.

Remove the large claws and set aside, then twist off the smaller ones. Some may be too small for eating, but if you are cooking a lot of crabs, put them back in the water with the shells for soup stock. Turn the crab on its back and with a pointed knife inserted at the base of the body (betweeen where the front pincers would be) push upwards until the body breaks away from the shells. This is called the 'apron' and, apart from the soft flesh in the middle which can be taken out with a teaspoon, it is discarded. Also discard the spongy fingers, known as 'dead men's fingers' that lie around the apron or remain on the main shell, any dark green matter encountered (not dark brown or pale greenish brown, only *dark green*) and a small sac that may be found lying in the top of the shell.

With a spoon take out all the meat from the big shell and put it into a bowl. Wash the shell, and push, with your thumbs, the natural markings which form a wavy line on the open side. This will break off and provide you with a natural serving receptacle. Crack the claws with a nutcracker (or with side-cutters for snipping flex) and take out all the meat, putting some aside to use for top decoration.

Mix the brown and claw flesh with a fork, then season well with salt and pepper and a few drops of Tabasco or Worcestershire sauce. Add about 2 tablespoons fresh white breadcrumbs for a large crab (or 1 tablespoon for a small one) or better still the same amount of sieved cottage cheese or cream or natural yoghurt. Add a good squeeze of lemon juice, then put back in the shell and garnish with the remaining claw meat.

Serve either with a sharp French dressing or wedges of lemon and brown bread and butter. Unless extremely large, allow one crab per person.

Crab's thumbs – *'Ordóga' (crúba) portáin*

These are the crab's large claws, called thumbs in Co. Kerry. Once I was returning on the train from a fish auction with a variety of fish and shellfish, and the guard, Mr O'Sullivan, came and sat in my compartment. 'What have ye there?' he said. I told him of the crab's claws I had bought. 'Ye mean crab's t'umbs', he said. 'D'ye know how to serve them?' Not giving me time to answer he told me. 'Ye take out the flesh, in one piece if ye can, then ye serve them with fresh mayonnaise, and a good plateful of newly dug potatoes and butter. They're gorgeous.' They were too, small butter-glistening potatoes, the size of pigeon's eggs, and the fresh crab's 't'umbs' with a fragrant lemony mayonnaise.

John Dory – *Deoraí*

This is a very fine fish with a large ugly head, which shouldn't put you off buying it. On account of the large head you will need to buy a third more to get good fillets from it than you would any other fish.

It bakes very well, and the fillets are excellent if lightly dusted with flour, then fried in oil until golden on each side and served with quite a lot of lemon.

Dublin Bay prawns in batter –
Piardóga i bhFuidreamh

This is a very popular way of serving Dublin Bay prawns which are often, alas, designated on the menu as 'scampi' which although a first cousin, is an Adriatic shellfish; this is the Norway lobster.

The batters can vary. Sometimes it is simply a matter of dipping the whole prawns in beaten egg, and then in breadcrumbs. The following batter is extremely light and crispy, and very good for fritters or for small pieces of chunky white fish, scallops, etc. Using beer in place of water for this batter will give an even lighter batter with a good flavour.

100 g (4 oz) plain flour
¼ teaspoon salt
1 tablespoon oil, preferably olive

oil for deep frying
1 large egg white

Mix the flour and salt with the oil, then add 150 ml (¼ pint) tepid water, or beer, beat well. The batter will be quite thick, but it should be smooth. Cover and set aside until needed; do not chill. Just before the batter is needed as the oil for deep-frying is heating up, beat the egg white until stiff and carefully fold it into the batter.

When the oil is very hot, drop in the battered pieces of fish, and cook on both sides until golden.

Fish cakes – *Iascmheallta*

Almost any fish can be used for these little cakes, but a good smoked fish, such as cod or haddock, is very pleasant. A cheaper white fish such as whiting can be used but will need more seasoning. Leftover cooked salmon or salmon trout is excellent too.

There is no set recipe for fish cakes, but the important point is to have the same amount of cooked, flaked fish as cooked, mashed potatoes. Mix these together very well, then add a good scattering of chopped herbs, such as parsley, chives, tarragon or fennel, and with a less flavoursome fish such as whiting, a pinch of ground mace or nutmeg. Season well with salt and freshly ground pepper and a drop or two of Tabasco if liked. Then add 1 egg, beaten, for every pound of the mixture, and mix thoroughly.

With floured hands, shape the mixture into little round or oval cakes and either roll again in flour (wholemeal is good) or dip into beaten egg and then in breadcrumbs. Fry the cakes on both sides in very hot shallow oil until golden. Serve warm.

Fish pie – *Pióg éisc*

This can be extremely good and it is a pity the title is not more attractive, although names such as 'Fisherman's pie' are now being used. The amount of seasoning depends on what fish is used. Smoked fish is excellent, but if a plain fish is used then more seasoning will be needed. Some grated cheese added to the sauce is a simple but good idea. A mixture of fish is pleasant and, when available, prawns or other shellfish added will turn it into a very good meal.

450 g (1 lb) smoked cod or haddock or any fish or fish combination
450 ml (¾ pint) milk
1 rounded tablespoon cornflour
2 tablespoons parsley, chopped
few drops of tabasco

200 g (7 oz) can tomatoes, drained or equivalent amount of peeled fresh tomatoes, chopped and drained
50 g (2 oz) grated cheese
450 g (1 lb) cooked mashed potatoes
butter

Poach the fish in milk to cover, then remove the fish and strain the liquid and put back in the pan. Remove any skin or bones from the fish. Cream the cornflour with a little of the milk. Add the rest to the pan. Bring to the boil, then add the creamed cornflour, stirring all the time to avoid any lumps.

Add the fish, the parsley, the tabasco and tomatoes and mix well, then add half the cheese and put the mixture into an ovenproof dish. Cover with mashed potatoes, scatter the remaining cheese over the top and dot with butter. Bake at 200°C, 400°F, Mark 6 for about 35 minutes, or until the top is peaking brown. Serves 4–6.

Gurnard with cheese – *Crúdan le cáis*

Gurnard, or gurnet, is another ugly fish with a large head, but all three varieties – grey, yellow and red – have a firm white flesh which makes them good for baking. They are also good for fish pie, which can be made without any crust, simply with cheese scattered generously over the top, as cheese and gurnard go well together.

Haddock baked in cider – *Cadóg, bácáilte i gCeirtlis*

Almost any white fish, such as cod or whiting, can be used rather than haddock for this.

1 tablespoon butter
2 tablespoons flour
salt and pepper
4 large fillets haddock
1 tablespoon parsley, chopped

Sprig of fennel or lemon thyme, or a bay leaf
2 shallots or 1 small onion, sliced
4 lemon slices
300 ml (½ pint) dry cider

Lightly grease an ovenproof dish with some of the butter. Mix the flour, salt and pepper, and roll the fish fillets in the mixture. Lay the floured fillets in the dish then add the herbs, shallot or onion and the lemon slices. Pour the cider in the dish and dot the fish with the remaining butter. Cover with foil and bake gently at 180°C, 350°F, Mark 4 for half an hour. Take off the foil and glaze for a few minutes under a hot grill, but not long enough for it to dry up. Serves 4.

Haddock with cream – *Cadóg le hUachtar*

This recipe is from a family manuscript dated 1893. Any filleted white fish can be cooked this way.

8 fresh haddock fillets (about 1¼ kg (2¾ lb))
2 tablespoons flour
salt and pepper
150 g (5 oz) butter, melted

300 ml (½ pint) cream
1 heaped teaspoon freshly made English mustard
parsley for garnish

Mix the flour, salt and pepper and dip the fillets in the seasoned flour, then roll them in the melted butter. Put them in a flat pan with any remaining melted butter and add the cream. Heat gently for not more than 5 minutes, until the fish is cooked and the liquid has reduced a little.

Put the fillets on to a warmed serving dish and keep hot. Stir the mustard in to the sauce and reduce it, stirring over high heat until it thickens slightly. Scrape around the edges so that all the essence is in the sauce. Pour over the fish and serve garnished with parsley. Serves 4.

Smoked haddock with eggs – *Cadóg dheataithe, le hubh*

This can be made with smoked cod rather than haddock but it will not be as delicate in taste.

1 large smoked haddock, about 1 kg (2¼ lb)
about 300 ml (½ pint) milk

2 large eggs
2 teaspoons cornflour

Put the fish into a large pan and cover with the milk. Bring to the boil and cook for 3 minutes, then turn over and cook the other side. Transfer to a warmed dish and remove the skin and bones. Divide into two portions and keep warm. Poach the eggs in the fishy milk and when ready, put one on top of each portion of fish. Then cream the cornflour with a little of the stock and add to the pan, stirring until it boils and thickens. Pour the sauce over the eggs and serve at once with brown bread and butter. Serves 2.

Hake with drawn butter sauce – *Colmóir le hAnlann ime thaosctha*

Drawn butter sauce is one of the oldest of sauces and used to be served with fish, vegetables and some meats. It is simply made and extremely good. Irish hake is a fine fish much liked by Spanish fishermen who come to Ireland to fish.

4 hake steaks or thick fillets, about
    1 kg (2¼ lb) in all
600 ml (1 pint) cider
sprig of fennel or parsley

Sauce

175 g (6 oz) butter
2 level tablespoons flour
salt and pepper

pinch of nutmeg
300 ml (4 pint) fish stock
squeeze of lemon

First cook the hake steaks by poaching them in the cider with the fennel or parsley for about 15 minutes or until they are cooked through. Lift out gently, remove the bones and keep warm on a serving dish while you make the sauce.

Melt half the butter, add the flour and seasonings and nutmeg and mix to a smooth paste. Add the stock gradually, stirring well over low heat, until it is creamy. Add the lemon juice, and the remaining butter in small bits, and stir well with a wooden spoon or whisk until all the butter is absorbed and the sauce is creamy and slightly thickened. Serve with the fish, but separately. Serves 4.

Baked stuffed herrings – *Scadáin bhácáilte le búiste*

Herrings have played an important part in the economy of all Celtic countries, providing much needed protein for the poor. Herrings are eaten fresh, salted, smoked (kippers), and potted, and are cooked in many ways. Unfortunately today, due to over-fishing of stocks, herrings are becoming scarce and the price is consequently getting higher. They figure in literature from very early on. Dean Swift wrote evocatively of the fisherwoman's cry when selling her Dublin Bay herrings:

> Be not sparing,
> Leave off swearing.
> Buy my herring
> Fresh from Malahide,
> Better was never tried.
> Come, eat them with pure fresh butter and mustard,
> Their bellies are soft, and as white as a custard.
> Come sixpence a dozen, to get me some bread,
> Or, like my herrings, I soon shall be dead.

Alfred Perceval Graves, Bishop of Limerick and grandfather of the poet Robert Graves, wrote in praise of the herring in 1846:

> Let all the fish that swim the sea,
> Salmon and turbot, cod and ling,
> Bow down the head and bend the knee,
> To herring, their King! – to herring, their King.

Stuffing

4 heaped tablespoons breadcrumbs
1 tablespoon parsley, chopped
1 small egg, beaten

juice and grated peel of 1 lemon
pinch of nutmeg
salt and pepper

8 herrings, cleaned
300 ml (½ pint) cider
1 bay leaf, well crumbled
salt and freshly ground black
    pepper

First make the stuffing by mixing the breadcrumbs, parsley, beaten egg, lemon juice and peel, and salt and pepper. Stuff the fish with the mixture. Lay in an ovenproof dish, close together, add the cider, crumbled bay leaf and salt and pepper. Cover with foil and bake at 180°C, 350°F, Mark 4 for about 35 minutes. Serves 4.

Herrings fried with oatmeal – *Scadáin friochta le min choirce*

This is good served with mustard sauce, or alternatively, the fish may be painted with mustard before being rolled in the oatmeal.

8 fresh herrings
100 g (4 oz) coarse oatmeal
salt and pepper

bacon dripping or oil
lemon for garnish

Take off the heads and tails, scrape the scales off and clean the fish. Mix the oatmeal with the salt and pepper, then roll the herrings in the mixture. Heat the dripping or oil and fry the fish on both sides, browning them well. Drain on paper before serving. Serves 4.

Jugged kippers – *Cipéirí*

The technique of salting and smoking fish was probably introduced in Ireland by the Norsemen, or Vikings, who founded all the principal cities of Ireland. Look for kippers which are pale in colour, for these have the best flavour. When you see deep copper-coloured ones this is often not the result of the smoking process but of a spray-dye.

Jugging is the cooking method for those who like the salt and fat taken out of their kippers. They are good served with scrambled eggs.

Find a deep jug big enough to enclose the kippers you want to cook. Take off the heads and put the fish, tails up, into the jug, then fill the jug with boiling water and cover it. Leave for 5–6 minutes, then drain well, and serve the kippers on hot plates with a knob of butter and a sprinkle of pepper on each one.

Kipper pâté

This is a simple modern dish made with a blender.

Blend equal quantities of boned and skinned kipper with cottage cheese, lemon juice to taste, and pepper. Put into little pots and cover with melted butter.

Ling – *Langa*

There is a Gaelic saying: 'Ling would be the beef of the sea if it always had salt enough, butter enough and boiling enough.' Up until a few years ago, you would see dried ling hanging in country shops, looking like stiffened shirts; the island people salted and dried it for use when the weather was bad. Now it has gone out of fashion, although it is still sold, and a good fish it is. It is the largest member of the cod family.

> Skerries has bracing sea air, clean sands and good fishing. They were selling dried ling in the little stone and thatched shop half-way down the street, and a large complete ling was hanging up. Along the coast a lot of this good fish is eaten, most of it cured, and such curing is done along the west coasts of Ireland.
>
> From *Irish Holiday* by Dorothy Hartley, 1938.

To prepare West Cork salt ling, first cut it into pieces, then soak it overnight. Then boil it in half milk and half water, with a sliced onion, for 30–40 minutes. If liked the liquid can be thickened with cornflour and served over the fish.

Lobster – *Gliomach*

Lobster was eaten a great deal in the past when it was plentiful and cheap. In 1788 a clergyman wrote, in *An Account of the Customs, Manners and Dress of the Inhabitants of the Rosses*:

> Their shellfish they got in the following manner; the men went to the rocks with a hook tied to the end of a strong rod; and with that they pulled from under the rocks, as many crabs and lobsters as they wanted; the lobsters commonly weighing from five to twelve pounds each.

The social historian, Dorothy Hartley, recalling the 1920s and early 1930s wrote:

> Years ago when I first visited the west (of Ireland), large lobsters averaged 9d each and bread and butter, lobsters and tea were staple diet.

Oh, that those day could return!

It is generally eaten cold in Ireland, with a salad. Cook them by the method given for crab, page 52, for a large lobster for 15–20 minutes, then leave to cool in the cooking water. To prepare it, the most useful tools are a sharp knife and a small instrument used for stripping electric flex, called side-cutters. These enable you to snip up the claws and open them, so that the claw flesh can be removed whole, something which is difficult if nut-crackers or a small hammer are used. The tail-end should be cut in half with a sharp heavy knife, and great care should be taken to catch all the juice which escapes from the shell. This should be combined with the 'cream' which coats the shell. Place the lobster meat on fresh, crisp lettuce and pour a little of the juice over to keep it moist. The rest can be incorporated into home-made mayonnaise to be served separately.

Dublin lawyer

This is a traditional method of serving lobster. It is extremely delicious. If possible make this dish with a raw lobster, that is one which has been killed just before cooking by plunging a sharp instrument into the cross on the head. However, a lightly cooked lobster can be used and will still be extremely good. This dish can be served with boiled rice if liked.

1 fresh lobster, about 1 kg (2¼ lb) cut in two down the centre	4 tablespoons Irish whiskey
3 heaped tablespoons butter	150 ml (¼ pint) cream
	salt and pepper

Remove all the meat from the lobster, including the claws; retain the shells for serving. Cut the meat into chunks. Heat the butter until foaming and quickly sauté the lobster chunks in it until just cooked but not coloured. Warm the whiskey slightly, then pour it over the lobster and set fire to it. Add the cream, mix with the pan juices and taste for seasoning. Put back into the half shells and serve hot. Serves 2.

Thackeray's hot lobster

From *The Irish Sketch Book*, 1843:

> You take a lobster, about three feet long if possible, remove the shell, cut or break the flesh of the fish in pieces not too small. Some one else meanwhile makes a mixture of mustard, vinegar, catsup and lots of cayenne pepper. You produce a machine called a *despatcher* which has a spirit-lamp under it that usually is illuminated with whiskey. The lobster, the sauce, and near half-a-pound of butter are placed in the despatcher, which is immediately closed. When boiling, the mixture is stirred up, the lobster being sure to heave about the pan in a convulsive manner, while it emits a remarkable rich and agreeable odour through the apartment. A glass and a half of sherry is now thrown into the pan, and the contents served out hot, and eaten by the company. Porter is commonly drunk, and whisky-punch afterwards, and the dish is fit for an emperor.

N.B. – You are recommended not to hurry yourself in getting up the next morning, and may take soda-water with advantage – *Probatum est.*

In fact although this seems quite a strong dish, it can be made very good if the strong condiments are merely wafted across the dish.

Pickled lobster – *Gliomach picilte*

This is a method from the eighteenth century, when so many foods were pickled, mainly as means of keeping them. This method is from Sara Power's manuscript book of 1746:

> Boyl your lobsters in Salt and Water till they slip out of their Shelles, take the tails out whole, and make your pickle of half white wine, and half water, put in whole cloves, whole pepper, two bay leaves, Musharooms, Capers and a branch of Rosemary, and a little Cucumbers, put in your lobsters, let them have a boyl or two in pickle, take them out, lay them to be cold, let the pickle boyl longer. Put in the bodys, it will give them a pretty Relish, when the Lobsters and pickles are cold put them in a long pot for use.

Mackerel – *Ronnach*

On the coasts, particularly at Wexford, freshly caught mackerel are gently boiled in seawater. The fishermen say they never taste better. This is called in Irish *ronnach i sáile.*

Mackerel can be cooked in any way as for herrings. Gooseberry and fennel sauce (see sauces section) was popular in the eighteenth century with grilled or fried mackerel.

Mullet – *Lannach*

Mullet is found all around the coasts of Ireland and is extremely good when either baked whole, *Lannach bacailte*, or cut into fillets, dusted with seasoned flour and fried in oil, *lannach friochta*. It must be freshly caught to be at its best. W. H. Maxwell in *Wild Sports of the West* wrote in 1832 of its excellence:

> We dined sumptuously. The flavour of a mullet, fresh from the water, neither injured by land-carriage nor spoiled by exposure to the sun, is exquisite.

Mussels stuffed with garlic – *Diúilicíní líonta le gairleog*

'Ri sea Diúilicíní ach ria tualaigh sea bairnigh.' ('Mussels are the food of kings, limpets are the food of peasants.')

Mussels have always been eaten in Ireland, usually by coastal dwellers, but they were also hawked around the streets of Drogheda and of course Dublin, as evidenced in the old song about Molly Malone who 'wheeled her wheelbarrow through streets broad and narrow'.

Today the mussels of Wexford are particularly large and succulent, a commercial mussel farm having been established there, but there are also many fine mussels in other parts of Ireland. This is a modern recipe given to me by the Irish Aquaculture Association.

450–700 g (1–1 ½ lb) shelled cooked mussels (2 ¼ litres, 4 pints) if bought in the shells
100 g (4 oz) butter
2 large cloves garlic, crushed
juice of ½ large lemon
salt and pepper
1 tablespoon parsley, finely chopped
lemon wedges for garnish.

Put the mussels into an ovenproof dish. In a saucepan heat the butter until just melted, add the garlic, then the lemon juice, salt and pepper and chopped parsley. Mix well and when amalgamated and very hot, pour gently over the mussels. Run the dish under a hot grill until peaking brown. Serves 4.

Mussels in white wine sauce

This is a very common way of cooking mussels and extremely good. Cider can be used in place of white wine.

60 mussels
1 large onion, or 4 shallots, finely chopped
½ bottle dry white wine
2 teaspoons flour
2 teaspoons butter
salt and pepper
2 tablespoons parsley, chopped
pinch of ground nutmeg

Wash and scrub the mussels well, discarding any that are open. Put into a large saucepan, add the onion or shallots and wine, cover and bring to the boil. Cook for about 5 minutes, shaking the saucepan from time to time, or until all the mussels are open. Strain the liquor into another saucepan. Remove the top shells and beards from the mussels and put into warmed soup plates; keep warm. Work the flour into the butter and add the pieces to the strained liquor. Boil it up stirring as it thickens. Season to taste, stir, add the parsley and pour over the mussels. Serves 3–4.

Periwinkles – *Miogáin*

These little shellfish, usually known as 'winkles', are called 'willicks' in the north of Ireland. They are usually boiled in salt water for about 5 minutes, then drained and cooled. To eat, the small black plaque which covers the opening is removed and the 'winkle' is extracted with a pin. They used to be eaten at all seaside resorts rather the way potato crisps are now. They are a toothsome little fish. When shelled they can be added to soups, sauces or garnishes.

Plaice with herbs and breadcumbs –
Leatóg le luibheanna agus grabhroga arain

Plaice is perhaps the most popular fish eaten in Ireland, usually sold in fillets, but extremely good if left on the bone, rolled in seasoned flour, either fried or grilled and then served with lemon.

700g (1½lb) plaice, skinned and boned
1 tablespoon butter
4 large ripe, peeled tomatoes, coarsely chopped
salt and pepper
1 tablespoon fresh herbs, chopped
or 2 teaspoons dried
squeeze of lemon juice
2 cups fresh breadcrumbs
1 tablespoon hard cheese, finely grated
1 large lemon cut in wedges.

Cut the fish into large pieces. Butter an ovenproof dish, and spread a layer of about a third of the chopped tomatoes on the bottom, then a layer of about a third of the fish chunks. Add salt, pepper, a sprinkle of herbs and a squeeze of lemon juice. Then put a thin layer of breadcrumbs over the top and repeat the operation. Before putting on the top layer of breadcrumbs mix in half the cheese, then sprinkle the rest over the top and dot with butter. Put into a hot oven, 200°C, 400°F, Mark 6, for about half an hour or until the top is crispy and slightly browned. Serve with the lemon wedges. Serves 3–4.

Plaice with mushrooms –
Leathóg bhallach le beacáin

4 plaice fillets
seasoned flour for dredging
100g (4oz) butter
225g (½lb) mushrooms, cleaned and thinly sliced
½ teaspoon garlic, minced (optional)
salt and pepper
parsley and chives, chopped

Roll the fish in seasoned flour. Heat the butter until foaming then put in the fish and brown quickly on both sides. Lower the heat, add the mushrooms and minced garlic, if liked, and fry gently until the fish is just cooked through and the mushrooms are soft. Taste for seasoning and serve sprinkled with the chopped parsley and chives. Serves 4.

Pollock with melted butter and chives —
Mangach le him leáite agus siobhais

This is the fish most often caught by amateur anglers.

1 whole pollock, about 1 kg (2¼ lb)
  cleaned
cider to half cover

175 g (6 oz) butter, melted
2 tablespoons chives, chopped

Put the cleaned fish into a baking dish and add enough cider to come half-way up the fish, cover with foil and bake at 200°C, 400°F, Mark 6 for half an hour. Remove the skin, head, tail and as many bones as possible. Put in a warmed dish with a little of the liquid and keep warm. Heat the butter until foaming and add the chives, mix well, then pour over the fish and serve. Serves 4.

Prawns — *Cloicheáin*

These are not to be confused with Dublin Bay prawns; the true prawn (*Leander serratus*) is much smaller and is good for prawn cocktail, for sauces or omelettes, for garnish or for making a paste. Cook them by boiling in salt water, or by steaming, for about 7 minutes.

Skate with brown butter —
Roc nó sciata, le hArán donn

Choose the thick centre cut of the skate (or ray) if possible, although this is a good fish in all its cuts. There are no bones, just cartilage, which makes it popular with children. Also it is useful for it improves with keeping for a few days as it is a game fish. On the Scottish islands, it was liked quite 'high' and to this end was often earth-dried, that is put under sods of earth for a few days.

4 centre cuts skate (or ray)
175 g (6 oz) butter, melted
2 tablespoons capers
1 lemon cut in wedges

Poach the fish in enough salted water to barely cover for about 20 minutes, turning it half-way through cooking. Lift out and keep warm on a hot dish. Meanwhile, heat the butter until foaming and then let it go on cooking until it become a pale brown, but don't let it become too dark. Add the capers and some of the caper liquid, and as soon as the capers are heated through pour them over the fish and serve with lemon wedges. Serves 4.

Poached salmon — *Bradán scallta*

Salmon is the king of fish in Ireland and has long been prized. It figures in many legends and was the main dish served at banquets given by the kings of Ireland, when it was cooked on a spit after being rubbed with salt and basted with butter and honey.

Legend has it that Fionn MacCumaill (Finn MacCool) ate the salmon which had eaten hazelnuts from the Tree of Knowledge, thus imparting that knowledge to the first person who tasted it when cooked.

A ninth-century anonymous poem called 'The Hermit's Song' describes the hermit wishing for 'Hens, salmon, trout and bees', and there is an old Irish saying which goes: '*Sláinte an bhradáin chugat.*' ('May you be as healthy as the salmon.')

At certain times of the year the rivers are alive with them, particularly under Salmon Weir Bridge, Galway town, when they lie packed like sardines. Arthur Young in his *A Tour of Ireland*, 1776–9, described seeing salmon leap at Ballyshannon: 'was delighted to see the salmon jump, to me an unusual sight: the water was perfectly alive with them.'

On St John's Day in midsummer, boats and nets are blessed and at Port Ballintrae, Co. Antrim, the salmon fishermen of the River Bush hold a communal dinner, known locally as 'The Salmon Dinner'. The menu is of fish soup, freshly caught salmon and the first digging of new potatoes with butter. An essential feature is the accompanying Bushmills whiskey.

Salmon is most usually poached in Ireland and served cold, but it is also baked, grilled, potted and cured, although it is no longer pickled.

If you don't have a large enough fish kettle to take a whole salmon, put the fish, well cleaned and de-scaled, on a large piece of double foil that has been rubbed with oil. Tuck a sprig of fennel or parsley into the gullet, spoon about 2 tablespoons of fish-stock, dry white wine or cider over the salmon and wrap the foil loosely around the fish, securing it well. Cook in a low oven, 150°C, 300°F, Mark 2, for about 15–20 minutes to the half kilo (pound).

If the fish is to be eaten hot, leave it in the unopened foil for 10 minutes, then serve. If it is to be eaten cold, leave in the foil to cool, then open the foil and remove the skin from the top and also any side fins. Chill slightly, but bring to room temperature before serving.

Baked salmon – *Bradán bácáilte*

Butter and cream figure extensively in Irish cooking, and both are used in making this delicious dish.

1 salmon, about 2 kg (4½ lb), cleaned and de-scaled	150 ml (¼ pint) dry white wine or dry cider
two sprigs parsley	300 ml (½ pint) double cream
3 heaped tablespoons butter	juice of 1 lemon
salt and freshly ground white pepper	

Trim the tail off the fish and put the parsley inside the cleaned gullet. Rub a little of the butter in an ovenproof dish and put in the fish; dot the rest over the salmon. Season, and pour the wine or cider around the dish, cover with foil and bake at 180°C, 350°F, Mark 4 for about 15 minutes to the half kilo (pound). After half an hour, take from the oven and baste slightly, then pour the cream over the fish, cover and put back in the oven to finish cooking.

When cooked, take from the oven, remove the skin and any side bones or fins. Put in a warmed serving dish and keep hot. Reduce the sauce on top of the stove, stirring all the time, add the lemon juice and taste for seasoning. Pour some sauce over the fish and serve the rest separately.

Grilled salmon steaks – *Bradán stéigeanna gríosctha*

First cover the grilling pan with foil, then rub thickly with butter and put under the grill to melt and heat up, but not to let colour. Dust the salmon steaks lightly with seasoned flour and turn them over in the hot butter before grilling. Cook for about 8 miutes depending on thickness until the fish will leave the bones easily. There is no need to turn the steaks when the pan has been heated enough before they are put on it. Serve with a pat of butter worked with chopped fresh parsley and a squeeze of lemon. Or if you want to combine tradition with taste, add some ground hazelnuts to the butter, thus emulating Finn MacCool.

Salmon mould – *Múnla bradáin*

This family recipe is an excellent way of making salmon go a long way. A tail end of salmon is good for this.

900 g (2 lb) salmon
150 ml (¼ pint) dry sherry
salt and pepper
cayenne pepper
900 g (2 lb) white fish such as cod or
   haddock

25 g (1 oz) fresh breadcrumbs
2 egg yolks
1 level tablespoon butter
600 ml (1 pint) aspic jelly or gelatine
parsley and cucumber slices for
   garnish

Skin and bone the salmon, then cut into 5-cm (2-inch) cubes. Marinate in the sherry with a little salt and pepper for about three hours. Fillet and skin the white fish, then either mince or chop fine in a food processor. Add the breadcrumbs, egg yolks, salt, pepper and a little of the marinade, just enough to moisten. Butter a large oven-proof dish, put in a layer of the white fish, then a layer of the salmon chunks and repeat, ending with the white fish on top. Dot with the rest of the butter, sprinkle over about 3 tablespoons of the marinade, cover and place in a pan of water. Cook in a moderate oven, 180°C, 350°F, Mark 4, for 1–1½ hours. Let cool then put a clean piece of paper over the top, and weight it lightly. Leave overnight. The next day, turn out carefully on to a serving dish and cover with aspic jelly or gelatine, garnish with parsley and cucumber slices. Serves 8–10.

Salmon on skewers – *Bradán ar bhriogúin*

This is another quite economical way of using salmon, and should be served with boiled rice. If you think this is a purely modern idea, as I did, then you will be pleasantly surprised by the following quote from a letter of Edward Willes to Lord Warwick, written about 1760:

> Entertained in an Assay House . . . we had a fresh Caught Salmon roasted in pieces on wooden scewers. The room was adorned a la Mode in Antient Irish Fashion . . .

450 g (1 lb) salmon, boned
3 tablespoons sherry, dry
225 g (½ lb) medium-sized
   mushrooms

4 bay leaves
175 g (6 oz) butter, melted
juice of 1 large lemon

Cut the salmon into largish chunks, pour the sherry over it and leave while preparing the other ingredients. Clean the mushrooms, then thread on skewers, alternating pieces of salmon with mushrooms, and placing a bay leaf at each end. Lay the skewers on a foil-lined grilling pan. Heat the butter and add half the lemon juice. Pour this liberally over the skewers and grill under moderate heat, turning to grill all sides, and basting with more butter, until the fish is cooked. Serve with the pan juices, boiled up with any remaining butter and the rest of the lemon juice. Serves 4–5.

Pickled salmon – *Bradán picilte*

This recipe stems from the days when salmon was very cheap, and was used extensively by sportsmen.

> A Sportsman's breakfast: First, a large bowl of new milk which instantly disappeared; then a liberal allowance of cold salmon soaked in vinegar – a very common dish this . . . and a bottle of port wine.
>
> From *The Sportsman in Ireland*, 1897.

900 g (2 lb) salmon fillets
300 ml (½ pint) white wine vinegar
1 small onion, sliced
2 carrots, sliced

1 sprig each of parsley, lemon thyme
   and tarragon
salt and pepper

Gently cook the salmon in water to cover for about 30 minutes, then lift out, keeping the cooking liquid. Put into a deep dish and let cool. Put the vegetables into a saucepan with the herbs, the fish liquor and the white wine vinegar, and season well. Boil up, and continue boiling until it has reduced by about one third. While still hot, strain over the salmon. Cover and leave for a few days in this pickle, turning the fish at least once a day. To serve, pour a little of the liquid over each portion of fish, and hand round brown bread and butter. Serves about 6.

Scallops baked with breadcrumbs – Muiríní bácáilte le grabhróga aráin

Scallops have always been immensely popular in Ireland, and if left will grow to a very large size. The method of fishing them in the eighteenth century was, to say the least, practical and uninhibited. The Reverend A. B. gives the following account of the Rosses, Co. Donegal, 1788:

> For scollops and oysters, when the tide was out, the younger women waded into the sea where they knew the beds of such fish lay; some of them naked; others having stripped off their petticoats, went in their gowns tucked up about their waist; and by armfuls brought to shore whatever number of scollops they thought requisite; the scollops weighing from two to four pounds each.

1 dozen large scallops, or 4 dozen smaller ones (called 'queenies' or 'closheens' in western Ireland)	4 tablespoons white wine or cider
	1 tablespoon lemon juice
2 heaped tablespoons butter	salt and freshly ground white pepper
2 cups fresh white breadcrumbs	parsley, chopped

Remove the scallops from the shell with a sharp knife and take off the black bag and any black filaments, taking care to save the liquor from the shells. Butter an ovenproof dish and sprinkle the bottom and sides fairly thickly with breadcrumbs, to about 1-cm (½-inch) thick. Cut each large scallop into 4 pieces (or the smaller ones into 2) combine with any red roes, the fish juice, white wine, lemon juice, a little chopped parsley, salt and pepper in the dish, then cover thickly with breadcrumbs. Dot lavishly with butter and bake at 200°C, 400°F, Mark 6 for about 40 minutes for the large scallops (or 25–30 minutes for the queenies). Serves 4–6.

Scallops in batter – Muiríní i bhFuidreamh

Both the large and small scallops are delicious cooked in a batter. First they should be cleaned and then boiled gently in water to cover for about 10 minutes for the large ones, or 5 minutes for the small ones. Drain the scallops and cut into convenient size pieces (no need to do this with the queenies), then dip into a light batter and deep-fry until golden. Serve with lemon wedges and tartare sauce. A nice variation on this is to wrap the scallop pieces in strips of lean bacon before battering and frying.

Scallop pie – *Piógmuiríní*

If scallops are very expensive this pie can be made combining scallops with any mixture of thick white fish, such as monkfish, turbot and halibut.

8 large scallops, or 4 scallops and an
    equal amount of any white fish
300 ml (½ pint) milk
salt and pepper
2 tablespoons butter
1 tablespoon flour

225 g (½ lb) mushrooms, sliced
3–4 tablespoons sherry or medium
    sweet white wine
About 450 g (1 lb) freshly made
    mashed potatoes

Clean the scallops and cut in half, then simmer in the milk for 15 minutes. Strain, reserving the liquid. Heat 1 tablespoon of the butter and stir in the flour, cook for about a minute stirring, then add the milk gradually, stirring all the time to avoid lumps. Season with salt and pepper, add the sliced mushrooms and simmer for about 10 minutes longer, then add the sherry and finally the scallops. When hot, transfer to an ovenproof dish and cover with mashed potatoes, making sure that they cover the fish right to the edges. Dot with the remaining butter and bake in a moderate oven, 180°C, 350°F Mark 4, for 20–30 minutes or until the top is peaking brown. Serves at least 4.

Shrimps – *Ribí róibéis*

The true shrimps are very tiny, and used to be popular seaside fare along with winkles. They should be steamed for about 5 minutes, then the shells picked off. The tiny shellfish are excellent for sauces and soups, for potting (covered with clarified butter), or as ingredients for omelettes or seafood pancakes.

Stuffed black sole – *Leathǒg dhubh le búiste*

There are two kinds of sole in Ireland, the most prized being the one called 'black sole'. The other, a much smaller, softer fish is known as 'lemon sole'. Black sole is usually painted with melted butter, and then grilled; this is called 'sole on the bone'. It is one of the best ways of eating this expensive and excellent fish.

In this more complicated dish, lift the top fillets off and remove the bone, then put inside a mixture of small shrimps or prawns, chopped scallops and mushrooms. Roll the stuffed fillets in flour and fry them on both sides in a combination of oil and butter until golden.

Lemon sole grilled with curd cheese – *Leathóg bhuí gríosctha le cáis ghrutha*

This very delicate fish can be turned in seasoned flour and then fried quickly until golden brown on both sides.

Grilling it with curd or cottage cheese is another excellent way to cook it. The fish should be filleted right across so that two whole fillets the shape of the fish are obtained. Ask the fishmonger to do this for you. In this dish the flavours of the buttery cream filling and the milky fish are extremely good together.

8 lemon sole fillets (4 fish)
1 tablespoon butter
4 heaped tablespoons sieved cottage or curd cheese

1 tablespoon herbs, finely chopped
salt and pepper
juice of 1 lemon
a little oil

Line the grilling pan with foil, then lay 4 of the fillets on the foil, retaining the pair of each. Lightly butter each one. Put the cottage or curd cheese through a sieve. Mix the herbs into the cheese, season lightly and add the lemon juice. Divide the cheese mixture among the 4 fillets, mounding it on top. Place the remaining 4 fillets over the tops of their matched pairs. Pour over a mere dribble of oil and put under a fairly hot grill to cook until the skin blisters slightly, then carefully turn the fillet pairs over; grill the other side. Serves 4.

Squid – *Scuid*

This is not generally found in fishmongers' but I am assured that it is one of the favourite fish in the Irish Naval Service. Only the small tender squid are used, and they are usually fried.

900 g (2 lb) young squid
seasoned flour
4 tablespoons oil

4 cloves garlic, chopped
1–2 tablespoons parsley, chopped
salt and pepper

Clean the squid and cut the body into thickish rings, and the tentacles into ½ inch pieces. Roll in seasoned flour, then put into a cold pan with the oil and fry over full heat for 8–10 minutes, stirring from time to time. Turn down the heat, cover, and simmer for another 15–20 minutes. Stir in the garlic and parsley towards the end of the cooking time, season and serve with wedges of lemon. Serves 2–3.

Taupe casserole – *Casaról mhadra éisc ghoirm*

This is a small shark, also spelled tope, caught in the west of Ireland and very good to eat when fairly young. It is usually sold skinned and boned. It is superb for soup, giving a fine flavour, and will stand quite long cooking. It can also be baked with canned or fresh tomatoes, herbs, onion and a little cider; cooked with a cheese sauce; or skewered with little strips of bacon, mushrooms and bay leaves. This casserole method is also extremely good.

900 g (2 lb) taupe fillets
seasoned flour
1 large onion, sliced
2 large leeks, cleaned and sliced
3 carrots, sliced
1 celery heart, sliced
50 g (2 oz) mushrooms

1 teaspoon mixed herbs such as
lemon, thyme and fennel
1 handful sorrel, if available
1 tablespoon parsley, chopped
salt and pepper
300 ml (½ pint) cider

Roll the taupe fillets in the seasoned flour then cut into largish cubes. Put into a casserole with all the other ingredients; stir well. Cover and cook in the oven at 180°C, 350°F, Mark 4 for about an hour, or until well cooked. Serves 4.

Taupe salad with parsnips –
Sailéad mhadra éisc ghoirm le meacain bhána

Parsnips in a fish salad in the old days were known as 'poor man's lobster' for the parsnip does acquire a fishy flavour and is roughly a similar texture to lobster. The salad can be made with any firm white fish.

3 medium-sized parsnips, peeled
and cooked
275 g (10 oz) taupe, cooked and
flaked
1 teaspoon anchovy essence

1 cup mayonnaise, preferably
home-made, with ¼ teaspoon dry
mustard added
lettuce leaves
lemon wedges for garnish

Cut the parsnips, when cooled, into rings and mix with the flaked fish and the anchovy essence. Then add the mustard mayonnaise and mix well. Arrange on crisp lettuce and serve with lemon wedges. Serves 4.

Turbot with seaweed – *Tubard scallta le feamainn*

A very old method of cooking fish is to poach or steam the fresh catch over seaweed. This gives a wonderful flavour, but the fish must be absolutely fresh and the seaweed well washed. Many is the time I have enjoyed this in the past, beside a fire made in a small hole dug in the sands. When the flames die down, it is covered with seaweed and the fish placed on top to cook for about half an hour, although longer will not hurt the fish. This is a difficult dish to make at home unless you live near the sea, but watercress or sorrel, or a mixture, can also be used instead of seaweed and also produces a fine dish, with a wonderful aroma. Mackerel, sea bass or any thick white fish can replace the turbot.

1 large bunch freshly gathered
seaweed, well washed
1 turbot
lemon juice
salt and freshly ground black
pepper

2 sprigs thyme
1 sprig fennel
150 ml (¼ pint) fish stock, chicken
stock or dry cider

Lay half the seaweed in an enamelled oval heatproof pot large enough to hold the fish. Rub the fish with lemon juice, inside and out, season with salt and pepper and lay it on top of the seaweed. Place the sprigs of herbs on top, then put the rest of the seaweed over the fish. Add the warmed liquid to the pan, cover and cook over a fairly high heat for about half an hour, or until the fish will come away easily from the bone if prodded with a fork.

When it is cooked, gently lift the fish on to a warmed serving plate, and serve with drawn butter sauce. Serves 3–4.

Whitebait – *Bánbhaoite*

Whitebait are the very small fry of the herring and sprat and when not much longer than 5 cm (2 inches) they are quite delicious eaten whole. I live by the sea, and a few years ago hundreds of these tiny creatures, being pursued by a shoal of much larger fish, leapt into the air to escape and into my garden, where we gathered them in buckets for a superb feast. Alas, they haven't done it again, but we still hope, given due warning by the darting terns and the agitated waters.

Heat oil for deep-frying. Dip the fish in milk and then shake them in flour in a large paper bag. Lower them into the deep oil and fry for 2 or 3 minutes until golden and crispy, then serve at once with brown bread and butter and lots of lemon.

Whiting in cheese sauce – *Faoitín in anlann cáise*

Whiting is one of the cheapest of our fishes. The deep sea whiting has much more flavour than the smaller ones. It can be coated with seasoned flour and fried or grilled, or it can be used for fish cakes, fish creams or fish pie. It is best served in a sauce, as here.

4 large whiting fillets	450 ml (¾ pint) milk
pepper	pinch of ground nutmeg
1 heaped tablespoon butter	50 g (2 oz) grated hard cheese
1 heaped tablespoon flour	

Put the fillets in an ovenproof dish and pepper them. Heat the butter, add the flour and cook for about 1 minute, then gradually add the milk, stirring all the time, until smooth and creamy. Add the nutmeg and cheese and stir until the cheese melts. Pour the sauce over the fillets and bake at 200°C, 450°F, Mark 6 for 25–30 minutes, or until the top is golden brown. Serves 4.

Freshwater fish

Fish that inhabit free-flowing waters with a gravel or sandy bottom can be scaled, but fish which live on the bottom of muddy waters should be washed but not scaled, and dusted with flour so that when cooked the floured skin can be peeled off.

In the last century and the early years of this one, potatoes were well scrubbed and put into a large pot, then a few herbs such as thyme or parsley were added and the fish put on top, either whole or cut up. The whole is cooked in sea water for sea fish and plain water for river fish. If the fish are small, then cook the potatoes first for about 10 minutes, so that both are ready at the same time. If you have a small onion or find wild garlic, of which there is plenty in Ireland, then add a little for added flavour. This method was used by both rich and poor, and with good fresh ingredients it is delicious. Here is an account of a fishing expedition in 1897 from *The Sportsman In Ireland*.

Here I will describe a morning repast. First a large iron pot slung by three sticks over a good clear turf-fire; well-washed, but not skinned potatoes, a perch, split and well-seasoned and a crimped trout, ['crimped' means slits out across the sides] of eleven pounds, hot even unto burning; plenty of lake water clear as crystal; and finally an infusion of the best Cork whiskey.

Bream – *Bran*

In France there is an adage: 'He that hath breams in his pond is able to bid his friends welcome.' It should be rubbed with flour before frying, and the skin removed before eating.

Carp – *Carbán*

There is not a lot of carp in Ireland but I have bought it here and very good it is too. It should not be scaled, but soaked for a few hours in water with some vinegar added, before cooking. Carp is best baked. I stuff mine with wild sorrel and butter, then wrap it in foil with some chopped onions, parsley and a little cider, and bake it for half an hour.

Crayfish – *Cráifisc*

These are little freshwater lobsters which inhabit Lough Derg and other big Irish lakes. I have a friend who is nimble at catching them by hanging over the lakeside at dusk with a funny little colander-shaped net, and endless patience. They are delicious when steamed for a few minutes, but make the most of any you find, for I have never seen them for sale, although I am assured they are commonly found in limestone parts of the country.

Marinated eels – *Eascanna*

Eels are very plentiful in Ireland and there are still some five fishing weirs on the River Bann, as well as a developing fishery for brown or feeding eels caught on Lough Neagh which is one of the most important feeding areas in Europe with its watershed of eight rivers and only one outlet to the sea by the Lower Bann. Most of them are exported to Holland and Germany.

Eels were an important item of diet for prehistoric man, also in medieval times, and in pre-Famine days they were sold both salted and fresh in the Bann valley. In Athlone town they were sold cooked with an onion stuck in their mouths.

> '. . . run to the eel-stream for a double-handful of mint. If Paddy's there and has an eel skinned, bring it up in a dock leaf to be jellied for brother's breakfast.' The eels were sold at sixpence or eightpence the dozen . . .
> *The Farm by Lough Gur*, Mary Carbery, writing about the 1870s.

Sean O'Faoláin writes about eel-catching in the lake at GouganeBarra, Co. Cork in the 1920s or early 1930s, in his short story, 'The Silence of the Valley'.

> To lure the eels a few random bits of guts has been thrown into the brown shallows at their feet and there swayed like seaweeds . . . 'Will you roast the eels for me tonight?' and over his shoulder the priest called, 'I will, Jo, after supper . . .'

Eels should only be bought freshly killed, and have the fishmonger skin it for you. If you must do it yourself, suspend the eel by strings from a strong hook and make a circular cut around the neck and sprinkle this with salt. With pliers ease the skin away for about ½ inch, and pull down evenly, holding the eel with a cloth. When finished take it down and cut into pieces. It does jerk about even when cut up, so leave it awhile in a covered pot if you are squeamish. Then marinate the pieces in a mixture of wine vinegar and oil with salt and pepper and a few bay leaves for about 2 hours. After that it can be grilled or baked with oil or butter, bay leaves and seasoning for about half an hour.

Stewed eels

Parboil the eels first and then put them into a white sauce and simmer for 40 minutes, then add 1 tablespoon each of chopped parsley and chopped chives.

Jellied eels

Simmer eels with herbs in water for 45 minutes, and they will jelly when cold.

Potted eels

This is an eighteenth-century method for soused or potted eel from Sara Power, 1746:

> Get a quart of White Wine, half a pint of Vinegar, some Lemon peel, nutmegs, Mace, some betten pepper, Cinnamon and Salt enough to season it, some bay leaves and boyl them up with the fish for above half an Hour. Then take out the Fish and put into a long dish and boyl up the flowings, when it is cold add a few slices of a lemon, pour it over and keep it close covered.

Perch fried in batter – *Péirse*

Perch is one of the best tasting of all freshwater fish and it is prolific in Irish lakes and rivers, especially in Lough Neagh. On the Tyrone side the young perch are called 'grunts', and used for soup. Care should be taken in preparing it as the fins have sharp spines which can sting badly; it is best to wear gloves when cleaning it. The large fish can be poached and served with parsley sauce, or baked, but the smaller ones are delicious skinned and fried. To skin, slip a knife under the skin just above the tail and then pull off quickly.

100 g (4 oz) flour	4–6 small perch
salt	about 4 tablespoons oil
1 egg yolk, beaten	parsley sprigs
about 4 tablespoons pale beer	lemon wedges

Mix the flour with a pinch of salt, then add the beaten egg yolk and beat until smooth. Thin it down with the beer, beating well, then leave to stand for about half an hour. Heat the oil. Beat the batter again, then dip the fillets into the batter, and fry in the hot oil on both sides, adding the sprigs of parsley to the pan. Serve with lemon wedges and the fried parsley.

Baked pike – *Gailliasc bácáilte*

Pike is much prized by European anglers who come over to Ireland but seldom eaten now by the Irish, although it was once a most popular dish.

There are frequent references to 'jack pike' in literature, and still many pike in our lakes, no doubt all the better-tasting for their diet of trout! The best pike to cook are those weighing 3 kg (6½ lb) or less. To make the flesh tender, a handful of salt should be pushed down the throat after catching and left overnight.

Make a stuffing of breadcrumbs mixed with herbs and a small chopped onion and bound with an egg. Stuff the pike and put it into a pan, brush with fat and cover it with rashers of bacon. Bake for about an hour in a moderate oven.

Poached pike – *Gailliasc scallta*

2½–3 kg (5½–6½ lb) pike
1 medium-sized onion, sliced
600 ml (1 pint) dry cider or white
  wine
1 bay leaf
sprig of thyme

sprig of parsley
6–8 whole black peppercorns
juice of 1 lemon
225 g (8 oz) unsalted butter

Clean the fish and scrape off the scales. Put into a large pan with the onion, cider or wine and the herbs and peppercorns. Cover with water and bring to the boil. Cover and simmer gently for about half an hour, then test to see if it is done. The flesh should leave the backbone easily. It may need another 10 minutes cooking. Lift out carefully on to a warmed dish and take off the skin. Divide into portions and keep warm.

Heat the butter until foaming, then add the lemon juice. Pour the mixture over the portions of fish and serve with horseradish sauce if liked. Serves 10–12.

Pollan – *Pollan*

Pollan is a relic of the Ice Age, a freshwater herring trapped in three deep lakes, Lough Neagh, Lough Ree and Lough Derg, thousands of years ago. A similar fish is found in the Scottish lochs Castle and Mill in Dumfrieshire, and Derwentwater and Bassenthwaite in Cumbria. There is also a possible link between it and a fish found in some deep Siberian Lakes. It is certainly closely related to the *gwyniad* of Wales. The zoological name is *Coregonus albula* and the first person to describe it in Ireland is W. Thompson in his book *Natural History of Ireland* (1849–56). It is a bottom-feeder, so is seldom seen. It lives on a type of small shrimp and is sometimes captured in nets at eel-weirs but is very rare. It is essential to cook them when very fresh, rolled in seasoned flour and then fried.

Baked tench – *Cúramán*

Tench is a difficult fish to scale and it is most easily cooked floured and baked and then the skin removed before eating. Scaled it can be put into a buttered dish with a little chopped shallot or onion, salt, pepper, parsley, and butter, and baked for about 25 minutes at 200°C, 400°F, Mark 6 basting once with the juices. Then add 3–4 tablespoons of cream and a squeeze of lemon juice before serving with plenty of good boiled potatoes.

Trout baked in wine – *Breac bácáilte i bhfíon*

Trout is very nearly everyone's favourite. There are several kinds, at least in Ireland: the lake or brown trout, the salmon trout which has pink flesh; and the rainbow trout. There is also a red trout in Blarney

Lake, similar to an Irish blunt-nosed char with pink spots and an orangey-red belly, an Ice Age relic, with which it could be confused. Both are members of the salmon family and very good to eat.

The writer W. M. Thackeray in *The Irish Sketch Book*, 1843, has a mouthwatering description of cooking freshly caught salmon trout at Lake Derryclare, Connemara, on hot turf ashes which were spread on the floor of a herd's cottage eaten 'with about a hundred weight of potatoes'.

> ... Marcus proceeded to grill on the floor some of the trout which we afterwards ate with immeasurable satisfaction. They were such trouts, as when once tasted, remain for ever in the recollection of a commonly grateful mind – rich, flaky, creamy, full of flavour. A Parisian *gourmand* would have paid ten francs for the smallest *cooleen* among them; and when transported to his capital, how different in flavouring they would have been! ... The world has not had time to spoil those innocent beings before they were gobbled up with pepper and salt ... sufficient to say they were red salmon trouts – none of your white-fleshed, brown-skinned fellows.

Trout can be fried in butter or grilled after being rubbed with butter or oil. Some cooks like to roll them in oatmeal before frying, but I feel that with fish of top quality, the simpler ways of cooking are the better.

This is a good recipe for rainbow trout (I don't think fresh salmon trout is improved by cooking in wine). Barely cover the fish with white wine, add some herbs and bake. The usual trout of 1 kg (2¼ lb) or less will need only about half an hour.

Sea-farmed trout in cucumber sauce – *Breac feirme mara le hAnlann cualar áin*

Sea-farmed trout should be gutted as soon as you get it home if this has not already been done. To do so, cut behind each gill in a slant-wise fashion and pull out the gut, upwards rather than downwards. Wash well to remove any blood, and dry the trout thoroughly.

This recipe is from the *Bord Iscaigh Mhara*, cookery advisers for the Irish Aquaculture Association.

2 tablespoons butter	150 ml (¼ pint) milk
4 trout, about 275 g (10 oz) each	150 ml (¼ pint) cream
4 spring onions, chopped	3 tablespoons white wine
1 small cucumber, thinly sliced	salt and freshly ground pepper
2 tablespoons flour	chopped parsley for garnish

Lightly butter an ovenproof dish and lay the cleaned and dried fish in it. In a saucepan heat the rest of the butter, add the chopped spring onions and the cucumber and soften for a few minutes but do not let colour. Mix the flour, milk, cream and wine together well and add to the pan; stir well until the sauce thickens and is smooth. Season to taste. Pour this sauce over the fish, cover with foil and bake at 200°C, 400°F, Mark 6 for about half an hour. Garnish with chopped parsley and serve. Serves 4.

chapter four

POULTRY AND GAME –
ÉANLAITH AGUS GÉIM

Poultry

Poultry has always been popular with the Irish. Even the poorest of people usually kept a few hens, for their eggs provided valuable protein. These birds lived on potato skins and household scraps and as they ran freely they also picked up insects, worms and other food, which gave them an excellent taste. When the hens had finished laying they ended up in the pot, sometimes along with a young rabbit or a piece of bacon. It is for this reason that many Irish recipes are for braised dishes; braising was a way of making old birds tender and edible.

Roast birds were usually reserved for special occasions such as a wedding or anniversary, for nobody wanted to kill off birds while they were still providing eggs. All kinds of wild birds were eaten, including gannets and puffins, as well as their eggs.

Goose was the Christmas bird, usually boiled or casseroled, but also stuffed and roasted. Turkeys were not common at Christmas until quite recently, although they were eaten at other times throughout the year. Duck was also a favourite, especially at Whitsuntide when the early peas were ready.

Braised chicken with ham – *Sicín is liamhás galstofa*

The Irish have always liked to include ham or bacon, if available, when braising a bird.

1 chicken, about 1½ kg (3½ lb), jointed
2 tablespoons oil or butter
225 g (8 oz) ham or bacon
1 tablespoon flour
600 ml (1 pint) chicken stock
12 shallots or small onions, sliced

225 g (8 oz) mushrooms
1 teaspoon fresh marjoram, chopped
4 wild garlic leaves, or 1 clove, chopped
salt and pepper

Skin the chicken, or leave the skin on and wipe it all over well. Heat the oil in a deep frying pan and add the ham or bacon cubes, then transfer with a slotted spoon to a casserole. Brown the chicken pieces in the same pan and then sprinkle them with the flour and cook, turning them over in the oil, for 1 minute. Add the stock gradually and stir until smooth. Then add the sliced shallots or onions, the herbs and the mushrooms. Stir well and season to taste. Transfer to the casserole and mix all up well. Bring to boiling point, then cook either over low heat on top of the stove, stirring occasionally, or in a moderate oven, 180°C, 350°F, Mark 4, for about 45 minutes, or until the chicken is well cooked. Serves 4–6.

Chicken and cabbage – *Sicín agus cabáiste*

This country dish must be made with young, tender cabbage to get the proper flavour, preferably a white-headed cabbage with close leaves.

1 chicken, about 1½ kg (3½ lb), jointed
½ lemon
459 ml (¾ pint) dry cider
salt and pepper

2 tablespoons bacon dripping or oil
1 small head white cabbage, shredded
1 medium onion, chopped
juice of ½ lemon

Wipe the chicken joints and rub with the half lemon. Put into a casserole or saucepan with the cider and seasonings, and simmer very gently for about 35–40 minutes. Meanwhile, heat the bacon dripping or oil and quickly fry the shredded cabbage and chopped onion to soften but not colour. Season well, then put the chicken joints on top, pour over the lemon juice and a little of the cooking cider, cover and cook gently for a further 15 minutes. Serves 4–6.

Chicken with cream sauce – *Sicín le hanlann uachtair*

1 chicken, about 1¾ kg (4 lb), jointed
seasoned flour
2 heaped tablespoons butter
1 thick slice streaky bacon, diced
1 level teaspoon tarragon

300 ml (½ pint) double cream
125 ml (¼ pint) chicken stock
salt and freshly ground pepper
watercress in sprigs for garnish

Take the skin from the chicken joints, and roll in the seasoned flour. Heat the butter until foaming and quickly fry the chicken until it is golden all over. Remove from the pan and fry the bacon in the same fat. Put the chicken and bacon in a clean pan and add the tarragon. Combine the cream and stock and add. Stir well over heat for a few minutes until the sauce has thickened. Season to taste and serve with sprigs of watercress to provide a good crisp contrast to the creamy chicken. Serves 4–6.

Chicken and ham in jelly –
Sicín is liamhás i nGlóthach

This 'mould' was a very popular dish in Victorian times and is still good as a summer dish or for a buffet. Turkey or leftover turkey can be used instead of chicken.

1 chicken, about 2 kg (4½ lb)	25 g (1 oz) gelatine
350 g (12 oz) lean ham or bacon, chopped	1 tablespoon parsley, chopped
	salt and pepper
2 hard-boiled eggs, sliced	small bunch watercress

Simmer the chicken in salted water to cover for 1–1½ hours until it is tender but not overcooked. Let it cool in the stock and then skin, take the flesh from the bones and chop. Put the bones back in the stock and cook quite hard for about 20 minutes so that the stock reduces. Strain and let cool and then remove any fat from top of stock.

Wet a 1.5-litre (2½-pint) dish or mould with cold water. Arrange in the mould layers of the eggs, ham or bacon and chicken, sprinkling chopped parsley over each layer and seasoning to taste. Heat about 750 ml (1¼ pints) of the stock. Dissolve the gelatine in it, making sure that it is all quite absorbed and free from lumps. Pour this mixture gently over the contents of the mould, cover with foil or a plate and leave for 4 hours in the refrigerator to set. To unmould wrap a very hot cloth around the outside of the mould, invert a serving dish on top and then turn both over quickly. Garnish with fresh watercress sprigs and slice to serve. Serves at least 8.

Pot roasted chicken with apples –
Sicín potrósta le húlla

For cooking a mature bird, this is a good method for the autumn when windfall apples are available.

1 chicken, about 2 kg (4½ lb)	2 teaspoons sugar or to taste
450 g (1 lb) cooking apples, peeled and cored	½ large onion, chopped
	2 tablespoons oil
pinch each of ground cloves, ground ginger and dried sage	flour for sprinkling
700 g (1½ lb) sausage meat	600 ml (1 pint) cider or apple juice
1 large onion, sliced	salt and pepper
juice and grated peel of 1 lemon	freshly cooked carrots and peas for garnish (optional)

Wipe the chicken over and remove the lumps of fat from the inside. Peel and core the apples and slice thinly. Combine half the sausage meat with the onion slices and about three quarters of the apple slices. Add the spices, lemon peel and sugar and mix well. Stuff the bird with the mixture and secure well. Heat the oil and quickly brown the chicken all over then sprinkle with flour and cook for another minute or two, turning it in the fat. Transfer to a casserole. Roll the rest of the sausage meat into little balls about the size of large walnuts and sprinkle them with flour. Chop the remainder of the apple slices and combine with the chopped onion and put around the chicken, then arrange the sausage meat balls on top.

Heat the cider or apple juice and pour into the pan. Cover and cook gently on top of the stove or in a low oven, 150°C, 300°F, Mark 2, for 1–1½ hours. To serve, lift the bird on to a warmed serving dish, arrange the balls around it and spoon a little of the pan juices over the chicken: serve the remainder separately or if a thicker sauce is required boil it up on top of the stove to reduce it slightly. The chicken looks attractive garnished with young buttered carrots and peas. Serves 6.

Pot roasted chicken country style – Sicín potrósta ar nós tuaithe

This family recipe dates from the turn of the century.

1 chicken, about 2 kg (4½ lb)	175 g (6 oz) bacon
100 g (4 oz) oatmeal	4 medium-sized onions, sliced
1 medium-sized onion, chopped	900 g (2 lb) potatoes
2 tablespoons butter or suet	seasoned flour
2–3 tablespoons stock	3 tablespoons dripping or oil
salt and pepper	4 medium-sized carrots, sliced

If there are giblets with the bird take them out, wash all but the liver (reserve that for another use, like pâté) and cover with water, add salt and pepper, bring to the boil and simmer for half an hour. Wipe the bird inside and out and remove any lumps of fat from the inside; sprinkle with salt. Mix together the oatmeal, chopped onion, butter or suet, stock, and seasoning, stuff the bird with this mixture and secure well. Heat the dripping or oil and lightly fry the bacon, then chop and put into a casserole. Quickly brown the bird in the same fat and put on top of the bacon. Soften the onion and briefly sauté the carrots then add to the casserole.

Strain the giblet stock and make it up to about ½ litre (1 pint). Heat and pour over the chicken. Cover and cook in a moderate over, 180°C, 350°F, Mark 4, for about an hour.

Meanwhile, cut the potatoes into thick slices and blanch them in boiling water or steam them for about 5 minutes, toss them in seasoned flour, and add them to the casserole, adding a little more of the giblet stock if needed. Cover with buttered wax paper and continue cooking for a further half hour, taking off the paper for the last few minutes for browning. Serves 4–6.

Chicken and leek pie – *Pióg shicín is cainneanna*

This is a delicious pie which forms a soft jelly when cold. It can also be made with rabbit, or with a mixture of chicken and rabbit.

175 g (6 oz) shortcrust pastry
1 chicken, about 1¾ kg (4 lb) jointed, chopped and boned
4 slices thick gammon or ham
4 large leeks well cleaned and chopped

1 medium-sized onion, or two shallots, finely sliced
salt and pepper
pinch of ground mace or nutmeg
300 ml (½ pint) chicken stock
125 ml (¼ pint) double cream

Make the pastry and leave it in a cold place to rest. Meanwhile, prepare the pie. In a deep 1–1.5-litre (2-pint) pie dish place layers of the chicken, the ham, leeks and onion or shallot, adding the mace, nutmeg and seasoning, then repeating the layers until the dish is full. Add the stock, then dampen the edges of the dish before rolling out the pastry to the required size. Place the pastry over the pie and press the edges down well. Crimp them with fork. Make a small hole in the centre. Roll out the scraps of pastry and form a leaf or rosette for the top. Place this very lightly over the small hole. Brush the pastry with milk, and bake in the centre of oven at moderate heat, 180°C, 350°F, Mark 3, for 25–30 minutes. Cover the pastry with damp greaseproof paper when partially cooked if the top seems to be getting too brown. Gently heat the cream. When pie is cooked remove from oven. Carefully lift off the rosette and pour the cream in through the hole. Put back the rosette and serve. Serves 4.

Spatchcock – *Éan luathbhruite*

This is a very old method of cooking a chicken quickly. The name comes from 'dispatch-cock' meaning a bird killed and cooked in a hurry. This recipe comes from the late Mr John Gamble, F.H.C.I. of the Greenan Lodge Hotel, Dunmurry, Co. Antrim who was well known for his traditional cooking.

1 chicken, about 1¼ kg (2¾ lb)
100 g (4 oz) butter, melted
1 heaped teaspoon dry mustard powder
1 tablespoon milk

2 heaped tablespoons fresh breadcrumbs
salt and pepper
watercress for garnish

Have the chicken slit in two right through the breast. If doing this yourself start with the back rather than the breast side, and cut with a heavy knife. Flatten each half well with the flat side of the knife to prevent the chicken from curling up when cooking. Place in foil-lined grilling pan (without the rack), bone side up, and season well. Pour half the melted butter over the chicken and cook under a fairly hot grill for 7–10 minutes, watching to see the chicken halves do not burn. Turn them over and grill the breast sides.

Meanwhile, mix the mustard with milk. When the breasts are browned brush them with the mustard mixture then sprinkle with the breadcrumbs. Baste with the buttery juices and put back under the grill at lowish heat, until the breadcrumbs crisp up and colour a little. Serve at once with the cooking juices poured over the chicken, and watercress for garnish. Serves 2–4.

Braised duck – *Lacha ghalstofa*

Duck used to be immensely popular; every farmyard had a few of the endearing creatures waddling around and duck eggs were much prized, both for boiling and baking. Since the advent of the factory-bred chicken, they are much rarer.

1 duck, about 2 kg (4½ lb)	2 small heads lettuce, chopped
2 tablespoons oil or butter	½ tablespoon mint, chopped
1 tablespoon seasoned flour	½ tablespoon parsley, chopped
600 ml (1 pint) stock, preferably made with giblets	1 egg yolk, beaten with 2 tablespoons cream
450 g (1 lb) freshly shelled peas	salt and pepper

Wipe the duck over inside and out, then rub with seasoned flour. Heat the fat and quickly brown the duck over, then put into a casserole. Pour off the excess fat and add stock, the chopped mint and the chopped parsley. Season to taste, bring to the boil and pour over the duck, cover the casserole and cook at 180°C, 350°F, Mark 4 for about 20 minutes. Add the peas and lettuce to the casserole, cover again and cook a further hour, or until the duck is tender. Remove from oven, take off the lid, add the nutmeg, and taste for seasoning. Over a very low heat stir in the egg yolk and cream mixture mixing well but not letting it boil. Serve the duck either whole or jointed on a large serving dish with the peas and lettuce around it and a little of the sauce poured over the top. Serve the rest of the sauce separately. Serves 4.

Stuffed and roasted duck – *Lacha líonta is rósta*

Sage and onion stuffing is the most traditional for duck.

1 duck, about 2 kg (4½ lb)	grated
600 ml (1 pint) giblet stock, or cider	1 teaspoon dried sage
175 g (6 oz) breadcrumbs	3 tablespoons milk
liver of the bird, chopped	salt and pepper
1 small onion, chopped or finely	

Mix well the breadcrumbs, chopped liver, onion, sage, milk, salt and pepper. Stuff the duck with the mixture and secure well, tucking the wing pinions under the bird. Prick the breast of the duck all over, and lay on a rack in the roasting pan. Put in a hot preheated oven, 200°C,

400°F, Mark 6, just above the centre of the oven, covered loosely with foil. Roast for half an hour. Then take the pan out and pour off all the fat, replace in oven and roast for a further hour and then pour off all the fat again, and sprinkle the breast with salt. Lower the heat to 180°C, 350°F, Mark 4, put the duck back in the oven and roast for a further half hour without the foil covering. By this time the skin should be crisp and golden, and the duck cooked.

Put the bird on to a warmed serving dish and keep warm. Place the roasting pan on top of the stove, pour off excess fat, add the stock or cider and boil up rapidly, stirring, then season to taste. Serve the gravy separately. Serves 3–4. It is traditionally served with apple or gooseberry sauce.

Duck stuffed with apples – *Lacha líonta le húlla*

Stuff the duck with peeled and chopped cooking apples mixed with a little sugar and a pinch of sage. Secure well, then prick all over and put the duck on a rack into a hot oven, 200°C, 400°F, Mark 6, for half an hour, pour off the fat, then remove the rack and add 600 ml (1 pint) warmed dry cider to the roasting pan. Return to the oven and cook for a further hour, lowering the heat to 180°C, 350°F, Mark 4 after 40 minutes. Cover with foil if the duck seems to be getting too brown. Serve with gravy made by reducing the pan juices by boiling rapidly on top of the stove. Serves 3–4.

Soused turkey – *Turcaí*

Turkeys were eaten in Ireland in the eighteenth century if not earlier. There are several turkey recipes in Sara Power's book of 1746. Here is one for sousing the turkey:

> Get a fat Turkey Cock of a year old, kill and hang him up for two or three days, then take out the bones, and get four nutmegs and the like quantity of Mace, some betten pepper, Cinnamon, and Salt enough to season it. Put all these in the body of the Turkey and a good piece of butter; boyl in half a pint of White Wine, and half a pint of Water, with the rind of the lemon.

Stuffed roast turkey with celery sauce – *Turcaí líonta is rósta, le hAnlann soilire*

Since the turn of the century turkey has been served for Christmas, stuffed and roasted as in other countries who keep that tradition. The slight difference is, however, that the most usual sauce served with it was not cranberry (although they do grow wild here on the bogs) but a rich celery sauce (see page 125).

1 hen turkey about 5.4 kg (12 lb)	2–3 tablespoons butter
450 g (1 lb) pork sausage meat	850 ml (1½ pints) 3 cups generous
225 g (½ lb) shelled chestnuts	giblet stock or dry cider

For the stuffing (body of the bird)

8 slices crustless bread soaked in ½ cup milk	1 teaspoon thyme, chopped
raw turkey liver, chopped	1 tablespoon seedless raisins or sultanas
2 bacon rashers, chopped	3 stalks celery, finely chopped
1 tablespoon parsley, chopped	salt and pepper

First make the stuffing by soaking the bread in the milk until it is absorbed, then combine all the other ingredients and mix well. Cook the chestnuts by first making a deep slit down one side of the shell, then covering them with water and boiling for 20–30 minutes. Shell them while they are still warm as it is easier, taking off both the shell and the skin. Mix these into the sausage meat and season well.

Then wipe the bird inside and out and sprinkle with salt. Put the seasoned sausage meat in the crop and secure well, then put the other into the body part. Put the bird into a roasting tin large enough to take all the bird so that a part does not hang over the side. If this happens the juices will drip and burn giving off an unpleasant smell. Rub the bird over with the butter, pour the warmed stock or cider around, cover with foil and put into an oven preheated to 350°F, 180°C, Mark 4. Cook for about 20–25 minutes to the pound, but check that it is not overcooking; if it is, lower the heat considerably. Baste at least twice during cooking and sprinkle with salt and pepper about half-way through. Remove the foil about half an hour before the finish to let it brown.

When cooked put on to a warmed serving dish and keep warm, then pour off any excess fat and reduce the pan juices by rapid boiling on top of the stove and taste for seasoning. Add a little more cider if needed. Leave the bird for at least 5 minutes before carving, as this makes it much easier.

While the bird is cooking make the sauce. Serves 10–12.

Boiled ham is traditionally served with turkey and chicken.

Boiled or braised turkey – *Turcaí beirthe nó galstofa*

Turkey was often served boiled or braised, invariably for 'Little' or 'Woman's' Christmas – *Nollag nBan*, the Feast of the Epiphany on January 6th.

This recipe makes a very moist and pleasant-tasting turkey.

1 turkey, about 4½ kg (10 lb)	1 celery heart, sliced
900 g (2 lb) pork sausage meat	sprig of fresh thyme, chopped
salt and pepper	2 tablespoons parsley, chopped
pinch of sage	1½ litres (2½ pints) giblet stock
225 g (8 oz) salt fat pork, diced	2 tablespoons butter
6 carrots, sliced	2 tablespoons flour
2 medium-sized onions, stuck with cloves	4–5 tablespoons thick cream

Wipe the turkey inside and out, then sprinkle with salt. Mix into the sausage meat the salt and pepper, mace or nutmeg, sage, thyme and half of the chopped parsley. Stuff the bird with the mixture and secure it well. Heat a large pan and put the diced salt pork into it. When the fat runs out of it quickly brown the turkey and the vegetables in the fat. Add two pints of the giblet stock and season to taste. Cover the pan and cook the bird very slowly for 3–4 hours. Turn at least once during cooking, and finish with the breast upwards. When it is nearly ready make the sauce. Heat the butter and when foaming add the flour, then gradually the stock, stirring well. When it is thick and smooth stir in the cream and the rest of the parsley. Taste for seasoning. To dish up, put the turkey on a large warm dish with freshly cooked root vegetables around it, pour over a little of the sauce and serve the rest separately.

To serve cold, skin the bird and pour all the sauce over it, leave it to get cold, then garnish as wished. Serves 12–14.

Braised goose with dumplings – *Gé ghalstofa*

Goose was the usual bird for the festive occasions in Ireland until this century, often boiled or braised, for it must be remembered that in the humbler homes there was no oven, just a big turf fire with hooks and jacks and large black pot (which accounts for the term 'to take pot luck'). There is an old saying in Ireland that if you eat goose on Michaelmas, September 29th, you will have good fortune all the year round.

> Now this young farmer partook of boiled goose in his own house on an average once a week – that is to say, every Sunday since Michaelmas. And a very savoury dish too, is goose and dumplings cooked this way. But then the goose was always dismembered before it was put into the pot with the dumplings.
>
> From *Knocknagow* by Charles J. Kickham, *c.* 1870s.

The Michaelmas goose is usually what is known as a 'green goose', that is it has been feeding on the stubble after the harvest is gathered, which makes it very good to eat. The way to choose a goose is given in Dean Swift's poem from *The Progress of Poetry*:

The farmer's goose, who in the stubble,
Has fed without restraint or trouble,
Grown fat with corn and sitting still,
Can scarce get o'er the barndoor still;
And hardly waddles forth to cool
Her belly in the neighbours pool:
Nor loudly cackles at the door;
For cackling shows the goose is poor.

The Irish Folklore Commission has an interesting account of how the Christmas goose was cooked over the turf fire around the turn of the century and possibly earlier, in County Clare.

The Christmas goose was cooked thus; put the goose into a pot half-filled with cold water; hang over the fire till the water boils; take off and place on iron bar and/or stand beside the fire with coals under for about one hour. Then place coals on top; baste from time to time; add parsnips to the side of the goose and put slices of bacon on top of the goose. The fire must be kept good for this cooking. The top (breast) side will be a beautiful golden brown when well done.

1 goose, about 4½ kg (10lb), jointed	2–3 medium-sized parsnips,
seasoned flour	chopped
2 tablespoons goose fat	1 head celery, chopped
2 large onions, stuck with cloves	pinch dried sage
5–6 medium-sized carrots, sliced	1 litre (1¾ pints) giblet stock

Dumplings

225 g (8 oz) flour	pinch ground nutmeg
100 g (4 oz) shredded suet	1 tablespoon parsley, chopped
1 teaspoon salt	

Wipe over the goose joints and prick the breast skin with a thin fork, then roll in seasoned flour. Heat the goose fat and turn the joints in it until they are brown all over. Transfer to a large heavy pot and brown the vegetables in the same fat. Arrange these round the goose and sprinkle with sage. Heat the stock and pour it into the pot, and after bringing it to the boil, cover and simmer for about 1½ hours.

Meanwhile, make the dumplings. Mix all the dumpling ingredients together, then add enough water to make a soft yet pliable dough. With floured hands roll it into small balls. Put the balls in the pot with the goose and cook for a further half hour adding a very little more liquid to the pan if necessary.

Serve the goose on a large warmed dish with the vegetables and dumplings arranged around the edges. Serves 10–12. It can be left whole and stuffed with cooked potatoes mixed with onion, chopped bacon, the goose liver and herbs.

Game

Formerly game was very plentiful in Ireland with a fine variety. From the earliest times it has been used for food by all classes of society. It is only recently that the price has risen so steeply as to make most of it outside the reach of the majority of pockets. Feynes Moryson in his *Itinerary* wrote in 1605:

> Ireland hath great plenty of Pheasants, as I have known sixtie served at one feast, and abound much more with Rayles: but Partridges are somewhat rare:

He also says:

> There be very many Eagles, and a great plenty of Hares, Conies . . . And of Venison . . . yet in many woods they have many red Deare . . .

W. H. Maxwell in *Wild Sports of the West*, 1832, tells of Bishop Beresford who 'Never went a step without four long-tailed black horses to his carriage, and two mounted grooms behind him.' The otter-killer remarks: '. . . och hone! It was he who knew how to live like a bishop . . . one time I went with a haunch of red-deer and a bittern to the palace, that never less than twenty sat down in the parlour, and, in troth, there was double that number in the hall, for nobody came or went without being well taken care of.'

Most game profits from being hung for a few days and all game should be marinated before cooking.

Marinade for game

This marinade will do for any game. Double the quantity for large joints.

2 tablespoons olive oil	a few juniper berries, crushed
150 ml (¼ pint) red wine	sprig of rosemary
150 ml (¼ pint) red wine vinegar	2 bay leaves
1 medium-sized onion, or 2 shallots, sliced	salt and pepper

Mix all the ingredients then put the meat to be cooked in the marinade for at least 4 hours, preferably overnight, turning from time to time.

Jugged hare – *Giorria casaróil*

Hare is still very reasonable in price in Ireland, but with so much coursing they are getting difficult to find in the wild. Young hares or leverets are the best buy. The way to tell a young hare is by the claws, for an old animal has blunt ones.

1 large hare, about 1½–2 kg (3–4 lb) jointed and marinated overnight
seasoned flour
100 g (4 oz) butter, or 4 tablespoons cooking oil
175 g (6 oz) bacon or raw ham, chopped
1 celery heart, sliced
4 medium-sized onions, sliced or 12 button onions
4 medium-sized carrots, sliced

1 tablespoon parsley, chopped
2 teaspoons thyme, chopped (or 1 teaspoon dried)
2 bay leaves
3 tablespoons redcurrant jelly
1 glass port wine (optional)
750 ml (1½ pints) stock
blood of hare (optional)
1 level tablespoon cornflour (optional)
salt and freshly ground pepper

Pat the hare dry and roll in the seasoned flour. Heat the butter or oil and brown the joints all over, then put into a casserole with the pan juices. Add the chopped bacon or ham, the vegetables and the herbs, and season to taste. Heat the stock and pour over the joints. Add 2–3 tablespoons of the marinade, cover and cook at 160–80°C, 325–50°F, Mark 3–4 for 2–2½ hours or until tender. Add the redcurrant jelly and wine if using it, half an hour before serving, and stir well. If using the blood to thicken (the poulterer will give it to you in a small carton if you ask) stir a few tablespoons of hot stock into it, then add to the casserole about 15 minutes before serving, but do not reboil. If you are not using the blood but want the gravy thicker, take out the hare joints, add the cornflour creamed in a little of the marinade, stir well and gently boil up until it thickens. Replace hare to reheat.

Braised rabbit – *Coinín galstofa*

Rabbit was the great food for country people for many years. Tomás Ó Crohan in *The Islandman* tells us of the many rabbits they caught on the Blasket Islands when he was young: 'When we had all come to the boat and put the game together, we had eight dozen rabbits – a dozen a-piece.' Maurice O'Sullivan in *Twenty Years A-Growing* writes of the same island and rabbit stew: 'We sat down to dinner, a savoury dinner it was – a fine stew of rabbits and plenty of soup.' Young rabbits, called 'graziers' in Ireland, can be roasted as with the body of the hare, wrapped in bacon.

1 rabbit, jointed and marinated
3 tablespoons oil
1 large onion, sliced
3–4 carrots, sliced
flour

pinch of powdered marjoram
salt and pepper
600 ml (1 pint) chicken stock, or half stock, half cider

Pat the joints dry. Heat the oil and fry the joints on all sides until brown. Lift them out and put into a casserole. In the same oil lightly fry the vegetables, add the marjoram, sprinkle a little flour over and stir. Add the stock gradually stirring until smooth, then stir in a few tablespoons of the marinade. Pour this over the rabbit, cover and cook in a moderate oven, 180°C, 350°F, Mark 4, for about half an hour, then lower the heat to 150°C, 300°F, Mark 2 for a further 1½ hours or until tender.

Rabbit pie – *Piog coinín*

The braise above can be used as the basis for a delicious rabbit pie. Take the meat when cooled from the bones, add 2 or 3 rashers chopped bacon, the stock to come up to within 2.5 cm (1 inch) of the rim of the dish, then cover with rich shortcrust or flaky pastry and cook for about half an hour.

Braised venison – *Oiseoil ghalstofa*

The venison party went off quite well, the haunch was perfectly cooked for little Biddy Rogers was engaged to baste it, so that Catherine was able to devote herself to her stove, the oven having been got over early in the morning.

From *The Irish Journal of Elizabeth Smith*, writing of Baltiboys House, Blessington, Co. Wicklow, 1849. Elizabeth Smith was the great grandmother of Ninette de Valois, the famous director of the Royal Ballet, who was born at Baltiboys House.

Venison is now becoming available again in Ireland at a reasonable price, owing to the culling of herds in Phoenix Park, Killarney, Powerscourt and other places. It is a rich, lean and delicious meat, about half the price of beef which in a way it resembles. All venison should be hung for several days before marinating and cooking. For venison double the amount of wine and omit the vinegar.

2½–3 kg (5½–6½ lb) of venison, haunch, saddle or shoulder, marinated for 2–3 days
2 tablespoons oil, preferably olive
3 tablespoons butter
225 g (8 oz) bacon, diced

2 large onions, roughly chopped
600 ml (1 pint) beef stock
1 tablespoon flour
2 tablespoons redcurrant jelly
150 ml (¼ pint) port wine
salt and pepper

Pat the venison dry. Combine the oil and 2 tablespoons of the butter in a heavy pan and when hot add the diced bacon and let it crisp up, then transfer it to a large casserole or roasting pan. Brown the joint in the same fat, and add to the casserole. Soften the onion and add to the casserole.

Boil up the marinade rapidly on top of the stove until it is reduced by half. Add the stock and reduce the mixture a little more, then add to the casserole, cover and put into a moderate oven, 180°C, 350°F, Mark 3, and continue to cook for a total cooking time of about 30 minutes to the pound, until the meat is tender. Take the meat from the roasting pan and put it on to a warmed serving dish to keep warm.

Work the flour into the remaining tablespoon of butter until it is absorbed. Heat the roasting pan juices and boil to reduce a little, then add the flour and butter mixture in little pieces stirring all the time until the sauce thickens slightly. Add the redcurrant jelly and the port, stir as it heats and finally taste for seasoning. Pour a little of the pan gravy over the joint and serve the rest separately. Serves 10–12 people.

Roast venison – *Oiseoil rósta*

After marinating the joint should be well larded, either with bacon rashers over it or plenty of good dripping or butter. Roast it in a hot oven, 220°C, 425°F, Mark 7 for half an hour, then with the heat reduced to 190°C, 375°F, Mark 5 for a total of 20 minutes to the ½ kilo (pound) with frequent basting. Reduce the marinade and halfway through the cooking time pour 1 or 2 cups of hot marinade over the meat to baste it. For well done meat increase cooking time by 20 minutes for every 1½ kilos (3 pounds).

Grouse – *Cearc fhraoigh*

There are now very few grouse in Ireland. To conserve them the shooting season, which starts on September 1st, is limited to one month. Perhaps the best place to find grouse are on the Wicklow moors at the foot of the Wicklow Hills, for heather covered slopes are their natural habitat. Poachers are said to be responsible for at least a part of the scarcity but the proximity to urban areas is another hazard.

Therefore if the odd brace of grouse comes your way treat them with the respect they deserve; serve them simply cooked, so that their exquisite flavour can be savoured and remembered.

Grouse have delicate skin so pluck them carefully and see that they have been hung for a week to ten days depending on the weather temperature. Young birds are easy to recognize by having clean claws and no moulting ridge. Grouse are not stuffed in the usual way, the old traditional method is to put a lump of fresh butter inside the birds mixed with some wild bilberries or *fraughans*, the natural food which gives them their beautiful colour.

2 grouse	2 grouse livers
3 heaped tablespoons butter	2 slices of bread large enough to go
2 teaspoons lemon juice	under bird
salt and pepper	300 ml (½ pint) red wine, warmed
handful of bilberries if available	2 teaspoons rowanberry or
6 slices of fat bacon	redcurrant jelly

Combine 2 heaped tablespoons of the butter, lemon juice, salt and pepper and the bilberries. Wipe the birds inside and out, then halve the butter mixture and put half into the body of each bird. Wrap the birds with the bacon, place in a roasting pan and cover with foil. Bake at 220°C, 425°F, Mark 7 for 15 minutes. Then remove the foil and baste with the warmed red wine. Lower the heat to 200°C, 400°F, Mark 6 for a further 10–15 minutes, then baste again and lift off the bacon. Meanwhile, fry up the grouse livers in a little of the remaining butter and toast the bread. Mash up the livers, butter the toast and spread with liver. Spread the bacon slices with the rowanberry or redcurrant jelly and roll them up. Lay a bird on top of each piece of toast, surround with the bacon rolls and serve.

Partridge with apple and onion purée –
Pairtrisc le hÚsc Úll is oinniún

Partridge, like grouse, is now rare in Ireland.

2 partridge
4 rashers streaky bacon
3 tablespoons chicken dripping or butter
300 ml (½ pint) dry cider
4 tablespoons lard or oil
450 g (1 lb) cooking apples, peeled and thinly sliced
450 g (1 lb) onions, peeled and thinly sliced
salt and pepper
pinch of ground cinnamon
150 ml (¼ pint) sweet white wine or sweet cider

Fry the rashers over the breast of the birds. Put the dripping or butter in a roasting pan and place the birds in pan. Cover with foil and roast at 200°C, 400°F, Mark 6 for 20 minutes, then take out the roasting pan, pour off excess fat and add the dry cider. Lower the heat to 180°C, 350°F, Mark 4 and continue cooking for a total cooking time of 20 minutes to the ½ kilo (pound). Remove the foil and let it cook a further 10 minutes to brown before serving.

Meanwhile, make the purée. Heat the lard or oil and add the apple and onion slices to stew over a low heat, with a lid, so that they soften but do not colour. When they are all soft, drain off any excess fat or oil, season with the salt and pepper add the cinnamon and lastly the wine or sweet cider. Continue to simmer over a very low heat until it is like a thick syrup. Serve the birds with the hot purée served separately. This purée is excellent with roast pheasant which is cooked as the partridge.

Pheasant with celery and cream –
Piasún agus soilire is Uachtar

There are still plenty of pheasants in Ireland for about 2 months from October. They should be hung, tail downwards, for at least 4 days and up to a week in cold weather. It is ready to cook if the tail feathers pull out easily. If not hung long enough the pheasant will be dry and tasteless.

1 well-hung hen pheasant
100 g (4 oz) butter
2 rashers bacon, diced
300 ml (½ pint) chicken stock
1 teaspoon parsley, chopped
pinch of tarragon
150 ml (¼ pint) port wine
2 celery hearts cut in rounds
1 large egg yolk, beaten
300 ml (½ pint) thick cream
salt and pepper

Wipe the bird over. Heat the butter and quickly brown the bird all over. Put the rashers in the pan and cook them a little to let the fat run out, but not to get crisp. Transfer to a casserole, and add the stock, parsley, tarragon, port, salt and pepper and bring to the boil, stirring all the time. Cover and place in oven at 200°C, 400°F, Mark 6 for 20 minutes, then add the celery. Cover again and continue cooking for about 20 minutes or until the bird is tender.

Remove from oven and put the bird and the celery on to a warmed serving dish and keep warm. Mix the beaten egg yolk with the cream, add 2 tablespoons of the hot stock and stir quickly. Add this mixture to the casserole stirring well as it heats up, but do not let it boil. Pour a little of the pan gravy over the bird and serve the rest separately. Serves 6.

Pigeons in Guinness – *Colúir i leann dubh*

Pigeons are plentiful at certain times of the year. They can be cooked in many ways.

2 plump young pigeons	thyme and parsley, chopped
4 tablespoons butter or oil	300 ml (½ pint) Guinness
seasoned flour	225 g (8 oz) mushrooms
1 large onion, chopped	squeeze of lemon juice
450 g (1 lb) carrots, sliced	salt and pepper
1 sprig each of marjoram,	

Wipe the pigeons over. Heat all but a small knob of butter and brown the pigeons quickly all over. Sprinkle some seasoned flour over them, turn them over heat for a minute, then transfer to a casserole. In the same fat soften the onion, carrots, and the chopped herbs, add the Guinness and 300 ml (½ pint) of water and boil up stirring well. Season to taste, then pour over the birds, cover and cook in a moderate oven, 180°C, 350°F, Mark 4, for 1½ hours. Meanwhile, wipe over the mushrooms and remove stalks, then bring to the boil enough water to cover them, salt it and add the knob of butter and a squeeze of lemon. Put in the mushrooms, bring back to boiling point, cover tightly, and boil for 5 minutes. Drain and add the mushrooms to the pigeons. Serves 4.

Pigeon pie – *Pióg cholúr*

This is a very old recipe for a dish that was once very popular. Originally the pigeons were put into the pie cut up, but still on the bone. I find this makes eating difficult. It is much easier if you cut off the breast and wing fillets and use these. The other parts of the bird can be made into casserole or soups.

225 g (8 oz) shortcrust pastry	1 hard-boiled egg, chopped
8 breast fillets from 4 pigeons	1 tablespoon parsley, chopped
225 g (8 oz) stewing steak cut in	pinch of marjoram
pieces	salt and pepper
seasoned flour	

Make the shortcrust pastry and chill until needed. Wipe the breasts over and put into a pan with the steak pieces, cover with salted water and bring to the boil, then simmer for half an hour. Remove from the stock, strain, and reserve the stock. Roll the pigeon and steak in seasoned flour and put into a deep 1-litre (2-pint) pie dish. Add the chopped egg, parsley, marjoram, salt and pepper then the stock, filling the pie dish to within an inch of the top. Dampen the edges of the pie dish, roll out the pastry to fit and put over pressing down the edges well. Make a small hole in the centre and cover it lightly with a rosette made from the trimmings. Brush with a little milk and put into a hot oven, 220°C, 425°F, Mark 7, for 15 minutes, then lower the heat to 180°C, 350°F, Mark 4 and cook for an hour covering the crust with paper if it seems to be getting too brown. Serves 4.

Plover — *Pilibín*

Plovers are plentiful in Ireland. There are two kinds, the golden plover which is the best to eat, and the grey plover which is good, but not as fine as the golden variety. Large flocks can sometimes be seen. It is a very small bird; one or two should be served per person depending on the course.

First wrap the birds well in bacon, or rub them well with butter, and roast in a hot oven, 220°C, 425°F, Mark 7 for about 15 minutes. They can be served on large *croûtons* of fried bread and a little red wine or port mixed with the pan juices boiled up on top of the stove and well seasoned can be poured over them.

Snipe cooked over turf — *Naoscach bruite os cionn móna*

The snipe is a very fat bird, but its fat does not cloy, and very rarely disagrees even with the weakest stomach. It is much esteemed as a delicious and well-flavoured dish, and is cooked in the same manner as woodcock.

From *Wild Sports of the West* by W. H. Maxwell, 1832.

Snipe is a very delicate small bird which can weigh as little as 50g (2oz). It is skinned, not plucked, and it is not drawn before cooking. Skin the birds by cutting off the wings and head, then rub the skin away from the breast and gently pull back. The skin will come off like a jacket. Get a turf fire hot, but see that there are no flames. Put the rack over to get hot, then put the birds whole on to the rack and grill for about 7 minutes each side. Allow 3–4 per person.

Wild duck with port — *Fia-lacha le pórtfhíona*

Wild duck must be hung for two or three days when a greenish tinge will come on the thin skin underneath. Widgeon, teal and woodcock can be cooked in the same way but will only need half the cooking as they are much smaller. Allow two wild duck for more than two people.

This recipe is adapted from *The Lady's Assistant* by Charlotte Mason of Dublin, 1778:

2 wild duck
4 tablespoons butter
300 ml (½ pint) port wine, warmed

juice of 1 orange or 1 lemon
salt and pepper

Rub the birds with the butter and roast in a hot oven, 200°C, 400°F, Mark 6, for 20–30 minutes. Add the warmed port, salt and pepper, and put back for 10 minutes. Take from the oven and add the orange or lemon juice. Put the birds on a warmed serving dish and keep warm while you boil up the juices to reduce a little. Serve with the juices poured over the birds.

Woodcock – *Creabhar*

This can be cooked in the same way as the wild duck with port, but it should only be roasted for 15 minutes, then put into either a chafing dish or a thick frying pan and cooking continued there. The intestines or 'trail' as it is called should be chopped up and put into the pan as well.

If the trail is too strong for you, then cook it separately for those who like it and serve on crustless fried bread with the bird mounted on top.

chapter five

MEATS – *FEOLTA*

Today meat is probably the favourite food of the Irish but this has not always been so, especially with regard to beef. Cattle were highly prized and cows were kept for their milk, from which were made curds and cheeses, and for their hides which were used not only for *curraghs* (hide boats) but also for utensils, clothing and shoes.

Stevens, describing Limerick in 1690 in his journal, observed: 'the people generally being the greatest lovers of milk I ever saw which they eat and drink in about twenty different sorts of ways and what is strangest love it best when sourest'. Unwanted bull calves were eaten, as were old cows past their milking period and animals killed or maimed by accidents. But generally the meat was eaten on great occasions and most of the good meat was exported.

When meat was eaten it was often mutton rather than beef, and of course the most general meat for many hundreds of years was pork or bacon.

The picture changed somewhat in the eighteenth century when the large houses had been established, and even the inns were serving food. Mr George Packenham, visiting his brother in Westmeath in 1737, found 'plenty of flesh, fish and fowl – the beef very large and sweet – and good French claret'. Mrs Delany, the English wife of Dr Patrick Delany, the Dean of Down, found the following at Newton Gore, near Killala on June 12th, 1732.

He (Mr Mahone) keeps a man cook and has given entertainments of twenty dishes of meat! The people of this country don't seem solicitous of having *good dwellings* or more furniture than is absolutely necessary – *hardly so much*, but they make it up in eating and drinking! I have not seen less than fourteen dishes of meat for dinner, and seven for supper, during my peregrinations; and they not only treat us at their houses magnificently, but if we are to go to an inn, they constantly provide us with a basket crammed with good things; no people *can be more hospitable or obliging*, and there is not only great abundance but great order and neatness.

However, these large meals were the privilege only of the landed gentry. Many thousands lived on a bare subsistence of oatmeal, milk and potatoes with eggs, old fowl, game or fish when available.

The meat dishes given in this book range from the humblest to those that were eaten only at the richer tables.

Beef

Beef stew with dumplings – *Mairteoil le domplagáin*

In Tipperary, which formerly was not a sheep-raising county, this was often called 'Irish stew' but genuine Irish stew is made with lamb or mutton. A little chopped bacon may be added to this, also a small swede, chopped, can be added if liked.

900 g (2 lb) stewing beef, shin or
    chuck, cut into cubes
seasoned flour
2 tablespoons beef dripping or oil
3–4 medium-sized onions, chopped
6 small carrots, sliced

1 bay leaf
1 sprig thyme
1 sprig parsley
salt and pepper
850 ml (1½ pints) stock

Dumplings
4 tablespoons flour
2 tablespoons fresh breadcrumbs
2 tablespoons grated suet
1 tablespoon mixed herbs, chopped

Roll the meat in seasoned flour. Heat the fat and quickly brown the meat. Put with the vegetables, herbs and seasoning into a saucepan. Add the stock, bring to the boil and simmer gently for 1–1½ hours, or until tender.

Meanwhile, make the dumplings. Combine the dumpling ingredients, roll into small balls and chill. When the meat is tender add the dumplings, bring back to the boil, and simmer, uncovered, for about 10 minutes, then serve. Serves 4.

Beef braised with Guinness—
Mairteoil ghalstofa le leann dubh

This was a nineteenth-century dish made originally with porter, a weaker dark beer than Guinness. A pale beer can be used if preferred.

2 tablespoons beef dripping or oil
2 bay leaves
1¼ kg (2¾ lb) stewing beef, cut into chunks
1 large onion, sliced

2 tablespoons seasoned flour
150 ml (¼ pint) Guinness
salt and pepper
225 g (8 oz) carrots, sliced
1 tablespoon parsley, chopped

Heat the fat and put in the bay leaves, then add the beef and brown quickly. Push aside and add the onion and just soften it. Sprinkle with the flour and let it brown, then add the Guinness and an equal amount of water, or a little more if needed, to barely cover. Season well and add the carrots. Bring to the boil, then cover and braise in a slow oven, 160°C, 325°F, Mark 3 for about 1½ hours. Check to see if it is drying up, and if so add a little more liquid. Check also for tenderness, and if necessary continue cooking a little longer. Before serving, sprinkle with the chopped parsley. Serves 4–5.

Beefsteak and kidney pie—
Pióg stéig mhairteola is duán

700 g (1½ lb) stewing beef, cut in cubes
350 g (12 oz) ox kidney, skinned, fatty core removed, chopped
2 tablespoons dripping or oil
1 large onion, sliced

1 beef stock cube
flour
pinch of ground marjoram
pinch of mixed spice
salt and pepper
225 g (8 oz) shortcrust pastry

Heat the oil and quickly fry the beef and kidney, turning to brown them all over. Take out and put into a saucepan. Soften the sliced onion in the same fat and crumble the stock cube into the pan with a sprinkling of flour. Add the marjoram, mixed spice and seasoning, mix well. Add about 600 ml (1 pint) of water and stir until it thickens.

Pour the mixture over the meat, bring to the boil, cover and simmer until the meat is tender, about 1½ hours. Transfer to a 1-litre (2-pint) pie dish, allowing the liquid to come no higher than 1 cm (½ inch) from the top. Dampen the rim of the pie dish, roll the pastry out to the right size, lay over, and press down the edges with a fork or a pastry crimper. Make a small hole in the top and cover it lightly with a small rosette, made from the pastry scraps. Brush with milk and bake at 200°C, 400°F, Mark 6 for 15 minutes, then lower heat to 180°C, 350°F, Mark 4, for a further 15 minutes. Serves 4.

If liked, mushrooms can be added just before putting on the pastry crust.

Beef olives

This was a popular eighteenth-century method which was also done with thin slices of corned beef, ham or pork. This recipe is adapted from *The Lady's Assistant* by Charlotte Mason, Dublin, 1778.

12 thin slices rump beef
2 heaped tablespoons fresh
  breadcrumbs
1 medium-sized onion, grated or
  finely chopped
grated rind of 1 lemon
1 tablespoon mixed fresh herbs,
  chopped
2 eggs yolks
salt and pepper
1–2 tablespoons cooking fat or oil
flour
600 ml (1 pint) beef stock

Flatten the beef slices by banging them with a rolling pin. Combine the breadcrumbs, onion, lemon rind, herbs, egg yolks and seasoning and mix well. Spoon a little of the mixture on to each slice of beef, then roll them up tightly and secure with a cocktail stick. Heat the fat and quickly fry the 'olives' all over. Drain off excess fat, sprinkle with flour and cook for another minute, add the stock and bring to the boil. Transfer to an ovenproof dish, cover and cook for about 1½ hours at 180°C, 350°F, Mark 4, until tender. Serve with some of the pan gravy poured over them. Serves 4–6.

Collard beef – *Mairteoil rothlaithe*

The name is a contraction of 'collared beef', possibly because it was often served cold surrounded by salad vegetables such as watercress, cucumber, and pickles. It was a popular dish in Ireland when I was a child and always served at Christmas.

1½–2 kg (3¼–4½ lb) silverside or
  topside
salt and pepper
4 rashers streaky bacon
½ teaspoon each allspice, whole
peppercorns, sage and thyme
a sprinkling of ground clove,
  nutmeg and ginger
2 bay leaves

Trim the beef of fat, bone and gristle and cut it across horizontally into three pieces and lay each one out flat. Sprinkle the first piece with salt and pepper and half the spices, then lay 2 bacon rashers on top. Place the second piece of beef over the bacon and repeat, placing the third slice on top. Press down well and wrap tightly, either in double foil or muslin, and secure well by twisting the foil or tying with twine if using muslin.

Put into a large saucepan and cover with water. Bring gently to the boil, then simmer for 3–4 hours. Cool slightly, then take out and remove the foil or muslin. Put into a dish which it just fits, put a plate over it and a weight on top. Chill then serve. Serves about 8.

Beef Galantine – *Rollóg mhairteola nó Galaintín*

450 g (1 lb) minced lean beef
225 g (8 oz) minced cooked ham or
bacon
2 hard-boiled eggs
100 g (4 oz) fresh breadcrumbs

1 teaspoon mixed herbs, chopped
pinch of nutmeg
salt and pepper
1 large egg or 2 small ones, beaten
3–4 tablespoons good beef stock

Glaze
15 g (½ oz) gelatine
150 ml (½ pint) beef stock
1 teaspoon browning

Mix the minced meats with the breadcrumbs and herbs and seasonings, then add the beaten egg and 3 tablespoons of the stock, and mix. Add a little more stock if it seems too dry. Grease a 700 g (1½ lb) loaf tin and bake, covered and placed in a roasting pan, half-filled with hot water, for 1½ hours at 180°C, 350°F, Mark 4. Meanwhile make the glaze: boil together in a saucepan the gelatine, stock and browning for 15 minutes. Cool to lukewarm and brush over the meat. Serves 4.

Pot roast of beef – *Mairteoil photrósta*

In many remote parts of the country today pot-roasting is still done as it was in our forefather's time, over hearth fires or open grates. The pot-oven was a flat-bottomed pot with a flat lid standing on three legs. Sometimes these pots were suspended over the fire on the crook and red turf embers were put on the lid. When there was a hearth fire the hot turf was raked to one side, the pot put over these and some more hot turf put on top, which gave it heat from both above and below.

Take a fairly lean piece of beef from the top rib, known in Ireland as the 'housekeeper's cut', trim it and tie around with twine. It is better to get a thick high joint for this method. Heat a little fat and quickly brown it on all sides, then put into a heavy saucepan with a bay leaf, about 3 whole cloves, some whole allspice, 2 or 3 sliced carrots and 1 large sliced onion. Season well, add about 2 cups of good beef stock and let it boil, then cover and simmer over low heat for 30 minutes to the pound or longer, until the beef is tender. Add stock if it runs dry, but only a very little, if the heat is low enough it should not be needed. It is essential that it cooks long enough to make the beef really tender.

Corned beef – *Mairteoil shaillte*

Corned beef is sometimes called 'salt beef'. Two cuts can be used – the brisket, which is fat and lean in layers, and silverside, or tail-end, which is all lean with just a small rim of fat. Pork can also be done in the same way.

Boil together 2½ litres (4½ pints) of water, 450 g (1 lb) coarse salt, 100 g (4 oz) brown sugar, 2 teaspoons saltpetre, 3 bay leaves and a pinch each of whole cloves, allspice and black peppercorns. Remove any scum that forms and simmer until it is clear. Then let it get quite cold. Rub 3–4 kg (6½–9 lb) meat with common salt all over, getting into the bone and seams if possible. Stand in a large glass or earthenware container and cover entirely with the pickling liquid. Cover and weigh down and leave for 3 days, turning every day. Take the meat from the liquid and rub again with salt, then put back and leave for another 4 days. In cold weather the meat can be left for several weeks if you choose, but will need a check to see if mould is forming. If it is, remove the mould and bring again to the boil with 4 heaped tablespoons more of salt, and 1 of sugar, added to the liquid. Then soak the meat overnight in this liquid. Discard the liquid before serving.

Corned beef and cabbage – *Mairteoil shaillte le cabáiste*

Probably the most famous of all Irish beef dishes, corned beef and cabbage is still a great favourite in the winter months. This is Mrs Sarah Kenny's recipe.

2 kg (4½ lb) corned beef, soaked overnight
1 teaspoon dry mustard
pepper
sprig of thyme

sprig of parsley
2 large onions, 1 stuck with cloves
2 large carrots, sliced
1 large cabbage, quartered

Put the meat into a large saucepan with the mustard powder and pepper and cover with cold water. Bring to the boil and remove any scum. Add all the other ingredients except the cabbage and bring back to the boil, then simmer for 50 minutes. Add the cabbage quarters, bring to the boil again, then simmer for another half hour. Serve with cabbage arranged around the meat. Serves 8.

Spiced beef – *Mairteoil spíosraithe*

Traditionally eaten at Christmas time in Ireland, usually on St Stephen's Day, spiced beef can be found then in most butcher's shops, sometimes tied with red ribbon or with a sprig of holly. It is eaten either hot or cold.

After soaking a corned beef overnight, pat it dry. Mix together 2 heaped teaspoons each of ground cloves, allspice and cinnamon, and a pinch of nutmeg. Rub this mixture well all over the beef, and leave for at least 4 hours.

In the bottom of a large saucepan put a bed of chopped onions, chopped carrots and mixed herbs. If you have a few beef bones add these too with the large rib bones chopped. Rest the spiced beef on top of this and barely cover with warm water. Bring to the boil, then simmer gently for 30 minutes to the pound. During the last hour add 300 ml (½ pint) of Guinness, bring back to the boil, and then simmer again for the remainder of the time. Serves about 8.

Roast beef with batter pudding – *Mairteoil rósta*

Batter pudding is the Irish version of Yorkshire pudding. The Irish like their meat quite well-cooked, which rather spoils a good joint of beef in my opinion. A largish piece of beef cooked in this way will have the best flavour; small joints are disappointing.

2 kg (4 lb) sirloin or best rib beef, bone in
2 tablespoons beef dripping or oil
black pepper

mixed herbs
240 ml (8 fl oz) cider, beef stock or red wine

Batter
4 rounded tablespoons flour
½ teaspoon salt
1 large egg

300 ml (½ pint) milk
boiling beef dripping

Preheat the oven to 200°C, 400°F, Mark 6. Heat the fat and quickly sear the beef on all sides to seal the juices in. Put into a roasting pan with the dripping or oil, and sprinkle the herbs and black pepper over the meat. Put into the hot oven and cook for half an hour.

As soon as the meat is in the oven, make the batter:

Sift the flour and salt and make a well in the middle. Add the beaten egg and half the milk and beat for about 5 minutes to form a smooth paste. Add the remaining milk and beat for a further 5 minutes (3 minutes will do with an electric beater). Leave in a cool place, uncovered, until required.

After the meat has cooked for half an hour, lower the heat to 190°C, 375°F, Mark 5. Baste, then continue to cook, for a total roasting time of 16 minutes to the pound for rare beef, 20 minutes for medium, or longer for well done.

Half an hour before the end of the beef roasting time cook the batter. Pour about 2 tablespoons of the hot beef dripping from the roasting pan into a fairly shallow tin about 7 inches square. Add a few drops of cold water to the cold batter and beat it for a moment then pour the batter into the fat. It should sizzle as it goes in. Put the tin right at the top of the hot oven for about 30 minutes.

When the beef is done take it from the oven and put on to a warmed serving dish and keep warm. Scrape down the sides of the roasting pan and add the cider, beef stock or red wine over heat. Stir well, season and boil up quickly to reduce.

Serve very hot with the roast beef and the batter pudding which should be served as soon as it has risen or, like a soufflé, it will fall.

Steak flamed with whiskey – *Stéig lasta le hUisce beatha*

This is often called Gaelic steak and I think it is comparatively modern. It is served in many restaurants.

Cook a fillet steak in a little butter in a very hot pan (do not use a non-stick pan, as you cannot get it hot enough). When cooked as wished, pour 2 tablespoons of warmed Irish whiskey over the meat and set it alight, then take out the meat and put it on to a warmed dish. Add 2–3 tablespoons of cream to the pan juices, mix well and boil up to reduce a little, then pour over. Serve at once garnished with watercress.

Wellington steak – *Stéig Wellington*

This was said to be a favourite of the Duke of Wellington, who was born in Ireland and it is sometimes also known as beef Wellington. It is good for a whole beef fillet and makes an excellent party dish.

450 g (1 lb) flaky pastry	chopped
1 fillet steak, about 1¼ kg (2¾ lb)	salt and pepper
450 g (1 lb) mushrooms, finely	175 g (6 oz) butter

Make the pastry first, and chill until needed. Trim the fat from the fillet, then season it, rub with butter and put at the top of a very hot oven, 220°C, 425°F, Mark 7 for 10 minutes. Heat the rest of the butter and sweat the mushrooms until they form a purée. Drain off any excess fat, then roll the steak in the mushrooms so that all surfaces are covered.

Roll out the pastry in a shape large enough to fit the steak and meet at the top. Lay the meat on it, bring up over the top to enclose the meat, dampen the pastry edges and squeeze together to secure. Brush with beaten egg, place on a baking sheet, put in a very hot oven 220°C, 425°F, Mark 7 for 15–20 minutes or until golden.

Bookmaker's sandwich – *Ceapaire geallghlacadóra*

This is an excellent dish to take with you for a busy day out, such as a race meeting or a fishing expedition. It is also most useful if you are doing something like moving house when it is difficult to get a proper meal.

1 long crusty loaf, Vienna style	freshly made mustard
1–2 tablespoons butter	salt and black pepper
450 g (1 lb) sirloin or fillet steak	

Slice the loaf in half lengthways and butter it well. Cut the steak in two lengthways, rub with butter and pepper it. Grill the steak under high heat but do not overcook. Put the meatstrips straight away on to the buttered half loaves. Season with salt and pepper and spread with mustard. Put the two halves of the sandwich together. Place on foil, wrap tightly and put a light weight on top. When cold cut into fairly thick slices and put back together and wrap again. The steak juices absorb into the bread and will keep it moist. Serves 3–4.

Ox kidney casserole – *Casaról dhuán daimh*

Ox kidney should only be used in casseroles or stews, as it is too tough to fry.

1 ox kidney, about 450–700 g (1–1½lb)	pinch of ground marjoram
seasoned flour	salt and pepper
1 large onion, sliced	about 600 ml (1 pint) beef stock, warmed
1 tablespoon chopped parsley	

Skin the kidney, cut in half and take out the fatty core. Cut the kidney into small cubes. Toss in the seasoned flour and put into the casserole with the onion and herbs. Season well, then add the warm stock. Bring to the boil and then put in to a 160°C, 325°F, Mark 3 oven, covered, and cook for 1½–2 hours, stirring once or twice during the cooking time, and adding a little more stock if the casserole is getting dry. Serves 3–4.

Oxtail stew – *Stobhach damheireabaill*

This is a very rich and nourishing stew which should be made ahead of time and left to get cold, then the fat removed from the top before the stew is reheated. It needs long, slow cooking or alternatively a pressure cooker will do it perfectly in 35 minutes at top pressure.

1 large oxtail, chopped	1 bay leaf
1 large onion, sliced	1 or 2 sprigs of parsley
1 tablespoon flour	salt and pepper
½ teaspoon powdered marjoram	about 600 ml (1 pint) beef stock

Trim as much fat as possible from the oxtail pieces. Heat the oil then quickly fry them all over, add the onion and soften it, then put in the flour and the herbs mixing well. Cook for 1 minute, then season and add stock to cover. (Add a little water if it is not enough.) Let it bubble up and transfer to a casserole, cover and cook in a slow oven 150°C, 300°F, Mark 2, for about 3 hours, then test for tenderness and continue cooking if necessary.

Let the stew get entirely cold, then remove the fat from the top before reheating thoroughly. Serves about 4.

Lamb

As roast beef is the traditional meat of England so roast lamb or mutton is the traditional meat of Ireland. Many travellers have remarked on its succulence and flavour. Madame de Bovet, a French traveller to Ireland in the late nineteenth century, who was most critical of the food, remarked after a party where the guests were served a baron of mutton that the delicious gravy was 'the only triumph of Irish cookery'.

Mrs Delany, the renowned hostess, was much more complimentary when writing about a curious mutton dish she was given during an elaborate picnic at a place called Patrick Down, seven miles from Killalla on July 4th, 1732.

> For our feast there was prepared what here they call a 'swilled *mouton*', that is, a sheep roasted whole in its skin, scorched like a hog. I never ate anything better; we sat on the grass, had a rock for our table; and though there was a great variety of good cheer, nothing was touched but the *mouton*.

Obviously an eighteenth-century barbecue!

Crusty roast lamb – *Uaineoil faoi chrústa*

1 shoulder of lamb, about 1½–2 kg (3¼–4½ lb)	700 g (1½ lb) potatoes, peeled and sliced
1 cup fresh breadcrumbs	1 large onion, sliced
pinch of mixed herbs	1 large cooking apple, peeled, cored and sliced
2 tablespoons butter, soft	
salt and pepper	300 ml (½ pint) chicken stock

Wipe the lamb over and cut criss-cross slits around the top. Mix together the breadcrumbs, herbs, butter, salt and pepper. Rub the mixture on to the top of the meat, pressing down well so that it sticks. Fill the bottom of the roasting pan with the vegetables and apple, mixing them and seasoning well. Put the joint on top, then pour the stock into the pan but not over the meat.

Cover loosely with a piece of foil and bake at 200°C, 400°F, Mark 6 for half an hour. Then lower the heat to 180°C, 350°F, Mark 4 and cook for a further 20–25 minutes to the pound. Take off the foil before the final half hour, and check that the vegetables are nearly cooked. Finish the cooking without the foil, to let the top get brown and crusty. Serves about 6.

Lamb with cabbage – *Uaineoil le cabáiste*

Very much a country dish, but a good one. Originally shoulder or gigot chops were used on the bone, but I find the bones tiresome when eating. Therefore I like to cut the meat off the bone into cubes. The bones can be used for stock.

4 large gigot (shoulder) lamb chops,
   boned and cubed
1 large onion, sliced
1 medium-sized white cabbage
salt

8 whole peppercorns
pinch of caraway seeds
600 ml (1 pint) lamb stock
2 tablespoons parsley, chopped

Trim the cabbage, cut into fairly thick shreds and put into ice water to freshen up. In a deep casserole put layers of the meat, the onion and the cabbage, well drained, finishing with the cabbage. Season each layer with salt and add the peppercorns and the caraway seeds. Pour in the stock, cover and braise slowly in a 160°C, 325°F, Mark 3 oven for about 2 hours or until all is very tender. Sprinkle thickly with the parsley before serving. Serves about 4.

Boiled mutton with caper sauce – *Caoireoil bheirithe agus anlann caprais*

This old dish is seldom seen today although it is extremely good. It is best served surrounded with small boiled potatoes and carrots sprinkled with chopped parsley.

1 leg joint of lamb or mutton, about
   1½–2 kg (3¼–4½ lb)
2 medium-sized onions, sliced
2 carrots, sliced

sprig of fresh thyme
sprig of rosemary
1 bay leaf
salt and pepper

Sauce

1 heaped tablespoon butter
1 heaped tablespoon flour
600 ml (1 pint) mutton stock or
   chicken stock, warmed

2 tablespoons capers with juice
salt and pepper
1 tablespoon cream

Remove any surplus fat from the meat, put into a deep saucepan and cover with cold water. Add the vegetables, herbs and seasoning. Bring to the boil and take off any scum, then simmer quite gently, covered, for about 30 minutes to the ½ kilo (pound), testing for tenderness.

When the lamb is almost cooked make the sauce. Melt the butter, stir in the flour and cook for 1 minute. Add the stock gradually stirring well to avoid lumps. Add the capers and the liquid and stir again, then add the seasoning and the cream; do not allow to reboil.

Put the meat on a warmed serving dish, and carve in fairly thick slices down the bone; cover with the sauce. Serves about 6–8.

Onion sauce instead of capers is also traditional.

Irish stew – *Stobhach Gaelach*

This dish is known all over the Western world, and is very likely one of the oldest Irish recipes in existence, but it is frequently spoilt by too much liquid. Other vegetables and barley are sometimes added but do not improve it.

1¼–1½ kg (2¾–3¼ lb) best end of
  neck chops
900 g (2 lb) potatoes, peeled and
  sliced
450 g (1 lb) onions, sliced

1 tablespoon parsley, chopped
pinch of thyme
salt and pepper
about 600 ml (1 pint) stock

Trim the meat of bone, fat and gristle, then cut into fairly large pieces. Layer the meat and the vegetables in a deep pan, seasoning each layer well, and ending with potatoes. Pour in the stock and cover with a piece of buttered foil, then the lid, and bake in a slow oven 150°C, 300°F, Mark 2 for about 2 hours. Or, if preferred, on the top of the stove, shaking the pan from time to time to prevent sticking. Add a very little more liquid if needed. Serves 4.

Lamb stew with barley – *Stobhach uaineola nó cuoireola*

This country stew can be made with beef or chicken rather than lamb or even with a mixture.

1¼ kg (2½ lb) neck of lamb
75 g (3 oz) pearl barley
1 large onion, sliced
3–4 small carrots, sliced

1 small swede, diced
salt and pepper
2 tablespoons parsley, chopped

Trim the meat and put into a large saucepan, cover with water and bring to the boil. Skim off any scum then add all ingredients except the parsley. Boil again, then simmer, covered, for about 1½ hours or until tender. Taste for seasoning before serving garnished thickly with parsley. Serves about 4.

Hotpot – *Prácás*

This is another recipe using cheaper cuts of lamb, and lamb's kidneys as well. It is a very succulent, fat-free dish, full of flavour.

4 lean mutton chops
6 lamb's kidneys
450 g (1 lb) potatoes, peeled and
  sliced

1 large onion, sliced
salt and pepper
300 ml (½ pint) good beef stock,
  without fat

Trim the chops of all fat and bone them, then skin, core and slice the kidneys. Layer the meat and kidneys with the vegetables in a deep ovenproof dish, starting and ending with potatoes, and seasoning well. Pour in the stock, cover with greased foil and a lid, and bake at 180°C, 350°F, Mark 4 for 1–1½ hours. Uncover for the last half hour to let the top brown. Serves 4–6.

Roast lamb with apples – *Uaineoil rósta le hÚlla*

This is a Tipperary dish from the eighteenth century. Tipperary was and still is the great apple-growing centre, and cider is made at Clonmel.

2 kg (4½ lb) boned loin or shoulder
  of lamb
juice and peel of 1 lemon
450 g (1 lb) cooking apples, peeled
  and thinly sliced
1 tablespoon sugar

3 whole cloves
1 tablespoon ground ginger
salt and pepper
2 tablespoons melted butter or oil
600 ml (1 pint) dry cider or apple
  juice

Rub the meat inside and out with the lemon juice and peel. Lay the apple slices over the inner side of the meat, sprinkle with sugar and cloves, roll up and secure well. Rub all over with the ginger, salt and pepper, put into a baking tin and brush all over with the melted butter or oil. Roast at 200°C, 400°F, Mark 6 for half an hour, then lower to 180°C, 350°F, Mark 4 and cook for a further hour and 20 minutes. Heat the cider and baste with it at least three times during cooking.

Drain off excess fat from the pan and boil the pan juices over high heat until reduced by about half; serve separately. Serves about 8.

Lamb shoulder in pastry –
Gualainn chaoireola i dTaosrán

350 g (12 oz) shortcrust or flaky
  pastry
1¼–1½ kg (2¾–3¼ lb) boned
  shoulder of lamb
6 tablespoons butter

1 tablespoon mixed chopped herbs
  such as parsley, chives and
  rosemary or marjoram
salt and black pepper
milk or beaten egg to glaze

Make the pastry and chill for at least 1 hour before using. See that the lamb is fairly free of fat, and securely tied; put in a baking tin and rub with about a third of the butter. Put into a very hot oven, 230°C, 450°F, Mark 8 for 20–30 minutes. Take out, and let cool a little in the baking tin.

Mix the remaining butter with the herbs, salt and pepper. Roll out the pastry to a piece large enough to wrap round the joint. Carefully remove the string from the lamb trying to retain the shape. Put it in the centre of the pastry, dampen the edges and draw the pastry up over the top and secure well by squeezing the pastry ends and edges together. Turn over so that the fold is underneath and put on a baking sheet. Decorate with pastry leaves made from the trimmings if liked. Prick all over the top lightly with a fork, then brush either with milk or the beaten egg.

Put into a hot, 200°C, 400°F, Mark 6, oven and cook for about half an hour or until the pastry is nicely browned. Turn the sheet around once during cooking so that both sides bake evenly. Serve, cut into fairly thick slices. Serves about 6.

Saddle of lamb

This is a large joint consisting of the 2 loins together from ribs to tail. It can weigh up to 4½ kg (10 lb). The kidneys are usually attached and cooked with it in their own fat, but I prefer to remove them and cook them separately, then use them as a garnish, as when left on they become too overcooked for my taste.

Rub the joint with butter, good dripping or oil, dust with pepper and tuck a sprig of rosemary inside. Roast in a very hot oven, 220°C, 425°F, Mark 7 for 20 minutes, reduce the heat to 200°C, 400°F, Mark 6 and cook for a total of 20–25 minutes to the ½ kilo (pound). When cooked drain the fat off and add a large glass of port wine to the pan juices, and boil up. Serve with mint sauce or redcurrant or rowan-berry jelly. Carve along the backbone.

Mutton pies – *Pióga caoireola*

These pies, also called 'Dingle pies' and somewhat like the Cornish pasty, are traditional in Co. Kerry and are still sold in Dingle and every August at Puck Fair in Killorglin. The 'king' of the fair is a large puck goat, much decorated and 'garlanded by greenery' which is hoisted high above the crowds on to a covered platform where he remains chained by the horns throughout the fair munching on cabbages.

Legend has it that it commemorates a time when the noise of a herd of goats led by the puck or billy ran into town and warned the Irish of the advancing English soldiers, but it is much more probable that the origins are far earlier than that and come from the Puck being a symbol of fertility and good luck. August 12th is the Old Lammas, and Lammas Day, August 1st, was formerly known in Ireland as 'Lewy's Fair' in memory of a pre-Christian deity, Lugh, the god of light. The main business of the Fair is the sale of livestock and it is also a traditional gathering place for all the travelling people, or 'tinkers'.

900 g (2 lb) self-raising flour
225 g (8 oz) butter
100 g (4 oz) lard or mutton dripping
1 heaped teaspoon salt
pinch of thyme
900 g (2 lb) lean mutton

salt and pepper
1 small onion, grated or finely chopped
2 teaspoons fresh mint, chopped, or 1 teaspoon dried

First make the pastry: mix the salt into the sifted flour, then rub in the fats and add about a cup of water, gradually, mixing well, until the dough is firm but not dry. Roll into a ball and chill.

Trim the meat of fat and gristle and if you can tell that it is tender use it raw, but if you are in any doubt, boil it in water to cover for half an hour, together with any bones you have trimmed off. Cut it into very small pieces, season well, and mix with the onion and herbs.

Roll out slightly more than half the pastry on a lightly floured surface, and cut into 6 circles about 10 cm (4 inches) across. Roll out the remaining pastry and cut into 6 slightly smaller circles. Put about a sixth of the meat mixture on each of the larger circles, dampen the outer edges, then lay a smaller circle on top of each. Press down and crimp with the prongs of a dampened fork. Make a small slit in the top of each to let the steam out and brush with a little milk. Put on to a greased baking sheet and bake at 180°C, 350°F, Mark 4 for 15 minutes. Lower the heat to 160°C, 325°F, Mark 3 and cook for a further 45 minutes if you used raw meat; if it was cooked then reduce the cooking time by 20 minutes.

Lamb's liver – *Ae uain*

Lamb's liver is considered the finest for frying in Ireland, although calves' liver, which is very good, is often much cheaper. It should be dusted with seasoned flour which has had a tiny pinch of sage mixed with it, and then fried fairly quickly on both sides in butter or oil. Care should be taken not to overcook as this ruins both the flavour and texture. Rashers of bacon are often fried and served with it.

Lamb's kidneys in their overcoats – *Duain sa tsaill*

This old Irish dish used to be popular for breakfast in the last century. It is by far the best way to get the true flavour of kidneys.

Put the kidneys still in their coats of suet in a baking tin into a very hot oven 220°C, 425°F, Mark 7 for about 30 minutes or until the outside is crisp and cooked. Break them open just before serving, on toast, with salt and pepper and a small nut of parsley or chive butter.

Stuffed lamb's hearts – *Croíthe líonta uan*

This good country dish is gaining in popularity again.

4 lamb's hearts
100 g (4 oz) breadcrumbs, soaked in a little milk
grated rind of 1 lemon
1 small onion, grated or finely chopped
1 teaspoon each fresh chopped thyme, parsley and marjoram (or ½ teaspoon dried)

salt and pepper
2 tablespoons fat or oil
about 1 tablespoon flour
1 large onion, coarsely chopped
1 stick celery, chopped
1 bay leaf
pinch of mace
600 ml (1 pint) stock

Wash the hearts and remove any fat, pipes or bits of gristle. Make a cut from the top down one side so that it forms a pocket. Combine the soaked breadcrumbs with the lemon rind, grated or finely chopped onion, thyme, parsley, marjoram, salt and pepper. Mix well, then stuff the hearts with it and secure. Melt the fat and quickly brown the hearts all over, shaking about a tablespoon of flour over them; let the flour brown a minute, then add the coarsely chopped onion and the celery. Turn them over in the fat over moderate heat then gradually add the stock to barely cover the hearts adding a little more water if necessary. Put in the bay leaf and mace, then transfer everything to a casserole, cover and cook in a slow oven, 160°C, 325°F, Mark 3, for 1½–2 hours. Serves 4.

Pork – *Muiceoíl*

The most important flesh meat eaten in ancient and medieval times, and very much later too, was pork or bacon. Many pig bones have been found in very large quantities in habitation sites dating from Neolithic times, and while many of these bones might have come from wild pig, there is no doubt that the pig has been a common domestic animal used for food in all periods of Irish history. There are constant references to oakmast, the prime food for fattening pigs since earliest times. Dr A. T. Lucas, in his learned paper 'Irish food before the potato', states: 'Another indication of the importance of pigs is the frequency with which swineherds are mentioned in early literature, and it is stated in the Laws that "swine must sleep in a sty secured with four strong fastenings by night, and must have a swineherd with them by day."' The remains of these *clochauns* can still be seen, and in some cases are still in use.

Not only fresh pork but also pork salted as bacon was a favourite food mentioned many times in sagas, stories and lives of the saints. In the twelfth-century *Vision of MacConglinne* it is referred to as *tinne* or *senshaille* and the references far outnumber any other meat.

Stephen Gwynn in *The Fair Hills of Ireland*, 1906, describes the method of dividing a pig's carcass in the early seventeenth century:

> The head, tongue and feet to the smith (the smith was thought to have magical qualities on account of his strength and skills, and was the first person to be invited to any function), the neck to the butcher, two small ribs that go with the hind-quarters to the tailor, the kidneys to the physician, the udder to the harper, the liver to the carpenter and sweetbread to her that is with child.

Dr E. Estyn Evans in his book *Irish Folk Ways*, 1957, says that the smith's right was maintained down to recent times. The popularity of pork and pork products has not waned up until the present day and almost every part of the pig is still used throughout Ireland in town and country.

Roast pork and apple sauce – *Muiceoíl rósta agus anlann úll*

Several different joints of pork are suitable for roasting, such as leg, shoulder or loin. It is really a matter of taste and pocket. The shoulder is usually boned and rolled and is a very sweet-eating part of the pig. The stuffing on page 116 can be used if wanted.

The special delight of some joints of pork is the crispy skin known as 'crackling'. This should be well scored by the butcher and an important part of the cooking is to see that the skin should *never* come into contact with the hot fat during cooking, or it will fry and become what in fact the Norman archers called '*cuir bouillie*', boiled leather. They used it to make breastplates to withstand the battleaxes and arrows of the enemy!

joint pork about 1.8 kg (4 lb)
600 ml (1 pint) cider, stock or water
salt and pepper

Put the pork into a roasting pan and place in a very hot oven 220°C, 425°F, Mark 7 without any added fat, and cook for 30 minutes, then take out and pour off the fat into a bowl. Lower the heat to 200°C, 400°F, Mark 6, put back into the oven with the cider, chicken stock or water, and cook for 30 minutes to the pound. About 30 minutes before it is ready remove from the oven and sprinkle salt over the skin and shake a few drops of cold water over the top, then put back and continue cooking.

This will give a very good crispy crackling and the sauce should be reduced on top of the stove and seasoned to taste. Serve with apple sauce (page 124).

Stuffed pork chops – *Gríscíní muiceola le búiste*

It is from the Irish that the word 'griskin' comes, meaning the best part of the loin. Some idea of the usefulness of the pig is given in this extract from *The Irish Journals of Elizabeth Smith*, 1840–50, of Baltiboys House, Blessington.

> *November 20th, 1842*
> A present from old Peggy, the back griskins of her pig ... it will be the most delicious bacon ever cured, but all the comfort that so small a weight of consumable material will give, the skin for a sieve, the lard for kitchen and the bones for soup, the blood for puddings, and the inmeats, a week's dinners, it will be a very merry Christmas ...

4 lean pork chops
black pepper
4 large onions, peeled and sliced
50 g (2 oz) butter
1 teaspoon sugar

1 tablespoon flour, seasoned
150 ml (¼ pint) warm milk
2 tablespoons cream
4 tablespoons breadcrumbs
1 tablespoon butter

Trim the chops and take out the small piece of bone, then put on to a grilling pan and dust with black pepper. Peel and slice the onions into a saucepan, just cover with water and bring to the boil, then simmer for 10 minutes. Drain, but reserve the liquid. Heat the butter in another pan, then add the onions and sugar and cook until they are quite soft. Beat with a fork to purée them. Add the flour and let it cook for a minute, then add the warm milk and enough of the onion liquor to make a thickish sauce. Season well, then add the cream.

Grill the chops well *on one side* only, transfer them cooked side down into a roasting pan and cover the tops with the onion sauce. Sprinkle breadcrumbs on top, then a dot of butter and pepper. Put into a hot oven, 210°C, 425°F, Mark 7, for about 20 minutes or until the top is crisply browned. If liked the chops can be grilled in the usual way and the sauce served with them, however the crispy topping is very good.

Pork císte – *Císte muiceola*

This traditional Irish dish is a kind of pork pudding not very often seen today, but is extremely good. The name is confusing, as *císte* can also mean cake in Irish, and some loaves of bread are also called cake, both in Irish and English. It is also made with lamb or mutton.

4 pork chops trimmed of fat
3 pork kidneys, or 225 g (8 oz) pork
  liver
2 medium-sized onions, sliced
2 medium-sized carrots, sliced
1 tablespoon parsley, chopped
pinch of thyme
salt and pepper

about 600 ml (1 pint) stock
225 g (8 oz) flour
salt
1 teaspoon baking powder
100 g (4 oz) grated suet
about 120 ml (4 fl oz) milk
2–3 tablespoons sultanas

Put the chops around the inside edge of a medium-sized flameproof pan with any bone-ends sticking upwards. Skin and chop the kidneys or liver and add, with the vegetables and herbs in the centre, season well and add just enough stock to barely cover the vegetables. Cover, bring to the boil, lower heat and simmer gently for about half an hour.

Meanwhile make the císte by mixing together the flour, salt, suet and baking powder and adding enough milk to make a firm dough. Add the sultanas and mix well. Roll out on a lightly floured surface to the size of the pan, place it on top, then press it down to meet the stew, even if the bones stick through, and to leave about an inch of space above it to allow for rising. Cover with greased wax paper and the lid and cook over low heat for 1–1½ hours.

When ready loosen the edges with a knife and cut into wedges, to serve meat, vegetables and the císte in each portion. Serves 4–6.

Brawn – *Toirceoil*

Brawn or pig's head cheese was a most popular dish all over Ireland, and still is, although nowadays, with the exception of farmer's wives, it is usually made commercially. Calf's head brawn was a favourite dish of my father's, served with cold caper and onion sauce, although it is more commonly served with a mustard sauce (see the Sauces section).

1 pig's head with tongue, soaked
   overnight if salted
2 pig's feet, split
1 onion, stuck with cloves
blade of mace

sprig of parsley
sprig of thyme
12 peppercorns
salt

If the pig's head has been salted and soaked overnight, scrape the outside. Put into a large saucepan with the pig's feet, the onion, mace, parsley, thyme and peppercorns. Barely cover with cold water, bring to the boil, then cover and simmer for at least 3 hours, or until the meat is beginning to come away from the bones. Lift the head out and take all the meat from the bones, remove the tongue and put into cold water, then skin it and trim off any gristle. Put the bones back in the stock and boil down to reduce, then strain and chill. Take any fat from the top when cold.

Pull the meat into pieces and put in a large deep dish or bowl and put the tongue, whole, in the centre. Press all down well, then pour, or spoon, enough of the stock (which will have jellied – warm it if necessary) to cover all the meat. Cover with a plate, and chill. When cold, put foil over the top and weight it down. Serve cold in slices, with a sauce. Serves 10–12.

Pork and apple casserole – *Casaról muiceola is úlla*

4 pork shoulder chops, trimmed
2 medium-sized onions, sliced
450 g (1 lb) cooking apples, peeled
   and sliced
½ teaspoon dried sage

1 heaped tablespoon brown sugar
300 ml (½ pint) cider
salt and pepper
700 g (1½ lb) potatoes, peeled and
   sliced thickly

Bone the chops and trim most of the fat, then put into a casserole with the onions, apples, sage, brown sugar and cider. Season to taste. Bring to the boil, then cover and simmer 1–1½ hours, or cook in a moderate oven 180°C, 350°F, Mark 4 for the same time, or until tender.

About half an hour before the pork is ready, cook the potato slices, drain and mash very well. Then take the meat from the casserole and strain the juices into the potatoes. Whip it in well, pile in a warmed dish and spoon the meat and vegetables over the mashed potatoes. Serves 4.

Stuffed pork steaks – *Stéigeanna muiceola*

The pork steak, known as the pork fillet or tenderloin in Britain and the United States, is a traditional cut in Ireland. It is very lean and can be roasted, grilled or braised, stuffed or not.

2 kg (4½ lb) pork steak
2 cups fresh white breadcrumbs
1 medium-sized onion, finely
    chopped
1 teaspoon grated lemon rind and
    juice of ½ lemon
pinch of ground mace or nutmeg

½ teaspoon sage
½ teaspoon thyme
1 tablespoon parsley, chopped
about 2 tablespoons milk
salt and pepper
50 g (2 oz) butter
1 cup stock or cider

Mix all the stuffing ingredients together and just moisten with a little milk: see that it is well absorbed and is in no way sloppy.

Pull off any streaks of fat from the outside of the pork steak then lay it on a board and cut with a sharp knife down the middle, but not all the way through. Pull the sides apart gently using your hands and the blunt side of the knife, until the gap widens out nearly flat. Score down the length, again not cutting through, so that when you have finished it presents a flattish rectangular shape.

Put the stuffing on to the flattened surface and either fold the pork over or roll up and secure well. Rub all over with butter and season lightly, then put into a roasting pan and add stock or cider, cover loosely with foil and cook at 200°C, 400°F, Mark 6 for 20 minutes, then lower the heat to 180°C, 350°F, Mark 4 for 45 minutes, basting once or twice, and turning if it seems necessary. Remove the foil before the final 15 minutes to brown the meat a bit.

To make the gravy, transfer the meat to a warmed dish and keep warm, then scrape down the sides of the pan, and boil up the pan juices rapidly on top of the stove, adding a little water if needed, and seasoning. Serves 6–8.

They can also be served as above with braised root vegetables and stock to cover for 1½ hours.

Pork pie with raised crust –
Pióg muiceola le crústa ardaithe

This pastry is the one usually used for pork pies, game pies and some raised fruit pies. All the pastry ingredients must be kept warm, and the pastry made quickly.

450–700 g (1–1½ lb) raw pork, finely
    chopped
salt and pepper
½ teaspoon chopped herbs
450 g (1 lb) flour
1 teaspoon salt

150 g (5 oz) lard
200 ml (7 fl oz) milk and water mixed
beaten egg for glaze
300 ml (½ pint) stock, which will jell
    when cold

Have ready a warmed, wide-bottomed, straight-sided jar 10–12 cm (4–5 inches) in diameter. Mix the flour and salt together. Mix the pork, salt and pepper and chopped herbs and set aside in a bowl, and make a well in the centre. Bring the lard and milk/water mixture to boiling point in a saucepan, and when the lard has melted, pour the liquid at once into the flour well. Mix quickly and thoroughly first with a wooden spoon, then with your hands. As you proceed keep it warm; on no account let it cool or it will become brittle. Roll into a ball and divide into a ⅓ piece and a ⅔ piece. Roll out the large piece in a circle, and stand the warmed jar in the centre; working quickly, mould the warm paste around the sides. When the mould is complete, carefully lift out the jar, and, holding the paste mould carefully, fill it with the raw pork mixture.

Roll out the top pastry to fit, dampen the edges and put it on as a lid, pressing gently to make sure it is firm.

Roll out any scraps to make a rosette for the centre. Make a small hole in the centre of the top and place the rosette lightly over it, not pressing it down. Brush all over with beaten egg, lift gently on to a baking sheet and bake at 160°C, 325°F, Mark 3 for 1–1½ hours.

Take the pie from the oven and cool a little, then lift off the rosette and using a small funnel pour in the stock, to fill the pie. Put the rosette back and leave to get cold in a cool place, not the refrigerator or the pastry may set hard.

Pig's feet crubeens – *Crúibíní*

Crubeens are a country dish which used to be a great favourite accompanied by brown soda bread and pints of stout. The 'Grunter's Club' at Listowel always served them after the races; and some pubs still serve them regularly. Usually the hind feet of the pig are used, as there is more meat on them than on the 'trotters'.

The country method is to boil them in water with an onion, a carrot, and some herbs and seasonings, for about 2 hours. They can then be eaten, either warm from the pot, or cold, taken up in the fingers and chewed, rather as one eats corn on the cob. A modern refinement is to split the foot in two, take out the bones, let it get cold, then brush it with mustard, roll it in beaten egg and then in breadcrumbs and either fry or grill on both sides. Serve with Michael Kelly's sauce (see Sauces section).

Tripe and onions – *Tríopas agus oinníuin*

A famous Saturday night dish, the most common method being to slice the tripe and cook it in milk with a lot of sliced onions, salt, pepper and a pinch of nutmeg or mace. It needs long, slow cooking – about 2 hours until tender. Just before serving, thicken it with 1 tablespoon of either flour or cornflour.

My family method is to add 225 g (8 oz) of chopped bacon or ham, and when cooked and thickened a little, pour thick cream over the dish, scatter breadcrumbs on top (perhaps with a little grated cheese mixed in), dot with butter and brown it just a little under the grill. Garnish with chopped parsley before serving. About 900 g (2 lb) of tripe and the same amount of onions will serve 4–6 people.

Sausages – *Ispíní*

> She (Peg Woffington) wrenched from her brow a diamond and eyed it with contempt, took from her pocket a sausage and contemplated it with respect and affection.
>
> Charles Read

(Margaret Woffington was an Irish actress born in Dublin in 1717, daughter of a washerwoman and a bricklayer, who rose to play Polly in John Gay's *Beggar's Opera* to enthusiastic audiences and became a much loved actress at Covent Garden, London, where she continued until she retired in 1757.)

Sausages have been an Irish favourite since as far back as the twelfth century, if not earlier. I would say that they are the single most popular item of food sold in Ireland. Very good ones can still be found in shops, but it is not difficult to make your own if you have an electric mincer, preferably one with a sausage filling attachment.

Get skins from your butcher if you're on good terms with him, or they can just be formed into sausage shapes or patties and rolled lightly in flour before frying. This is a basic recipe, but it is essential that you have at least a quarter of the meat weight in fat. Smoked sausages can be obtained by using lightly smoked and salted pork, in this case omit the salt from the recipe.

700 g (1½ lb) lean pork
225 g (8 oz) pork fat, without gristle
1 teaspoon salt
½ teaspoon ground allspice
freshly ground black pepper
pinch of dried sage or marjoram

25 g (1 oz) dried white breadcrumbs
 (optional)
ground ginger, mace, nutmeg,
 cloves and cayenne pepper
 (optional, for spicier sausages)

Mince the meat and fat twice, then mix very well and season. Add the herbs and the breadcrumbs and spices if using. Form into shapes or fill skins.

Sausages in beer or cider

Lightly brown the sausages under a grill or in a pan. Then fry some onions in a little oil and add the sausages. When they are cooked, pour off excess oil, add a sprinkling of flour, and either 1 cup of cider or pale beer. Simmer, mixing well for about 5 minutes and serve with mashed potatoes.

Dublin coddle – *Codal Duibhlinneach*

Combining two of the earliest Irish foods, this has been a favourite dish since the eighteenth century. It is said to have been much liked by Dean Swift.

8 thick slices ham or bacon
8 large pork sausages
4 large onions, sliced
900 g (2 lb) potatoes, peeled and
sliced
salt and pepper
4 tablespoons parsley, chopped

Bring to the boil 1 litre (1¾ pints) of water and drop in the bacon and sausages, cut into large chunks. Cook for 5 minutes and drain, reserving the liquid. Put the meat into a large saucepan or ovenproof dish; mix with the sliced onions and potatoes, season well, and add about half the parsley. Add enough of the reserved stock to barely cover, lay greased paper on top, then a lid and either simmer gently or cook in a low oven 150°C, 300°F, Mark 2 for about 1½ hours until the liquid has reduced very much and everything is cooked but not mushy. Serve hot with soda bread and Guinness. Serves 4–6.

Blood puddings – *Putóga fola*

These are probably one of the oldest foods made with a product of meat. They exist all over the Western world, particularly in Celtic countries. Traditionally they were made with sheep's blood but nowadays pig's blood is more usual. In Cork it is called *drisheen* (spelled *drisín* in Irish) and it is larger in diameter than the usual black pudding. White puddings are made with finely minced boiled liver and lights without the blood. Black and white pudding, sliced and fried, forms an essential part of the Irish breakfast, with fried rashers of bacon, sausages, eggs and potato cakes. Tansy was the herb traditionally used to flavour the puddings; today it is usually thyme. At my home these puddings were often made with turkey or goose blood and they were superb.

> At night time when the carcass was cold ... Ben Meagher came for the salting of the pig. On such a night the whole house was seething with activity: ... getting ready the breadcrumbs, the oatmeal, the allspice, the chopped onions for the filling of the puddings.
>
> From *The Big Sycamore* by Joseph Brady.

1 litre (1¾ pints) pig's or sheep's
  blood
2 teaspoons salt
600 ml (1 pint) milk, or half milk and
  half cream
1 cup oatmeal
1 cup breadcrumbs or wheatmeal
225 g (8 oz) kidney suet, finely
chopped
1 level teaspoon ground allspice
1 level teaspoon black pepper
1 medium-sized onion, finely
  chopped
1 teaspoon fresh tansy or thyme
  leaves, chopped, or ½ teaspoon
  dried

First salt the blood to keep it liquid, then add all other ingredients, mixing well. Leave to stand for about 1 hour, then put into large sausage casings, or if large sausage casings are not available, then put into a well-greased ovenproof dish, cover with greaseproof paper or foil. Cook standing in another pan half-filled with water in a 150°C, 350°F, Mark 3 oven for 1–1½ hours. When cool cut in squares and serve either hot or cold.

Boiled ham or bacon – *Liamhás nó bagún beirithe*

Irish ham and bacon has been renowned for centuries and is still sought after. In the eighteenth century Limerick ham was given its characteristic flavour by being smoked over branches of juniper, a shrub growing freely in that county. In Ireland only the leg of the pig is called ham; all else is bacon, which is used in a variety of ways. Both ham and bacon which has been cured need to be soaked before cooking.

Soak the meat overnight in cold water, then drain, and scrape the skin with a knife. Put into a large pan, barely cover with fresh cold water or cider, or a mixture of both, with a teaspoon of sugar, a sprig of parsley or a stick of celery if available, and half a lemon. Bring to the boil, then lower the heat and just let the water tremble for 25 minutes to the ½ kilo (pound). Let it cool in the stock and when ready, take out and peel off the skin. Cover with either brown sugar with a good pinch of ground cloves, or a mixture of half breadcrumbs and half brown sugar with cloves, or breadcrumbs mixed with a few chopped herbs and a little grated lemon peel. Press all down well. Serve with either parsley sauce (the old-fashioned country preference) or lemon sauce, which is also excellent (see Sauces section).

Ham or bacon with cider in raisin and celery sauce – *Liamhás bruite le ceirtlis in anlann risíní is soilire*

2 kg (4½lb) piece of ham or bacon
1 large onion stuck with cloves
sprig of parsley
½ lemon
1 litre (1¾ pints) dry cider
pepper
2 tablespoons brown sugar

3 tablespoons breadcrumbs
½ teaspoon ground mace
1 heaped tablespoon butter
1 heaped tablespoon flour
50 g (2 oz) raisins or sultanas
2 stalks celery, very finely chopped

Soak the ham or bacon overnight, then drain and scrape the skin. Put into a large saucepan with the onion, parsley, half lemon, pepper and cider. Bring to the boil, then simmer for 25 minutes to the pound. Cool, then lift out the ham or bacon and peel off the skin; preserve the stock.

Mix the brown sugar, breadcrumbs, mace and a little stock just enough to moisten; add a little pepper. Press the mixture and put the ham or bacon on to the top and put into a baking pan with about 2 cups of the stock. Bake in a moderate oven, 180°C, 350°F, Mark 4, for 30–40 minutes. Meanwhile, make the sauce. Melt the butter in a pan, add the flour and cook, stirring for a minute, then add 2 cups of the stock gradually, stirring, and when smooth add the raisins or sultanas and chopped celery (do not let the celery cook too much, for its crunchiness should contrast with the ham). Serve the ham with the sauce. Serves 6–8.

Braised ham with apples and honey – Liamhás galstofa le hÚlla is mil

This can be made either with very thick slices of cooked ham or with ham steaks.

4 thick ham slices or ham steaks
2 tablespoons butter
2 large cooking apples, peeled and sliced
1 medium-sized onion, sliced

1 tablespoon brown sugar
pinch of ground cloves
2 tablespoons honey
300 ml (½ pint) cider

Trim the ham slices or steaks to leave only a little fat. Heat the butter and fry the apples and onion slices until soft but not coloured, then put the ham on top, add the brown sugar and cloves, and trickle the honey over. Finally pour in the cider, bring to the boil, then simmer, covered, for about 15 minutes or until all is well cooked. Enough for 4.

Veal

Veal is not eaten by the Irish very much, due in the main to a superstition that only sick calves were killed. I think it is fair to say that veal was eaten, usually, only by people who had travelled in France and England.

Some eighteenth-century menus mention fillet of veal but it was, and still is, an unusual meat. Mrs Delany of Delville, Glasnevin, in 1744, gives a dinner in which the first course consists of:

Turkey endove (endives); boyled neck of mutton; greens; soups, plum pudding; roast loin of veal and venison pasty.

And the second course also contained the veal sweetbreads; partridge; collared pig; creamed apple tart; crabs; fricassée of eggs and pigeons.

Veal needs long slow cooking for joints, but fairly fast cooking for cutlets or fillet slices.

Braised veal – Laofheoil ghalstofa

700–900 g (1½–2 lb) shoulder veal
about 4 rashers of bacon
1 medium to large onion, sliced
2–3 medium carrots, sliced
½ teaspoon tarragon
grated rind of 1 lemon

300 ml (½ pint) generous chicken stock
salt and pepper
1 tablespoon potato flour or arrowroot

Tie the meat up into a convenient shape, then put about 3 rashers around and over it. Line a casserole with the onions, carrots, herbs, the remaining bacon rasher, chopped, and salt and pepper. Put the meat on top of this, then add the stock. Do not cover, but put into a moderate oven, 180°C, 350°F, Mark 4, for 1½ hours. Baste from time to time, adding a little more stock if needed. The veal should be browned. When it is ready, take from the pan and keep warm. Add the potato flour or arrowroot mixed with a little water to the stock, stir and bring to the boil. Paint some of this thickened stock over the top of the veal and put back into the oven for 15 minutes to heat up. Serves about 4.

Veal cake – *Císte lasfheola*

A recipe from Geraldine FitzMaurice, 1831, good for a cold dish.

450 g (1 lb) pie veal, minced or finely chopped
350 g (12 oz) ham or lean bacon, chopped
1 tablespoon parsley, chopped
½ teaspoon celery seeds
300 ml (½ pint) non-fatty stock or consommé
2 hard boiled eggs, sliced
salt and pepper

Put a layer of sliced eggs on the bottom of a 1-litre (2-pint) ovenproof basin, then add the meats sprinkling with parsley and celery seeds. Pour stock into the basin until the meats are covered. Cover the basin either with a lid or foil then stand the basin in an ovenproof pan. Fill the pan with hot water so that the water comes about half-way up the sides of the basin and put it in a moderate oven 180°C, 350°F, Mark 4 for about 1½ hours. Remove from the oven and let it get quite cold before unmoulding by wrapping a hot towel around the basin and inverting it on to a serving plate. Cut the cake in wedges or slices and serve with a salad. Serves about 6.

Veal with cucumber – *Laofheoil le cúcamar*

4 slices fillet of veal
1 medium-sized cucumber
100 g (4 oz) butter
4 tablespoons cream
salt and pepper
1 tablespoon parsley, chopped

Beat the veal until flat, then peel the cucumber and cut into 25 cm (1 inch) pieces. Put the cucumber into salted water and boil for 10 minutes, then drain and keep warm. Melt half the butter, add the veal and brown quickly on both sides, then take them out and keep hot. Scrape the pan well to get the meat essences and add the cream and seasoning. Boil for a few minutes to thicken, then draw to the side and add first the rest of the butter, in small pieces, and then the cooked cucumber. Let them heat, then put the veal on top, cover and simmer for 15 minutes, then serve at once garnished with parsley. Serves 4.

Veal kidneys – *Duáin laonna*

Veal kidneys are very delicate in taste and are excellent cooked in this nineteenth-century way.

2–3 veal kidneys, depending on size
75 g (3 oz) butter
1 tablespoon juniper berries
450 g (1 lb) potatoes, parboiled and

sliced
salt and pepper
3 tablespoons white wine

Take the skin and fatty core from the kidneys and slice very thickly. Heat half the butter and at the same time put the juniper berries in a slow oven to 'sweat'. When the butter is foaming add the kidneys, turn once, then add the half-cooked potato slices. Season well, then add the wine, cover and cook over gentle heat for 10 minutes. Take the juniper berries from the oven and add to the kidneys with the rest of the butter in small pieces, shaking the pan. Cover and cook again gently for 5 minutes. Serves 4.

Veal sweetbreads in cream sauce – *Briscíní milse laofheola in anlann uachtair*

Sweetbreads should first be soaked in cold salted water for 3–4 hours, blanched in boiling water for 5 minutes, then the skin and membrane removed, and the sweetbreads cut to uniform size. They can then be dipped in beaten egg followed by breadcrumbs and fried in butter with lemon, or made into a casserole with mushrooms and bacon. This old method is very good too.

4 tablespoons butter
1 medium-sized onion, sliced
3 level tablespoons flour
600 ml (1 pint) milk
300 ml (½ pint) cream
3 tablespoons dry white wine or
  sherry

2 tablespoons chopped fresh herbs –
  parsley, lemon, thyme, mint, wild
  garlic leaves, lemon balm and
  chives
1 kg (1¾ lb) sweetbreads, blanched
  and cut to uniform size

Melt half the butter and soften the onion, add the flour and stir until mixed. Then add the rest of the butter and work it in. Add the milk, stirring to form a thick sauce, then add the cream, wine, herbs and seasoning; mix. Add the sweatbreads and bring to the boil, then simmer, covered, for about 1 hour or until very tender. Serve with fried *croûtons* of bread around the dish. Serves 4.

Kid – *Meannán*

Male kids are often eaten in the country in Ireland, and they can be cooked as for lamb or mutton. It is probable that the original Irish stew was made from kid. Country kid stew, *Stobhach tuaithe meannáin* in Irish, can be prepared like mutton stew and dumplings are often served with it. Very young kid can also be roasted.

chapter six

SAUCES – *ANLANNA*

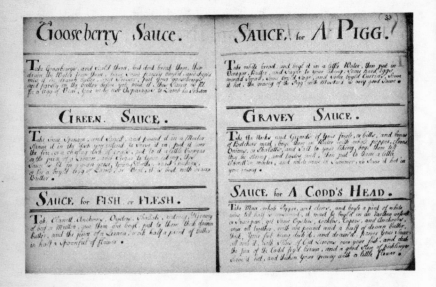

Anchovy sauce for fish – *Anlann ainseabhaí*

The following sauce, particularly good with herrings, and with mackerel, come from *The Lady's Assistant*, Charlotte Mason, 1778 adapted slightly for modern kitchens.

Beat together 2 egg yolks, a good pinch of ground nutmeg, pepper and salt. Add 3 level tablespoons flour, 1 finely chopped 225 g (8 oz) anchovy, melted butter and 1 cup water. Mix very well then heat up and let it gently come to the boil, stirring all the time until thick. Add a little more water if it seems too thick. Finally add 1 teaspoon mustard and a good squeeze of lemon juice.

Apple sauce – *Anlann úll*

This is good with pork, duck, goose, mackerel and some game.

450 g (1 lb) cooking apples	pinch of ground nutmeg or
about 1 tablespoon sugar	cloves
	1 rounded tablespoon butter

Peel, core and slice the apples and cook in about 4 tablespoons of water until they are quite soft. Either sieve or mash well, and heat them up again. Add sugar to taste, the nutmeg or cloves and the butter, cut into small pieces. Serve hot.

Bread sauce – *Anlann aráin*

Serve with roast chicken, turkey and roast game birds. Bread sauce is perhaps the only sauce from medieval times still in use.

Before the Normans introduced the saucer for sauces, thick slices of hard bread known as 'trenchers' were used as plates and a too-liquid sauce would sink into it so a thickener was needed. Almost all early sauces were thickened with breadcrumbs, mainly I think because with primitive cooking methods breadcrumbs were easier to manage than flour which if overcooked can become pasty as we all know, or egg yolks, which require careful handling at just the right temperature.

Bread sauce was first recorded in Scotland in the eighteenth century and was no doubt brought to Ireland by the many Scottish settlers who arrived in the seventeenth and eighteenth centuries.

1 medium-sized onion, peeled and stuck with 4 whole cloves
450 ml (¾ pint) milk
small blade of mace or pinch of nutmeg
a dozen peppercorns

8 rounded tablespoons fresh white breadcrumbs
1 rounded teaspoon butter
2 tablespoons thick cream
salt and white pepper

Put the cloved onion into a saucepan with the milk, mace or nutmeg and the peppercorns. Bring slowly to the boil, then remove at once from the heat, cover and leave to infuse for about half an hour. Strain the milk into another saucepan and stir in the breadcrumbs. Put over a gentle heat, stirring all the time, until the mixture boils and becomes quite thick. Season to taste, then add the butter in small pieces and finally the cream. Serve warm, but do not let it boil after the cream is added. Serves 4.

Caper sauce for brawn – *Anlann toirceola*

Mix together 1 mashed hard-boiled egg yolk, 1 tablespoon grated or finely chopped onion, 1 tablespoon capers and 2 tablespoons chopped parsley. When well mixed gradually add 2 tablespoons oil (olive oil is best) and 2 tablespoons of white wine vinegar. Stir well.

Celery sauce for Christmas turkey

Turkey has been served for Christmas in Ireland since the turn of the century (before then goose, beef or pork took precedence). It is stuffed and roasted as in other countries that keep that tradition, but with the slight difference that the most usual sauce served with it is not cranberry (although cranberries do grow wild here in the bogs) but a rich celery sauce.

Simmer chopped celery heart in chicken stock with pepper for about 15 minutes or until quite soft. Drain and reserve.

Make a white sauce (see recipe, page 134) and purée the celery with it in a liquidizer. Add a pinch of nutmeg, some cream and taste for seasoning. Keep warm until serving.

Cheese sauce – *Anlann cáise*

For serving with hard-boiled eggs, fish, cauliflower, potatoes, vegetable marrow.

Make a white sauce (see recipe, page 134) adding 3–4 tablespoons grated cheese after the liquid is added and begins to thicken.

Cucumber sauce – *Anlann cúcamair*

Serve with cold fish, especially salmon.

1 small cucumber
150 ml (¼ pint) double cream
2 teaspoons fresh tarragon,

chopped or tarragon vinegar
salt and white pepper

See that all ingredients are very cold before starting. Peel and grate the cucumber. Put in a sieve to drain. Beat the cream until thick, then add the tarragon or tarragon vinegar, beating all the time. Season to taste and just before serving mix the cucumber in. Serves 4.

Drawn butter sauce – *Anlann ime thaosctha*

For turnips and young green cabbage there was always provided a jug of drawn butter.

From *The Big Sycamore* by Joseph Brady.

Serve with fish, meats and vegetables.

175 g (6 oz) butter
2 level tablespoons flour
salt and pepper

pinch of nutmeg
300 ml (½ pint) stock or water
squeeze of lemon

Melt half the butter, add the flour and seasonings and nutmeg and mix to a smooth paste. Add the water or stock gradually, over low heat, stirring well until it is creamy. Add the lemon juice and the remaining butter in small bits and stir well with a wooden spoon or a whisk until all the butter is absorbed and the sauce is creamy and slightly thickened.

You can keep this hot for about half an hour over hot, but not boiling, water, and it should be well beaten before serving. Serves 4.

Drawn butter (2)

This is melted butter, about 100 g (4 oz) with a good squeeze of lemon juice added or a few drops of white wine vinegar, and a pinch of nutmeg. A small amount of this, with a small jug of very thin English mustard, so that it is of pouring consistency, is excellent with cod, whiting, etc.

Gooseberry and fennel sauce – *Anlann spíonán*

Serve with mackerel. With the fennel omitted it goes well with pork, duck, game, goose or veal. This recipe is adapted from *The Lady's Assistant* by Charlotte Mason, 1778.

225 g (8 oz) gooseberries
2 tablespoons sugar
1 tablespoon butter

2 tablespoons fresh fennel, chopped
or 1 tablespoon dried

Cook the gooseberries in about half a cup of water and when boiling add the sugar and let them simmer gently until burst open but not overcooked. Then add the butter in small pieces and finally the fennel.

Green sauce – *Anlann glas*

This charming little recipe is from Sara Power's handwritten manuscript book of 1746:

Take some Spinage and Sorrell and pound it in a Mortar, strain it in the dish you intend to serve it in, put it over the fire, or a chafing dish of coals. Put to it a little Vinegar or the juice of a Lemon, and Sugar to your liking. Then put it to a sauce of Drawn Butter, or put in enough Butter to moisten it well. This sauce is fit for a Green Goose, Young Duckes, roast Chickens, or for a Boyl'd Legg of Lamb or Veal.

Hollandaise sauce – *Anlann ollannach*

This is not a traditional Irish sauce but it has been used here since the eighteenth century. For serving with asparagus, fish, especially poached salmon.

225 g (8 oz) butter
2 tablespoons white wine vinegar or
  lemon
2 tablespoons water

salt and white pepper
1 tablespoon water
3 egg yolks
lemon juice

All ingredients should be at room temperature.

Divide the butter into small pieces and in a heavy saucepan put the vinegar and 2 tablespoons water with a little pepper. Cook over a high flame until reduced by half. Take from the heat and add the cold water. Add the egg yolks and whisk briskly until thick and creamy, then lower the heat (or put over hot water) and whisk until thick, adding the butter pieces one at a time and make sure each piece is melted before adding the next. Lift the pan from time to time, and when it is all used up add the lemon juice and season to taste. Keep in a shallow pan of warm, not hot, water, and beat before using.

Horseradish sauce – *Anlann raidisí fiáine*

This is the traditional sauce to serve with boiled or roast beef, smoked trout or smoked mackerel.

3 tablespoons grated horseradish
2 tablespoons sugar
½ teaspoon powdered mustard

2 tablespoons white wine vinegar
salt and pepper to taste
150 ml (¼ pint) cream, whipped

Mix the other ingredients together thoroughly and then add them gradually to the whipped cream, stirring until completely combined.

Lemon sauce – *Anlann liomóide*

Serve with ham or bacon. With chicken stock instead of ham stock it is also good with boiled chicken.

Melt 1 heaped tablespoon butter in a saucepan and add the same amount of flour, mix well and cook stirring for 1 minute. Add 2 cups of hot ham stock and stirring well to avoid lumps bring to the boil, then add the grated peel and juice of 1 large lemon, stir again and serve hot.

Mayonnaise – *Anlann maonáis*

Though originally a French sauce, mayonnaise has been, for several centuries, a traditional sauce in Ireland for serving with shellfish, salmon, chicken and hard-boiled eggs.

2 egg yolks (without a vestige of
   white)
300 ml (½ pint) olive oil

2 teaspoons tarragon vinegar
lemon juice (optional)

All ingredients should be at room temperature.

Begin beating with a whisk or food mixer to break up the membrane around the yolks, then, while continuing to beat add, very slowly at first, very small quantities of oil. If the oil is added too quickly, particularly at the beginning, or if the yolks are from eggs just taken from the refrigerator and they and the mixing bowl are cold, the mayonnaise will not thicken and will 'crack'. No amount of beating, however vigorous, will restore it once this has happened but there is a simple way out of the difficulty; take another egg yolk and a mixing bowl, both at warm room temperature and start to beat the warm yolk, adding, little by little, the 'cracked' mayonnaise until the whole has been combined and is thickening normally. As more oil is added and the mayonnaise begins to thicken the oil can be added in increasing quantities until quite large amounts can be added at a time provided a strong beating action is maintained. When the sauce has attained the consistency of 'summer country butter' the vinegar and/or lemon juice can be added, little by little. This will have the effect of thinning the sauce, but adding the remainder of the oil will bring it back to its proper thickness again. Lastly add the seasoning and, if it is to be kept for some time, whisk or beat strongly while adding 2 teaspoonfuls of boiling water.

Variations
A little horseradish can be added for beef; juices and coral (lobster roe boiled with the lobster) from a lobster; chopped fresh herbs with white fish; and capers, chopped gherkins and a little white wine vinegar with some chopped parsley makes an adequate tartare sauce for fish.

Michael Kelly's sauce

Serve with crubeens (pig's feet), calf's head, boiled tongue, or tripe.
   Michael Kelly, born in Cork c.1790, was an Irish composer who became director of music at the Theatre Royal, Drury Lane, in 1822.
   Mix together 1 tablespoon brown sugar, 1 teaspoon each of dry mustard powder and freshly ground black pepper, and stir in 2 tablespoons garlic vinegar. Blend, then gradually mix with 1 cup of melted butter.

Mint sauce – *Anlann miontais*

This is the traditional accompaniment for lamb and hogget (lamb over 1 year old) all over Ireland. Many varieties of mint with differing fragrances grow readily in all parts of Ireland. If using the exquisitely aromatic Eau de Cologne mint, a word of caution, it is so powerful in flavour that it should be limited to only a small leaf or two, mixed in with more ordinary varieties, and be very finely chopped indeed.

2 tablespoons mint, finely chopped
2 tablespoons sugar
2 tablespoons white wine vinegar

Dissolve the sugar in 2 tablespoons of hot water, add the vinegar and pour the mixture over the mint. Cool and serve cold in a sauce-boat, with a spoon so that those who help themselves may stir it up.

Mushroom ketchup – *Ceitseap beacán*

The Irish Folklore Commission have noted that mushroom ketchup was eaten with boiled potatoes like gravy and indeed there is no more delicious accompaniment for good, dry, 'floury' potatoes. It should be stored in small bottles, as the delicate fragrance is soon lost once a bottle is opened. The best mushroom ketchup is made from the mature mushrooms known in Ireland as 'flats', those that have opened out fully to expose the gills which are dark in colour.

salt
mushrooms
black peppercorns

blade of mace
allspice berries

Take a large deep ovenproof jar with a cover and stand it close to a source of heat such as a stove or fireplace. Cover the bottom with a thin scatter of salt and spread a layer of mushrooms over that. Give another scatter of salt and make another layer of mushrooms and so continue until the jar is full. Set a lid on top that will keep dust out but still allow the air to circulate. Leave for three weeks or longer, pressing the mushrooms down from time to time. The moisture from the air and the salt will draw the juices from the mushrooms. When they have been soaking thus for three or four weeks, put the whole jar into an oven with the lid properly in position. Allow it to come to the boil, taking care that it does not boil over. Let boil gently for 20 minutes, then take it out of the oven. Strain the cooked liquor through a chinois or a fine sieve, letting it drip but not pressing it through. Measure, and for each 600 ml (1 pint) add 12 g (½ oz) whole black peppercorns, 6 g (¼ oz) whole allspice berries, and two good-sized blades of mace. Bring to a brisk boil, then pour into sterilized small bottles.

Mustard sauce for fish – *Anlann mustaird*

2 teaspoons French mustard
2 teaspoons English mustard
600 ml (1 pint) white sauce, freshly
  made (see recipe, page 134)

Combine the mustards and the white sauce stirring well, and serve with fish or vegetable dishes. Particularly good with grilled or fried herrings.

Mustard sauce for brawn – *Anlann mustaird*

Mix together 1 teaspoon English mustard, 2 tablespoons brown sugar, 4 tablespoons of oil and 3 tablespoons of white vinegar. Add salt, pepper, a pinch of ground cloves and another of nutmeg, and stir well.

Onion sauce – *Anlann oinniún*

This is traditionally served with boiled or roast mutton, pork or hard-boiled eggs. If making it to serve with mutton, de-fatted mutton stock can be used in place of warm milk.

2 large onions
600 ml (1 pint) milk, warm
pinch of powdered mace or nutmeg
50 g (2 oz) butter

2 tablespoons flour
salt and freshly ground white
  pepper

Peel and slice the onions. Melt half the butter in a saucepan and before it reaches the frothing stage put in the sliced onions. Soften over low heat, on no account letting them become in the least degree browned. When the onions have softened, add the milk, the mace or nutmeg and seasoning to taste. Let simmer gently for 10–15 minutes, then pour off the liquid. Reserve the liquid keeping it hot. Melt the remaining butter in a clean saucepan and stir in the flour to form a smooth roux, then gradually add the hot cooking liquid stirring carefully to avoid lumps forming. Chop the cooked onions very finely and add them to the sauce and serve, unless a very smooth sauce is desired, in which case it can be liquidized for 30 seconds at high speed, then reheated. It should be served in a warmed sauce boat.

Parsley sauce – *Anlann peirsile*

Perhaps the most widely used traditional sauce in Ireland, this is a most appetizing accompaniment for boiled ham, poached salmon and many other fish and meats. Bad parsley sauce is not of recent origin as witnessed by the comment of a French visitor to Ireland in the nineteenth century, Madame de Bovet, who reported that on the table, 'were four of those boiled fowls which would be excellent were they not dishonoured by a white paste with parsley in it, the national sauce!' It is the duty of all the Irish to uphold the national honour by preparing it as it ought to be prepared! The stock used should be determined by the dish with which the sauce is to be served: if a fish dish, a fish stock; if ham, a ham stock; if mutton, a mutton stock.

2 tablespoons butter (preferably country butter)	3 tablespoons parsley, finely choppped
2 tablespoons flour	salt and freshly ground pepper
300 ml (½ pint) good stock	300 ml (½ pint) milk

Melt the butter in a saucepan and before it froths, stir in the flour and continue stirring as it cooks for a minute, then, as you gradually add the stock and the milk, blend continuously to ensure that no lumps form. Continue cooking until the sauce is of a creamy consistency, and finally add the chopped parsley and season to taste. When properly made this sauce should have the consistency of thick cream even when cold.

Port wine sauce – *Anlann pórtfhíona*

This is excellent with game, particularly with venison or wild duck though it is also very good with hot tongue. Madeira can be used rather than port if preferred.

2 tablespoons butter	2 teaspoons parsley, chopped
1 tablespoon shallot, finely chopped	salt and freshly ground black pepper
4 tablespoons port wine	
300 ml (½ pint) chicken stock	1 heaped teaspoon of butter worked with the same amount of flour

Heat the butter and soften the shallot in it, not letting it brown. Add the port, bring to the boil and continue to boil until reduced by half. Add the stock, seasoning, parsley and lemon juice. Add the flour/butter mixture in small pieces, blending carefully to avoid forming lumps after each piece is added. Continue to cook for a few minutes after the last piece is added. Serve in a hot sauce boat.

Redcurrant jelly – *Glóthach cuiríní dearga*

This is good with game and all cold meats.

1½ kg (3¼ lb) redcurrants, cleaned
white sugar (preferably preserving
   sugar)

Put the currants (there is no need to take the small stalks from them) in a saucepan and add cold water to just cover them. Bring to the boil, continue boiling until soft but no longer.

Turn into a jelly-bag or muslin and leave to drip overnight without squeezing. Measure the juice and pour it into a large saucepan. For every 600 ml (1 pint) of juice add 450 g (1 lb) of sugar. Bring to the boil, stirring, to ensure that the sugar is completely dissolved, and boil briskly until it reaches a temperature of 104°C, 220°F or until a few drops on a cold plate jell. At that point pour at once into sterilized and heated jars and seal.

Rowanberry jelly – *Glóthach chaora caorthainn*

'The Wry Rowan', a sixteenth-century poem, concerns 'a tree whose berries are good to taste, which is named the wry rowan'. These are the berries that give us perhaps the finest of all jellies for eating with cold meats.

2 large cooking apples
1½ kg (3¼ lb) rowanberries
white sugar (preferably preserving
   sugar)

There is no need to peel or core the apples, simply chop them and put them with the rowanberries, into a large saucepan and barely cover them with cold water. Bring to the boil and continue boiling for 40 minutes, then turn into a jelly-bag or muslin and leave to drip overnight. Measure the liquid and put in a large saucepan. For every pint of the dripped juice add 450 g (1 lb) sugar. Bring to the boil, stirring to make sure that the sugar completely dissolves, and boil briskly until it reaches a temperature of 104°C, 220°F, or until a few drops on a cold plate jell, then pour at once into sterilized and heated jars and seal.

Crab-apple jelly – *Glóthach fhia-úll*

This is particularly good with pork.

1½ kg (3¼ lb) crab-apples
white sugar, preferably preserving
  sugar

Quarter the crab-apples (there is no need to peel or core them) and put them in a large saucepan with just enough water to cover. Bring to the boil and continue cooking until they are softened, then turn into a jelly-bag or muslin and leave to drip overnight. Measure the liquid, and put in a large saucepan. For every 600 ml (1 pint) of the dripped juice add 450 g (1 lb) sugar. Bring to the boil, stirring to ensure that the sugar completely dissolves; continue at a good rolling boil until it reaches a temperature of 104°C, 220°F or until a few drops on a cold plate jell, then pour at once into sterilized and heated jars, and seal.

Cream salad dressing – *Anlann uachtair sailéid*

This unusual dressing was probably introduced into Ireland by the Palatines, refugees fleeing French Catholic persecution who settled in Ireland in 1807, bringing with them many culinary innovations to the Irish scene, including the making of sauerkraut and the use of marigold petals as a herb. They became famous for their cider and for the introduction of new agricultural methods. Today most of their descendents live in the vicinity of the Limerick and Kerry border. A well-known Palatine name is Switzer.

2 teaspoons dry mustard
2 teaspoons sugar
2 hard-boiled eggs
2 teaspoons malt vinegar

300 ml (½ pint) sour cream or fresh
  cream combined with the juice of
  ½ lemon

Pound the dry ingredients and the eggs together until they are thoroughly blended, then gradually add the vinegar and the sour cream or cream/lemon juice mixture, and blend until perfectly smooth. Pour over salad and serve at once.

Sorrel sauce – *Anlann samhaidh*

The use of sorrel in Irish cookery goes back to pre-Christian times; this recipe dates at least from the Middle Ages. It is excellent with pork, veal or white fish.

225 g (8 oz) fresh sorrel
1 tablespoon white wine
75 g (3 oz) butter
pinch of powdered mace

Chop the sorrel finely and put into a saucepan with the other ingredients. Bring to the boil and allow to simmer for 15 minutes, then beat well with a fork or liquidize; serve hot.

Watercress sauce – *Anlann bhiolar uisce*

Watercress was greatly appreciated in ancient times in Ireland and is many times mentioned in the literature, particularly in the story of Sweeney the Mad.

Certain streams were noted for the deliciousness of their watercress. It makes a splendid sauce for the stronger flavoured freshwater fish such as salmon and pike.

generous bunch of watercress
600 ml (1 pint) fish stock
2 tablespoons butter
2 tablespoons flour

2 tablespoons cream
salt and freshly ground white pepper

Remove the watercress leaves from the stalks. Cook the stalks in the fish stock until tender, then strain and discarding the stalks reserve the liquid. Melt the butter in a saucepan and add the flour; cook, stirring for 1 minute. Gradually add the hot stock, stirring continuously to avoid lumps forming. When the sauce has thickened, add the finely chopped watercress leaves, season to taste.

White sauce – *Anlann bán*

A plain white sauce is traditionally served with boiled cauliflower and other boiled vegetables in Ireland. The consistency should be that of a thick pouring cream. If stock is used, it should be appropriate to the meat or fish dish that will be served with the vegetables.

4 tablespoons butter
2 tablespoons flour
salt and freshly ground white

pepper
450–600 ml (¾–1 pint) scalded milk, thin cream or stock

Melt the butter in a saucepan and stir in the flour. Cook for a minute, stirring well, then gradually add the milk, cream or stock, and continue stirring while the sauce cooks for about 5 minutes. Serve hot. Makes ½ litre (¾–1 pint).

White sauce variations – *Anlanna bána éagsúla*

From this one basic sauce many other sauces can be made such as:

Anchovy – *Anlann bán ainseabhaí*
Add 1 level tablespoon anchovy essence to the above white sauce, or 4 mashed, drained anchovy fillets.

Caper – *Anlann bán caprais*
Add 2–3 tablespoons capers with not more than about 1 teaspoon of the juice.

Cheese – *Anlann bán cáise*
Add 3–4 tablespoons grated hard cheese.

Egg – *Anlann uibhe*
Add 2 finely chopped hard-boiled eggs.

Lobster – *Anlann bán gliomaigh*
Add about 100–175 g (4–6 oz) finely chopped lobster, or about two-thirds of that and some lobster coral (lobster roe, boiled), about 1 tablespoon.

Mushroom – *Anlann bán beacán*
Add 75 g (3 oz) sliced mushrooms.

Mustard – *Anlann bán mustaird*
Add 1–2 tablespoons of mild made mustard, or 2 teaspoons of the hotter made English mustard.

Onion – *Anlann bán oinniún* (see page 135)

Parsley – *Anlann bán peirsile* (see page 135)
Other herbs such as chervil, tarragon, chives, or a mixture can be used instead of parsley.

Shellfish – *Anlann éisc shliogaigh*
See Lobster above. Crab – anlann bán portáin, prawn – anlann bán cloicheán, or shrimp or scallops can also be used.

Watercress – *Anlann bán bhiolar uisce*
Add 1 bunch finely chopped watercress without the stalks. If liked the stalks can be first chopped and blanched and some of the water used in place of the milk for the basic sauce.

Savoury butters – *Imeanna leasaithe*

Butter is such an intrinsic part of Irish cooking that many variations are found, in which other ingredients are incorporated in butter, worked in well, then cut into pats and chilled. The most usual savoury butters have the following combined with 100 g (4 oz) of butter:

Anchovy: 2–3 mashed, drained anchovies or 1½ teaspoons anchovy essence, sometimes with a squeeze of lemon juice added, usually served with fried fish;

Chives: 2 tablespoons chopped, served with steaks, chops or fish;

Hazelnuts, 50 g (2 oz) skinned and pounded with a squeeze of lemon juice added, served with grilled salmon steaks;

Parsley, 2 tablespoons finely chopped (leaves only) with a squeeze of lemon juice added, served cold with steaks, chops, grilled fish or grilled mushrooms or baked potatoes;

Watercress, about 1½ bunches with stalks discarded, finely chopped, with a little lemon juice if liked, served with grilled fish or steak.

Dessert sauces

The most traditional of these sauces is probably the custard sauce, which uses all the dairy products so beloved of Irish cooks.

Brandy sauce – *Anlann brandaí*

A great deal of brandy was formerly drunk in Ireland and quantities were put into puddings and sauces for them. This sauce was served with steamed or boiled puddings and latterly with Christmas pudding.

2 rounded teaspoons cornflour
300 ml (½ pint) cream or milk
1 tablespoon sugar

2 egg yolks, well beaten
4 tablespoons brandy

Cream the cornflour with a little of the cream or milk, and bring the rest of it to the boil. Take off the heat and stir in the creamed cornflour mixture. Bring back to the boil and cook stirring constantly for 5 minutes, then stir in the sugar and take off the heat. When slightly cooled, stir in the beaten egg yolks and brandy. Put over boiling water and stir or whisk until it thickens slightly. Serve warm. Makes about 300 ml (½ pint).

Brandy butter

Brandy butter has been eaten with Christmas pudding and with mince pies since the late nineteenth century.

Cream 175 g (6 oz) butter with 4 tablespoons sugar until well mixed, then add a pinch of grated nutmeg and about 3 tablespoons brandy; work this in until it is absorbed. Chill and serve spoonfuls on the hot pudding or pies.

Burnt sugar or caramel sauce – *Anlann siúcra dhóite nó caramail*

This goes back to very early times. Made as here, with the cream, it is served over ice cream and cream desserts. It is also made without the cream and used to line the mould for a baked custard.

75 g (3 oz) sugar
150 ml (¼ pint) double cream

Put the sugar into a dry saucepan. Place over moderate heat and stir while the sugar melts and when it turns a golden brown take off the heat. Add 4 tablespoons of cold water at once, taking great care, as it will boil rapidly and may sputter, so stand back a little. Put over gentle heat and stir until it becomes a thin caramel liquid. Pour into a basin and leave until cold, then whip the cream very lightly and add the cold caramel to the whipped cream in a thin stream stirring until smooth and creamy. Serves about 4.

Chocolate sauce – *Anlann seacláide*

Serve with ice cream or cold vanilla pudding.

175 g (6 oz) sugar
50 g (2 oz) cocoa powder

Stir the sugar into 150 ml (¼ pint) water over low heat and when it is completely dissolved bring to the boil and let it boil for 1 minute, stirring. Take off the heat and whisk in the cocoa powder. Keep mixing until the sauce is very smooth. It will seem a bit thin at first but if allowed to cool for 15–20 minutes, being stirred from time to time, it will thicken to the right consistency. Serves 4–6.

Cider and lemon sauce –
Anlann ceirtlise is liomóide

Cider is a Celtic drink and has been made in Ireland for centuries. Originally this sauce would have been simply cider and honey, but this version has evolved through the ages. It is excellent served over fresh fruit salads, ice cream or steamed puddings.

2 lemons
225 g (8 oz) honey or sugar
150 ml (¼ pint) dry cider

Grate the rind of the 2 lemons, then squeeze the juice. Put into a saucepan with the sugar and cider, stir well and heat slowly to dissolve the sugar. When completely dissolved, raise the heat and bring to the boil. Let it boil, without stirring, for 15–20 minutes until syrupy. Serve warm or cold. Makes 300 ml (½ pint).

Custard sauce – *Anlann custaird*

This is possibly one of the oldest of all sauces for serving with sweet things, for it is simply a mixture of eggs, sugar and milk, all readily available in early days. It is an essential part of the traditional Irish sherry trifle and should always be home-made, as the packaged variety bears little resemblance.

1 heaped tablespoon vanilla sugar
1 large egg and 1 egg yolk
300 ml (½ pint) milk

Beat together the egg, egg yolk and sugar until well blended and fluffy. Heat the milk and gradually stir it in, then put over boiling water and heat, whisking or stirring with a wooden spoon until it thickens, but on no account let it boil. It is ready when it coats the back of the spoon and falls in ribbons. It will appear thin but it will thicken as it cools slightly. Serve at once in a warmed jug, or if it is wanted cold, cover with damp greaseproof paper cut to fit and placed directly on top of the sauce to prevent a skin forming. Makes slightly over 300 ml (½ pint).

Honey sauce – *Anlann meala*

This was popular in the eighteenth century and is an easy and excellent sauce for serving with steamed puddings, milk puddings and sweet omelettes.

225 g (8 oz) honey, preferably heather honey
juice and finely grated rind of 1 lemon
juice and finely grated rind of ½ orange
1 rounded teaspoon butter
1 large egg, beaten, or 150 ml (¼ pint) thick cream

Mix the honey with 300 ml (½ pint) water in the top of a double boiler over hot but not boiling water; stir until well blended. Then add the fruit juices and grated rinds and mix well. Add the butter in little pieces and finally the well beaten egg or the cream. Cook over the hot water, stirring constantly for about 7 minutes or until it has thickened slightly. Serve warm. Makes about 600 ml (1 pint).

Irish Mist sauce – *Anlann 'Irish Mist'*

Irish Mist is a liqueur made from Irish whiskey, honey and herbs. This is a modern sauce, very useful for serving over ice cream, pancakes or steamed puddings.

2 tablespoons marmalade or apricot jam
4 tablespoons orange juice
50 g (2 oz) glacé cherries, chopped in half
small pinch of ground cinnamon
4 tablespoons Irish Mist, warmed

In a small saucepan, combine the marmalade, orange juice, cherries and cinnamon, and heat, stirring. Keep hot while you serve the ice cream or whatever pudding, then take the hot sauce to the table. Add the warmed Irish Mist and ignite it. As it burns pour over the ice cream or pudding and eat at once.

Jam sauce – *Anlann suibhe*

Serve with steamed puddings or with rice pudding. Almost any jam can be used according to taste: apricot is a good choice as its taste blends well with most things.

Mix together 3 tablespoons jam, 4 tablespoons white wine and 2 tablespoons sugar, and heat for 5–10 minutes over gentle heat. A dash of whiskey added before serving is very good.

White wine sauce – *Anlann fíona ghil*

This was a most popular eighteenth and nineteenth century sauce served usually with steamed or boiled puddings, particularly those made with dried fruits.

1 tablespoon cornflour	1 tablespoon brown sugar
150 ml (¼ pint) sweet white wine	grated peel of ½ lemon
1 tablespoon butter	

Mix the cornflour and wine well over heat, bring to the boil and let boil for 5 minutes. Add the butter in little pieces, then the sugar and finally the lemon rind. Serve hot. Makes about 150 ml (¼ pint).

chapter seven

VEGETABLES – *GLASRAÍ*

Vegetables and wild plants such as watercress (*biolar*), nettle (*neantóg*), sorrel (*samhradh*), and garlic (*gairleog*), known as *creamh* in early documents, have been known and eaten in Ireland since prehistoric times, and later on they figure in the lives of the Saints and in the Brehon Laws. Other members of the onion family (*Allium*) such as the leek and onion, both wild (*A. babingtonii*) and crow garlic (*A. vineale*) were used in the special localities they were found in, mostly sandy or rocky places from Donegal to Clare for it is the wild leek and crow garlic which is found in the southern part of Ireland. All of these were mainly used as flavourings, which is the way we use most of them today. Many other wild plants such as goosefoot (*Chenopodium*), orach (*Atriplex patula*) called *ceathram coatrach* in Ireland, both spinach-like plants, were eaten but are now quite forgotten. They were boiled, then pounded and mixed with butter.

Some variety of parsnip or carrot called *meacan* appears to have been eaten from early times.

The potato was not generally used until probably the late seventeenth century.

Peas and beans are included in the foods on which toll might be levied in the Charter granted by Edward III to New Ross in 1374; they were possibly first cultivated in monastic settlements soon after the Norman invasion. The cabbage so beloved of the Irish, is indigenous to Asia and did not arrive in the British Isles until the sixteenth century; Sir Arthur Ashley of Wilburg St Giles in Dorsetshire is reputed to have been the first to plant them from seed brought from Holland. However, the most delicate member of that family, sea-kale, had been known (and still is) as strand cabbage in Donegal, where it grew in the sandy soil.

Another vegetable which must not be forgotten, grown in Ireland since the Norman conquest, is the globe artichoke, a member of the thistle family. It grows freely in Ireland. Its abundance was remarked by Dionysius Massari, Dean of Fermoy in 1645. In early manuscripts they are called 'harty choakes'.

A ninth century poem says:

Is leighas air gach tinn
Cheamb 'us a Mhàigh
Ol 'an flochair gid
Bainne ghobhar ban.

(Garlic with May butter
Cureth all disease
Drink of goat's white milk
Take along with these.)

Artichoke pie – *Pióg bhliosán*

Lady's Kelynge's recipe book of 1683 mentions 'Harty Choak Pye'.

225 g (8 oz) shortcrust pastry	½ orange, sliced thinly
25 g (1 oz) butter	12 dates, stones removed
25 g 1 oz) flour	2 hard-boiled eggs, sliced
300 ml (½ pint) milk, or a little more	pinch of nutmeg
10 artichoke bottoms	pinch of ginger
175 g (6 oz) stoned white grapes	salt and pepper
½ small lemon, sliced thinly	milk or beaten egg for glazing

Trim the stalk of the artichokes close to the head. Put them into a large saucepan of boiling water with a clove of garlic, a sprig of parsley, a small sliced carrot, salt, peppercorns and a little lemon rind. Simmer for 20–30 minutes depending on size (test with a fork where the stalk was cut off: for this dish it should still be a little firm). Remove all the leaves and scoop out the 'choke'.

Make the pastry, roll into a ball and chill for at least 1 hour before using. Heat the butter, add the flour and cook for 1 minute, stirring, then gradually add 300 ml (½ pint) milk, stirring all the time to avoid lumps. Use a little more milk if needed, but do not make the sauce too thin. Put the artichoke bottoms into a deep pie dish along with the grapes, lemon and orange slices, dates and hard-boiled egg slices, putting the eggs in the corners and on top. Sprinkle with the nutmeg, ginger, salt and pepper. Cover with the sauce, seeing that it goes right down to the bottom. Roll out the pastry to fit the dish. Moisten the edges of the dish and put the pastry on, pressing the edges down well. Prick lightly all over, brush with a little milk or egg, and bake at 200°C, 400°F, Mark 6 for 15 minutes; reduce the heat to 190°C, 175°F, Mark 5 and cook for a further 15–20 minutes. Serve hot. Par-boiled Jerusalem artichokes can be used instead of globe artichokes.

Sugared beetroot – *Biatas siúcraithe*

Beetroots should be well scrubbed and then boiled in water to cover for 45 minutes to 1 hour, depending on their size, after which the skins are rubbed off. It is important to see that the skin is not damaged before cooking.

This recipe comes from Co. Kerry: it is served hot and is delicious with red meats or with bacon.

3 medium-sized beets, cooked, peeled, and still hot	2 level tablespoons sugar
3 tablespoons butter	good pinch of salt

Heat the butter with the sugar and salt, stirring together. Slice the beets and pour the butter mixture over them, mix well.

Beetroot and potato – *Biatas agus práta*

This is served hot and is very good with cold meats.

2 tablespoons butter	salt and pepper
3 medium-sized cooked beets, peeled and sliced	1 teaspoon sugar
2 small onions, sliced	1 tablespoon white wine vinegar or tarragon vinegar
2 tablespoons flour	700 g (1½ lb) mashed potato, kept hot
300 ml (½ pint) milk mixed with 2 tablespoons cream	

Heat a little of the butter and soften the onions in it, but do not let them colour. Heat the rest of the butter, add the flour and cook for about 1 minute, stirring, then add the milk and cream mixture stirring all the time. Season well. Add the sugar and the vinegar and cook for about 1 minute, stirring, then add the beet slices to heat in the sauce.

Make a circle of the hot mashed potatoes on a warmed serving dish, put the beetroot and sauce in the middle, and serve hot.

Pickled beetroot – *Biatas picilte*

Beetroot has been pickled for centuries and is still very popular in Ireland.

For 6 large beetroot, cooked, peeled and sliced, you will need about 1 litre (1¾ pints) white malt vinegar, 1 tablespoon each of whole cloves and ground allspice, a blade of mace, 1 teaspoon black peppercorns and 1 heaped tablespoon sugar. Boil this up and then let it stand until it cools. Put the sliced beetroot in jars that have screw tops and fill up the jars with the pickling liquid, strained, and then screw the tops on tightly.

In the eighteenth century the pickle was more elaborate. This is from Sara Power, 1746:

> Make a pickle of salt and water and also some Clarrett with it and boyle it, when it boyles put in your beetroots and parboyle it and let it cool. Then mix some Vinegar and some of the same pickle, and keep it in it, or else keep it in Vinegar and Clarrett mix'd, you may use either as you like, so cover and keep for use.

Brussels sprouts – *Bachlóga Bhruiséile*

They are extremely good if sliced celery (small pieces about 1 cm (½ inch) long) is put in after they have been cooking for 5 minutes. They should stay crunchy to contrast with the sprout. If celery is not available then sprinkle heavily with celery salt before serving. They should never be overcooked, but retain a 'bite'.

Cabbage with Bacon – *Cabáiste agus bagún*

Cabbage is perhaps the favourite vegetable in Ireland; it is certainly the one most used. The young spring greens are the early green cabbage before it has hearted. It is tender and sweet. Then there is the 'white' cabbage which is pale in colour and very tightly knit; this is the cabbage that will stand the longer cooking of boiled meat dishes and it is also very good shredded for a salad. 'Red' cabbage is another variety for which lengthy cooking is appropriate. There is also the green Savoy cabbage with a crimped leaf, it stands up well to frost so it is sown for the winter crop. It is slightly tougher than the other varieties.

1 large or 2 small Savoy cabbage	4 allspice corns
8 rashers streaky bacon	about 300 ml (½ pint) bacon or
salt and pepper	chicken stock
4 cloves	

Cut the cabbage in half and boil for 15 minutes in salted water. Drain, soak in cold water for 1 minute, then drain well and slice. Line the bottom of a casserole with half the bacon rashers, then put the cabbage on top, and add the seasonings. Add enough stock to barely cover, then put the remaining rashers on top. Cover, and simmer for an hour until most of the liquid is absorbed. Serves 4.

Creamed cabbage – *Cabáiste le hanlann uachtair*

This dish was a favourite in the Limerick and Tipperary districts when I was young, but it is undoubtedly very much older.

143

1 white or young green cabbage
about 1 kg (2¼ lb)
2 tablespoons butter
2 level tablespoons flour

pinch of grated nutmeg
600 ml (1 pint) creamy milk or thin
cream
salt and pepper

Trim the cabbage and remove the tough stalk, cut into eighths and blanch for 5 minutes in boiling salted water. Drain very well, then cut into thin strips. Heat the butter, stir in the flour and cook for 1 minute, then gradually add the milk then the nutmeg, stirring well to avoid lumps. Add the cabbage and bring back to the boil. Cover and cook gently for 15 minutes, stirring from time to time. Serve the cabbage, still a little crunchy, in the creamy sauce. Serves 4–6.

Dressed cabbage – *Cabáiste le hanlann ime*

This is a very old dish, cabbage with drawn butter.

An early seventeenth-century manuscript instructs: 'Take a large quantity of the worts and shred them and put butter thereto, and seethe them and serve forth – and let nothing else come nigh them.'

My aunt's method was as follows. Melt about 2 tablespoons of butter in a heavy pot, then add the cabbage around in this until it is all covered with the butter. Add about 3 tablespoons bacon stock or water, cover and cook gently for about 20 minutes. By this time the liquid is nearly absorbed and the cabbage cooked. Then she added a good pinch of ground nutmeg or mace, just a sprinkling of flour, stirred in well, then another 2 tablespoons of butter, or sometimes good bacon dripping, melted over the fire with the cabbage and tossed in it. Pepper was sometimes added if needed. This method was used for all kinds of cabbage and was delicious.

Scotch cabbage – *Cabáiste Albanach*

In Kerry this was known as *Cabáiste Scaits.* and many things were called 'Scotch', in this case with some reason as cabbage seeds were often imported from Scotland. As early as 1777 Arthur Young in his *A Tour of Ireland* 1776–79 writes:

He has not for five or six years past been without a small field of Scotch cabbages. The seed he sows both in March and Autumn for use at different seasons . . . His people were all of the opinion that a good acre of cabbage will go as far as two acres of turnips . . .

This was written about Johnstown, bordering on the Shannon. This recipe comes from the Irish Folklore Commission.

The tough outer leaves of white cabbage are taken off and the rest is finely chopped. If young this is done without first blanching, if older it is blanched first, then chopped finely. The cabbage is cooked in sour cream with a good pinch of salt.

Cabbage salad – *Sailéad cabáiste*

This obviously comes from the Palatines, see page 133. Arthur Young in *A Tour of Ireland* 1776–79 says that:

Mr Oliver planted a colony of Palatines 15 year ago, from about Rathkeale (Tipperary), 66 families in one year. The benefit of them has been introducing much tillage . . . they drill their potatoes, and on stubble land worn out. House their cattle, feeding them with hay and raising thereby dung . . . They live partly on sour crout (sic) . . .

I have not heard of sauerkraut being made for many years in the Limerick region but certainly shredded cabbage mixed with the sour cream dressing on page 133 is very popular. The cabbage should first be refreshed in ice-cold water before shredding.

Colcannon – *Cál ceannann*

This is traditionally eaten in Ireland at Hallowe'en or All Hallows' Day, October 31st. Until quite recently this was a fast day, when no meat was eaten. The name is from *cal ceann fhionn* – white-headed cabbage. Colcannon should correctly be made with cooked, finely chopped kale (a member of the cabbage family) but it is also made with white cabbage; an interesting version is the Irish Folklore Commission's which gives it as mashed potatoes mixed with onions, butter and milk with a boiled white cabbage in the centre. Colcannon at Hallowe'en used to contain a plain gold ring, a sixpence, a thimble or button; the ring meant marriage within the year for the person who found it, the sixpence meant wealth, the thimble spinsterhood and the button bachelorhood.

450 g (1 lb) kale or cabbage	cream
450 g (1 lb) potatoes	pinch of mace
2 small leeks or green onion tops	salt and pepper
about 150 ml (¼ pint) milk or	about 100 g (4 oz) butter, melted

If using the kale, strip from the stalks or likewise remove the stump of cabbage before cooking in boiling salted water until tender but not overcooked. Drain very well and chop finely. Meanwhile, cook the potatoes and while they are cooking chop the leeks or onion tops and simmer them in milk or cream to cover for about 7 minutes. Drain the potatoes, season and mash them well then stir in the cooked leeks and milk, adding a little more milk if needed.

Finally, blend in the finely chopped kale or cabbage (modern cooks will find a blender or food processor ideal for this.) Add the mace and taste for seasoning. Heat the entire mixture gently, then pile into a warmed dish. Make a small well in the centre and pour in the melted butter. Serves about 6.

Red cabbage with bacon – *Cabáiste dearg le bagún*

Red cabbage is often served with game, especially venison, and it is also served with all sorts of pork. If liked a large cooking apple, peeled, cored and sliced, can be added with the cabbage.

1 tablespoon butter
1 large onion, sliced
100 g (4 oz) bacon or ham, sliced
1 medium-sized red cabbage, shredded finely
300 ml (½ pint) stock

4 whole cloves
pinch of allspice
salt and pepper
1 level tablespoon sugar
1–2 tablespoons red wine or wine vinegar

Heat the butter and just soften the onion in it with the bacon. Add the cabbage stock, spices, salt and pepper, then add the sugar and the wine or vinegar. Bring to the boil, cover and let it simmer gently for about 2 hours or until quite soft. Red cabbage is one vegetable which can take a lot of cooking and is only improved by it. Taste for seasoning before serving. Serves 6–8.

Carrots with cream – *Cairéid le huachtar*

Carrots have been eaten since prehistoric times, not only as a vegetable, but often made into a sweet pie or pudding, and also a cake.

This is a popular old farmhouse recipe from the days when cream was both cheap and plentiful.

450 g (1 lb) young carrots
salt
½ tablespoon thick cream

2 tablespoons butter
pepper

Clean the carrots, slice them and cook well in boiling salted water until they are quite soft. Drain, and mash well. Warm the cream and butter together and add to the carrots with a little pepper; mix well. Heat gently and serve. Serves 4.

Sugared carrots with mint –
Cairéid siúcraithe le miontas

For a totally different flavour, chopped parsley can be used in place of the mint, if fresh mint cannot be obtained.

450 g (1 lb) young carrots
2 level tablespoons butter
pepper

squeeze of lemon
1 tablespoon fresh mint, chopped

Prepare the carrots by scraping. If small leave them whole, otherwise cut them in half. Boil in salted water until tender; drain well. Melt the butter in a saucepan, add the carrots and shake the pan to coat them with butter. Add pepper to taste and a good squeeze of lemon. Finally add the mint, mix well and serve. Serves 4.

Carrot pie or pudding – *Plóg nó maróg chairéad*

This eighteenth-century recipe from Sara Power's handwritten book of 1746 gives a good idea of how carrots were used as a sweet dish.

> Take half a pound of butter, the yolk of 10 eggs, half a pound of powder sugar, and one spoonful of orange flavour water, beat your eggs well and beat your butter either to cream or melt it in Oyle, then take well colour'd carrots, boyle, and pare them well, so mix and beat all together, put it in a dish and do the brim with puff paste, bake it an hour, you must pound the carrots.

I make a sort of flan like this, using 350 g (12 oz) mashed cooked carrots, 2 tablespoons butter, 4 egg yolks, or two whole eggs, a little sugar to taste, 1 teaspoon orange flower water (obtainable from chemists) and about 1 cup of creamy milk or thin cream, the mixture is poured into a 22.5–25 cm (9–10-inch) flan case lined with pastry and baked for 30 minutes. It makes a delicious first course or last course. Serves 4.

Pickled collyflowers – *Cóilis picilte*

These days cauliflower is usually boiled until tender but not soft, drained, then served with a cheese sauce or white sauce. In the eighteenth century cauliflower was often pickled. There are several recipes for it; this simple one is from the manuscript of Cicely Darcy, c. 1740.

> Take these that are cleanest and whitest, cut them from the stalks the length of your finger, put in a cloath and boyle them in water and milk for ten minutes, then take them up and set them by till they are cold. Make a pickle of white wine vinegar, a little whole white pepper, a bay leafe, a nutmeg divided into quarters, cloves and mace, boyled well together, let this stand till it is cold, and then put in your Collyflowers, they will be fit to eat in 3 days.

Braised celery – *Soilire galstofa*

1 medium-sized head celery	salt and pepper
1 medium-sized onion, sliced	4 rashers streaky bacon, chopped
300 ml (½ pint) chicken or bacon stock	2–3 tablespoons breadcrumbs
sprig of parsley	1 tablespoon butter

Clean the celery and cut into short pieces, then put into a saucepan with the onion, the stock, parsley and salt and pepper. Sprinkle the chopped bacon over the top, cover and cook over medium heat for about half an hour, or until tender. Scatter the breadcrumbs and the butter in small pieces on the top and bake, uncovered, in a hot oven, 220°C, 425°F, Mark 7, until crisp and brown. Serves 4.

Braised and stuffed cucumber – Cúcamar líonta agus galstofa

Cucumber was often stuffed and braised in the eighteenth century. Choose large cucumbers. Peel them, cut off one end only and with a large knife or spoon scoop out the seeds. Fill the space with minced cold meat mixed with chopped garlic and herbs, or use herbed sausage meat. Put a carrot in the end as a stopper and bake covered, in a little stock, in a moderate oven for about 1 hour. Serve cut into rings. Serves 4.

Kale with cream – Cál le huachtar

Kale is a good winter vegetable which withstands frost. It is known in Mayo and Donegal as 'Raggedy Jack' on account of the serrated leaves. It needs to be stripped from the tough part of the stalk, and wants longer cooking than cabbage.

This was my father's favourite method and is delicious with any pork or red meat.

Wash 1 kg (1¾ lb) kale and strip the leaves from the stalk, then put into briskly boiling salted water. Cook until tender, 20–30 minutes, drain well and chop finely. In a saucepan combine 2 tablespoons butter, 2 tablespoons thick cream and a pinch of nutmeg, salt and pepper, and then add the kale and about 2 tablespoons of stock. Mix well and cook until it is well heated and the sauce is slightly reduced. Serves about 4.

Leeks in cream sauce – Cainneanna in anlann uachtair

Leeks are one of the oldest vegetables in Ireland and are used for soups, flavourings in stews and as a vegetable.

12 medium sized-leeks	150 ml (¼ pint) cream
300 ml (½ pint) milk	1 egg yolk, beaten
salt and pepper	8 rashers bacon

Clean the leeks well and trim them, leaving on some of the green. Cook them whole in the milk with seasoning for about 20 minutes or until soft throughout. Drain, reserving the cooking liquid and keep the leeks warm. Combine the beaten egg yolk with the cream and stir this mixture into the hot milk; mix well, and heat gently, stirring until it thickens, but not letting it boil. Meanwhile, grill the bacon. Pour the cream sauce over the leeks, and serve with the grilled bacon. Serves 2–4.

Mushrooms – Beacáin

Mushrooms have been an Irish favourite for many centuries, and still hold a popular place in Irish kitchens. There are many varieties which grow wild, the most common being the field mushroom and the delicate and beautifully apricot-coloured chanterelle which abounds around September and October. It is like a parasol, so easy to distinguish. Many people say it is tough and needs long cooking, but they cannot have tried the chanterelles which grow near me. These need only the lightest of cooking in butter, which will become apricot-coloured too. Generally speaking never pick a mushroom with white gills beneath the cap or one which exudes a yellow juice when cutting. These are dangerous. If you want to explore your woodlands then get a good book about mushrooms with colour photographs to make quite sure. A delicious fungus commonly called Jew's Ear (*Auricularia auricula*) which is brownish in colour and vaguely ear-shaped grows on the trunks of dead elder trees. It should only be gathered in wet or damp weather when it expands. Then it should be dried slowly and kept in a screw-top jar. This is the very expensive Chinese fungi, and to use it take about 2 tablespoons; soak in boiling water for half-an-hour, then add to a casserole or stew dish and cook for about 1 hour. It is delicious and I often add some to a casserole of chopped pork or lamb, with root vegetables which we call 'Chinese-Irish stew'. Do not attempt to cook like ordinary mushrooms as it will be rubbery. See also First courses and Sauces.

A welcome and beloved visitor was Countess de Salis who used to come on foot across the hills in her red colleen-bawn cloak . . . for her we picked the earliest mountainy mushrooms; nothing was too good for this friend . . .

From *The Farm by Lough Gur* by Mary Carbery.

Puffballs – *Bolgáin (Lycoperdon)*

Theses are perhaps the most delicious and very delicate and the size varies from about 5 cm (2 inches) across to the giant one which reaches enormous proportions. They must be picked and cooked when very fresh, otherwise the inside is nothing but dust. The cooking methods vary depending on the size. Small ones can be dipped in egg and breadcrumbs, or batter, and fried in butter or oil. Those the size of an egg can be rolled in seasoned flour, then casseroled in milk with a very little onion and a bay leaf, the milk thickened after cooking, and the whole garnished with parsley, and in earlier times a few barberries were scattered over, the scarlet colour looking most attractive. Really large ones should be sliced and egg and breadcrumbed then served with lemon wedges.

Mushrooms with cream – *Beacáin le huachtar*

450 g (1 lb) mushrooms	juice of 1 lemon
2 heaped tablespoons butter	1 tablespoon flour
salt and pepper	150 ml (¼ pint) double cream
minced garlic	1–2 tablespoons parsley, chopped

Prepare the mushrooms and take out the stalks, then chop them finely and put at the bottom of an ovenproof dish. Sprinkle salt over, also a little pepper and minced garlic, but not too much. Then add the lemon juice. Put the mushroom caps on top, gill side upwards and fill each cap with butter, then leave in a warm place. Meanwhile, mix the flour into the cream very thoroughly and then pour this over the mushrooms. Cover and bake at 220°C, 425°F, Mark 7 for about half an hour. Serve garnished with parsley. Serves 4.

Nettles – *Neantóga*

Nettles are cooked like spinach; also used for soups. See index.

Onions baked in their jackets – *Oinniúin bácáilte ina gcraicne*

Onions and many members of the onion family have been mentioned in Irish literature since the beginning of our recorded history. Dean Swift had this to say about onions in 1795:

> They make the blood warmer,
> You'll feed like a farmer;
> For this is every cook's opinion
> No savoury dish without an onion.
> But lest your kissing should be spoiled,
> Your onions must be thoroughly boiled:
> Or else you may spare
> Your mistress a share.
> The secret will never be known:
> She cannot discover
> The breath of her lover,
> But think it as sweet as her own.

Choose onions of the same size. Put them unpeeled into a baking pan with about 1 cm (½ inch) of water. Put on the middle shelf of a preheated oven, 180°C, 350°F, Mark 4, and bake for about 1 hour for medium-sized onions; squeeze to make sure they are cooked. Serve on side plates, with the skins peeled down but still adhering, with salt, pepper and butter.

Onions with bacon – *Oinniúin agus bagún*

Peel 6–8 medium-sized onions and put into a casserole. Add 1 medium-sized sliced carrot, a little chopped thyme, a bay leaf and some parsley, a pinch of mace and 2 whole cloves. Add about 4 slices of chopped streaky bacon. Put in a hot oven or cook on top of the stove until the bacon melts, then add about 1 cup of chicken stock, enough to half cover the onions. Cover and cook at 180°C, 350°F, Mark 4 for about 1 hour.

Parsnip and apple purée – *Taos meacan bán us úll*

An account written in 1673 says: 'The Irish feed much also upon parsnips . . .' They are used a lot in stews and casseroles, but usually they are simply boiled, then drained and mashed with butter and pepper.

Here fairly tart apples are used as a contrast to the sweet parsnip. Prepare equal quantities of each by peeling and chopping. Then cook them separately, the apples in very little water, and if sharp with a little sugar added, but not too much. Drain and combine the apples with the cooked and drained parsnips, mashing or blending very well. Add butter, pepper and pinches of ground cinammon and cloves.

Parsnip cakes – *Cácaí meacan bán*

These are excellent with pork, ham, bacon and sausages.

450 g (1 lb) parsnips	1 large egg
2 large tablespoons flour	8 rounded tablespoons
pinch of ground mace	breadcrumbs
2 tablespoons melted butter	oil for frying
salt and pepper	

Peel and slice the parsnips, then boil in salted water until tender. Drain and mash them well. Add the flour, mace, melted butter, salt and pepper, then form into little flat, round cakes. Dip into the beaten egg, then into breadcrumbs and fry in hot oil until brown on both sides. Serves about 4.

Parsnip chips – *Sceallóga meacan bán*

Serve with beef or beefsteak dishes, lamb chops or grilled hamsteaks.

Peel the parsnips and cut them into long fingers, soak in cold water for an hour, then boil for a few minutes. Drain, pat dry and roll them in flour. Fry in deep fat as you would potatoes, until golden all over.

Peas – *Piseanna*

See Soups.

Boiled potatoes – *Prátaí beirithe*

The potato that Sir Walter Raleigh is reputed to have brought from America and planted on his estate at Youghal was the sweet potato. The Virginian potato, as the one we use today is called, did not arrive until much later.

It is thought that in early days only the poor ate them, the majority being used to feed the pigs we were famous for, and also to fatten poultry. A manuscript of the Royal Irish Academy, 1814, says:

Seldom was potatoes used at the farmers' or cottiers' table unless during the winter or close season of the year, and this at dinner only. However by the late eighteenth century potatoes had taken over from oats and barley as a staple diet because the land had been parcelled up into small acreage, not large enough to grow a cereal crop for a family, but large enough to grow sufficient potatoes to feed them after a fashion.

Sam McAughtry, the Irish writer and broadcaster, recorded some elderly people in his native Belfast recently. This is part of a recording he made of Geordie Devine from the Tiger's Bay area of Belfast, where he still lives.

I was reared in Sailortown: Little Ship Street. We left there and came up to this street in 1906 . . . You hear people talking about the hunger in these times, but we got grub nearly all the time. You could have threepence worth of beef cuttings . . . and Mercer the baker down near York Street sold the stale bread . . . Then there was a place down there at Mountmollyer Avenue where you could have got a pennyworth of jam, bring your own jampot, of course. You could have got buttermilk for twopence a quart, but bear in mind it was buttermilk. It used to come in the wee runlets, and the bung was took out and the buttermilk was emptied into the big barrel and when you went into the grocers shop he dropped a scoop down and filled your jug. You took that with your potatoes, and I'm telling you, you weren't hungry.

St John's Day, June 21st, was the traditional day for digging up and eating the first new potatoes. In Co. Antrim on this day the salmon fishermen had a salmon dinner with the first new potatoes. To get the best vitamin content from potatoes, it is best to cook them the old Irish way, that is, in their skins. They are usually served on side plates for the diners to peel at the table, then transfer them to the dinner plate to be buttered and seasoned. New potatoes are cooked in boiling salted water; old potatoes are started in cold water. When tender they are drained and covered with a cloth to finish in their own steam. A small crack, known as 'laughing potatoes', means they are ready to serve.

Stuffed baked potatoes – *Prátaí líonta agus bácáilte*

For four people choose four potatoes which are fairly large, unmarked and of roughly the same size. Scrub them well, then prick them all over just before baking on the middle shelf in a moderate oven, 180°C, 350°F, Mark 4 for an hour or longer, until they are soft when squeezed between finger and thumb.

Remove from the oven and while they cool slightly, prepare the stuffing. Combine in a bowl 3 rashers of bacon, fried until crisp and then chopped or crumbled; 3 tablespoons grated cheese; 1 tablespoon chopped parsley. Split the potatoes down the middle, taking care not to damage the skins. Scoop out the potato and put into the bowl with the other ingredients: add 2 tablespoons butter, 2 tablespoons cream, salt and pepper and mix very throughly. Put the mixture into the potato shells, sprinkle a little more cheese on top and heat in a hot oven, 200°C, 400°F, Mark 6, for about 20 minutes.

Boxty cakes or bread – *Bacstaí*

Boxty on the griddle, Boxty in the pan,
If you don't get Boxty, you'll never get a man.

Boxty is traditional to the northern counties such as Cavan and Donegal, in the form of cakes, bread, dumplings, pancakes and puddings. Mr Patrick Gallagher, born in Cleendra, Donegal in 1873, recalled just before his death at the age of 92 that when he was a child boxty bread was often served instead of oat bread, with milk and salt, and called 'dippity'.

450 g (1 lb) raw potatoes	salt and pepper
450 g (1 lb) freshly mashed cooked potatoes	60 ml (2 fl oz) melted butter or bacon fat
450 g (1 lb) self-raising flour	about 150 ml (¼ pint) milk
2 teaspoons baking powder	

Peel the raw potatoes and grate them into a basin lined with a napkin or cloth. Wring them tightly over the basin, catching the liquid. Put the wrung-out grated potatoes into another basin and spread with the cooked mashed potato. When the starch has sunk to the bottom of the raw potato liquid, pour off the top and add the starchy part to the potato mixture. Sift the flour with the baking powder, and add; mix well and season to taste. Add the melted butter or bacon fat and mix in. If the mixture seems too soft, add some milk gradually.

Turn out on to a floured surface and knead lightly, then shape into 4 flat round cakes. Mark a cross on each one, to let them rise properly and so that they will divide into farls when cooked.

Put on to a greased baking sheet and bake at 160°C, 325°F, Mark 3 for 30–40 minutes. Serve hot, split, with butter.

Boxty pancakes – *Pancóga bacstaí*

450 g (1 lb) raw potatoes	1 level teaspoon baking powder
175 g (6 oz) flour, sifted	2 large eggs, beaten
1 teaspoon salt	about 150 ml (¼ pint) milk

Peel and grate the raw potatoes and combine with the sifted flour, salt, baking powder, beaten eggs, and finally just enough milk to make a batter of dropping consistency. Drop in spoonfuls on to a hot greased griddle and serve hot with butter.

Cally, poundies or pandy – *Brúitín*

These three names are given to similar versions of one dish: mashed new potatoes with onion, milk or cream, seasoning and butter. It is usually eaten with a spoon. Another dish traditional to northern counties, called 'champ' is also similar but with other additions such as nettle tops or chives.

> There was an old woman
> who lived in a lamp
> she had no room
> to beetle her champ.
> She's up with her beetle
> and broke the lamp
> and then she had room
> to beetle her champ.
>
> Traditional rhyme.

The beetle was the large wooden vessel used for mashing, or pounding the ingredients together.

1¾ kg (3¾ lb) new potatoes
salt
300 ml (½ pint) milk

1 medium-sized onion, or 4 spring onions, finely chopped
125 g (4 oz) butter

Scrape the new potatoes and wash, then put them into boiling water and simmer gently until they are soft. Drain and put them back in the pan over a very low heat, covered with a cloth, to dry out, then sprinkle with salt and mash well. Put the milk in a saucepan with the chopped onion and simmer for 5 minutes. Add to the mashed potatoes and mix well; it should be soft but not sloppy. Put over very low heat to dry out, and serve with a lump of butter on each portion, or make a well in the middle and pour in the butter, melted. Serves 6–8.

Potato cakes – *Cáicíní prátaí*

There are several kinds of potato cakes. This one is like a scone and is eaten hot from the oven with butter. Sometimes the cakes are sprinkled with caraway seeds before baking. This dough can also be used to line a baking tin for a savoury flan.

2 heaped tablespoons butter
225 g (8 oz) self-raising flour
salt

175 g (6 oz) freshly mashed cooked potato
3–4 tablespoons milk

Mix the butter into the flour and add a good pinch of salt. Combine with the mashed potato and add enough milk to make a soft, slack dough. Roll out on a floured surface and cut into rounds about 8 cm (3 inches) in diameter. Put on to a lightly greased baking tray and bake at 220°C, 425°F, Mark 7 for 20–30 minutes. Serve hot, split open and spread with butter. Makes 9 cakes.

There is another form of potato cake made in a larger shape and cooked in a heavy frying pan. It is a very old country method.

225 g (8 oz) cooked mashed potatoes
about 40 g (1½ oz) flour
25 g (1 oz) butter

1 large egg, separated
2 tablespoons chopped mixed peel, optional

Mash the potatoes in a bowl, then add the flour gradually: the exact amount will be determined by the flouriness of the potatoes, but it should form a firm dough. Add a little over half the butter, melted, the the egg yolk well beaten and finally the stiffly beaten egg white. Well butter a heavy frying pan and put the mixture in evenly. Cover and cook over a moderate heat until it is cooked through, about 25–30 minutes.

Finely sliced onions can be used instead of the peel.

Fadge

Fadge is the northern Irish name for this potato-cake dish, usually served with bacon and eggs for breakfast. The cakes can be stored in a tin for re-use.

1 kg (2¼ lb) freshly mashed cooked
   potatoes
2 tablespoons melted butter or

bacon fat
4 tablespoons flour, or more
salt

Add the butter or bacon fat to the mashed potato and then work in the flour and mix well. (You may need a little more flour if the potatoes are not very floury.) Add salt to taste, then turn out on to a floured surface. Roll out to 1 cm (½ inch) thickness, then cut into large rounds or triangles. Have ready a heated, lightly greased griddle or heavy pan. Prick the potato cakes on both side and fry for about 3 minutes on each side. Makes about 12 cakes.

Potato and leek purée – *Taos prátaí is cainneann*

Onions can be used for this dish instead of leeks if preferred. It is delicious with roast lamb.

450 g (1 lb) potatoes
4 large leeks
1 tablespoon butter

150 ml (¼ pint) single cream or milk
salt and pepper
pinch of nutmeg

Peel the potatoes and cut them up. Clean the leeks thoroughly and cut them up, including some of the green parts. Cook them all together in salted water; drain. Press through a sieve, or liquidize, to make a purée; dry this for a minute over low heat, then add the butter and cream or milk, and beat well. Season to taste and add the nutmeg, stir briskly and serve hot. Serves about 4.

Potatoes and onions – *Prátaí agus oinniúin*

This is an old Irish country dish which was often served for supper with a glass of buttermilk.

1 large onion, or 2 small ones
4 medium-sized potatoes, cooked whole

about 2 tablespoons butter or bacon dripping
salt and pepper

Peel the onion, then put into boiling water for 2 minutes. Take out and cool slightly, then slice finely; pat dry. Peel the cooked potatoes and slice them fairly finely. Heat the butter or fat in a frying pan and fry the onion until just softened, but not coloured, then add the potato slices and brown them all together. Half-way through cooking add salt and pepper. Serve hot. Serves 2–3.

Potato pie – *Pióg prátaí*

This is Sara Power's 1746 recipe for a very grand potato dish. I have made it and found it delicious.

Boyle and peel your potatoes, pound and break them thro' a sieve, then weigh a pound of them and put to it half a pound of butter, half a pound of powder sugar, a little brandy and the yolk of 6 eggs. Beat them some time, your dish being ready, paste on the top and bake an hour.

There is yet another version in Selina Newcomen's book dated 1717. She lived at Mosstown, Co. Longford.

Potato pie [afterwards it says 'Try this.'] Half a pound of well boyld potatoes made fine with a spoon; quarter of a pound of melted Butter, three quarters of a pound of sugar, a few bitter Almonds pound'd. Six Eggs, the yolks and white beat separately. Mix your ingredients as you do for a Cake and when nearly mix'd add a Glass of Whiskey. Put your puff paste round your dish, three quarters of an hour will Bake it.

Potato and apple pudding – *Maróg phrátaí is úll*

2 heaped tablespoons butter
225 g (8 oz) self raising flour
salt
175 g (6 oz) freshly mashed cooked potatoes
3–4 tablespoons milk

5 medium-sized cooking apples
brown or white sugar to taste
2 whole cloves
juice of ½ lemon
2–3 tablespoons cider

Mix the butter into the hot mashed potatoes, add a good pinch of salt and the flour and mix well, then add enough milk to make a soft, slack dough. Roll out and line a 750 ml (1½ pint) basin with some of it, reserving enough for the lid. Fill with the apples, peeled and cored and finely sliced, and sweeten to taste with sugar. Add 2 whole cloves, the lemon juice and the cider (or water) taking care not to make it too wet. Dampen the pastry edges, lay the lid on and press down. Cover with foil and secure well. Steam, or cook set in boiling water up to the rim, for 2–2½ hours. Serve cut in wedges with cream or home-made custard. Serves 4–6.

Fishermen's potatoes – *Prátaí iascairí*

This is an old fisherman's trick from the west of Ireland to cook potatoes without a pot. On the beach dig a pit about 5 cm (2 inches) deep. Put the potatoes in their skins into the pit and shovel sand back over them. Light a fire on top. It is said the potatoes will be well cooked in a little over half an hour.

Sea-kale with cream – *Praiseach thrá is uachtar*

This most delicate of vegetables used to grow wild in the sand of the beaches of Donegal, where it was known as 'strand cabbage'. It can be obtained from good greengrocers in the spring. It is usually simmered in salted water like asparagus for about 15 minutes, until just tender at the bottom end, then well drained and served with melted butter or drawn butter.

Trim about 450 g (1 lb) sea-kale, then rub over with a cut lemon and blanch for about 5 minutes in boiling water. Drain well, then put into a shallow ovenproof dish with about 2 tablespoons of minced onion or shallot. Barely cover with single cream or creamy milk, cover with foil and bake at 180°C, 350°F, Mark 4 for about 10 minutes. Take from the oven and pour off the sauce into a small saucepan. Beat 2 egg yolks with 2 tablespoons of cream, add to the saucepan and beat very gently, stirring all the time, to just under boiling point. Season slightly, pour over the sea-kale and serve, or if liked the top can be browned slightly under the grill. Serves 2–3.

Pickled samphire – *Cabáiste aille, picilte*

Rock samphire (*Crithmum maritimum*) can be found very often growing on the tops or sides of cliffs. It is a small fleshy-leafed branching plant which has an unusual flavour. It figures a lot in old cookery manuscripts, sometimes chopped and put into a cream sauce, but mainly pickled. It can also be steamed until tender and served with melted butter. The taste, slightly resinous, is one which I find attractive.

Pick the tops and buds and pack them in a wide-mouthed jar. A few tiny pickling onions can be added, they will acquire a most delicate flavour. Make a spiced vinegar of 1 litre (1¾ pints) white vinegar, 1 heaped teaspoon pickling spices, 1 bay leaf, 2 allspice berries and about 1 tablespoon of sugar. Bring to the boil, then cool, strain and pour over the samphire buds until quite covered. Tie down and store in a cool place. This pickle will last for some time.

It can also be preserved in lightly salted water.

Rutabaga pudding – *Svaeid*

Swede, or rutabaga, is a very popular winter vegetable in Ireland. It is usually peeled, cut into cubes and boiled in salted water until tender, then drained and mashed well with salt, pepper, butter and a pinch of ground ginger. The name 'rutabaga' used to be common around Limerick, and it is by this name that it is still known in the United States, no doubt taken there by Irish immigrants. This is an old-fashioned winter dish, well worth trying.

450 g (1 lb) swedes	1 teaspoon salt
3 tablespoons fine breadcrumbs	1 teaspoon sugar
3 tablespoons milk	1 large egg, well beaten
2 teaspoons melted butter	

Clean, peel and cube the swede, and cook in boiling water until tender, then drain well. Mash thoroughly, then add all the other ingredients. Put into a 750 ml (1½ pint) casserole and bake at 180°C, 350°F, Mark 4 for 1 hour. A pinch of cinnamon or a pinch of ginger may be added. Serves 4.

Stuffed marrow – *Mearóg*

Vegetable marrow was a latecomer to the British Isles not arriving until the nineteenth century. It was first used for chutney–mainly as a substitute for mangoes. Medium-sized chunky marrows are often stuffed with minced leftover meat as here.

1 medium-sized marrow	chopped
225 g (8 oz) minced cooked meat	1 small egg
2 tablespoons fresh breadcrumbs, white or brown	salt and pepper
	1 tablespoon tomato purée
1 teaspoon mixed chopped herbs	600 ml (1 pint) stock
1 small onion, grated or finely	grated cheese for topping

Peel the marrow, then cut in half lengthways and take out the seeds with a spoon. Put into a large fireproof dish, half full of boiling water and simmer for 5–10 minutes, until soft but not mushy. Meanwhile, mix together well the meat, breadcrumbs, herbs, onion, egg, salt and pepper. Put the marrow halves into an ovenproof dish and fill with the mixture. Combine the tomato purée with the stock and pour the liquid into the pan. Sprinkle the tops with a little grated cheese, cover with a lid or foil and bake in a moderate oven 180°C, 350°F, Mark 4 for about 40 minutes. Serves 4.

Sea vegetables

Carrageen, dulse and sloke are three gifts to Irish kitchens from the sea. Carrageen (*Chondrus crispus* or *Chondrus mamillosa*) is a branching mucilaginous seaweed found on rocks in Ireland. It is either dark purple or green when growing, but is usually sold dried and bleached. It is also known as 'Irish moss' or 'sea moss'. Its very gelatinous quality makes it good for thickening soups, for use in jellies, both sweet or savoury (it does not taste at all marine when properly prepared). It has a high vitamin content and nowadays it can be bought in many health shops. See index for recipes.

Dulse – *Duileasc*

Dulse (*Palmaria palmata*), also called 'dillisk', or 'dillesk', is a reddish-brown seaweed found on all the coasts of Ireland. It is usually sold dried. Added to fish or vegetable soup, it requires long slow cooking, but it can also be eaten raw.

Wash the dulse well removing any little bits of sand, grit or shell, then soak in cold water for 2–3 hours. Drain, and simmer in stock or milk for 2–3 hours until tender. Drain again and put back in the pan, add pepper and a good knob of butter and reheat a little before serving.

Sloke – *Sleabhac*

Sloke (*Porphyra umbilicalis*), known in Wales as 'laver' and also known as 'sea spinach', is a greenish-coloured seaweed found on rocks all over Ireland.

Wash well to remove all sand and grit, then soak for a few hours, and drain well. Layer in a casserole with dots of butter, pepper and salt, and add about 2.5 cm (1 inch) of water or less to keep the sloke from burning during long slow cooking. Bring to the boil, lower the heat and simmer very gently for 3–4 hours, stirring from time to time. Serve hot or cold with lemon juice or a little vinegar.

chapter eight

PUDDINGS – *MARÓGA*

Líne ugae, mil, meas, melle,
    Dia dod–roíd;
ulba milsi, mónainn derca,
    derona froích.

Eggs in clutches and God gives mast
    honey, heathpease;
sweet the apples and the berries
    of bog and heather

Anonymous tenth-century poem, *Ata Uarboth Dam I Caill* (*The Hermit*). Translated by James Carney.

Since the very earliest times, fruit served with honey as a sweetener has been a great part of the Irish diet. Many of these fruits were wild, but the apple was cultivated in pre-Norman times for they are specified in the regulations governing the food of the Culdees: 'In the case of apples if they be large, five or six of them, with the bread, are sufficient, but if they are small, twelve . . .' Even earlier, in the Laws of the fifth century an absconding tenant had the right to compensation for 'any that his own hand had planted'.

    The wild fruits most often mentioned are cherry, raspberry, blackberry, strawberry, elderberry, bilberry or whortleberry, cranberry, rowanberry, sloe, and of course apples and crab-apples. Nuts, too, are a fruit and the indigenous hazel nut occurs in both legend and fact.

Pastry making seems to have come to Ireland with the Normans, so many of these fruits were made into pies or mixed with the thick rich golden cream so freely available. They were cooked with honey to give added sweetness of a sort which can never be obtained with sugar, for it gives a lovely wild taste. Many of the fruits were made into wines and later on, into a thick paste, almost like a fudge, which kept very well.

In large houses the stillroom, where the wines, preserves and some sweet dishes were made, was always the province of the lady of the house. It is for this reason that some of the carefully hand-written recipe books of the eighteenth century which I own consist largely of sweet dishes and preserves of one kind or another.

Mrs Delany, the wife of the Dean of Down, wrote from Clogher in a letter dated August 2nd 1748, after going for a sketching walk in Longford's Glinn: 'I gathered four sorts of fruit – raspberries, cranberries, strawberries and nuts, of which there are a great plenty, the raspberries were particularly high-flavoured.' She grew a lot of imported fruits too, for back in Dublin she wrote in September 1750 from her home: 'I have just been gleaning my autumn fruits – melon, figs, Beury pears, grapes, filberts and walnuts. Walnuts are indeed but just come in with us. I loaded my basket and filled my hands with honeysuckles, jessamine, July flowers and pippins.'

All Irish people have a very sweet tooth and will spend hours making elaborate puddings and decorating cakes for the delectation of themselves and their families. The boiled suet puddings in winter, filled with dried fruit, or served with jam, cost next to nothing: they simmered over the fire and were a warming meal in the hard days of winter, especially during the years of hardship.

However, there are many lighter sweet dishes, some made with carrageen, which are delicious and at the same time full of vitamins. Almost all of the following recipes are still being made all over Ireland and enjoyed by all the generations of the family.

Almond cream – *Uachtar almóinní*

This was a favourite eighteenth-century pudding when almonds were used in cooking in many ways, usually after being pounded in a mortar.

4 heaped tablespoons ground
  almonds
300 ml (½ pint) double cream
1 heaped tablespoon fresh
  breadcrumbs

3 eggs, separated
2 heaped tablespoons sugar
2 tablespoons almonds, coarsely
  chopped

Mix the ground almonds with the cream, breadcrumbs, egg yolks and sugar very well in the top of a double boiler or over a very gentle heat, stirring as it heats. Do not let it boil. When it has thickened slightly, take off the heat and cool.

Whip the egg whites until stiff. Gently fold them into the cooled mixture, then spoon it into serving dishes and garnish with the chopped almonds. Chill, and serve cold. Serves 4.

Almond pudding – *Maróg almóinní*

This is similar to the almond cream but is more like a soufflé.

½ tablespoon butter
300 ml (½ pint) single cream
40 g (1½ oz) fresh breadcrumbs
50 g (2 oz) sugar
4 heaped tablespoons ground

almonds
4 drops almond essence
3 eggs
1 heaped tablespoon split or chopped almonds

Butter a 1-litre (2-pint) soufflé or ovenproof dish well. Gently warm the cream to well under boiling point and pour over the breadcrumbs in a bowl; leave for about 7 minutes. Add the sugar, ground almonds and almond essence and mix well.

Separate 2 of the eggs and beat 1 whole egg with the 2 yolks and add to the mixture. Whisk the 2 egg whites until stiff and fold in gently, seeing that they get down to the bottom. Sprinkle with split or chopped almonds then bake at 200°C, 400°F, Mark 6 for 25-30 minutes, and serve at once. Serves 4.

Apples – *Úlla*

Apples were so important that in the Brehon Law, or Laws of the Fianna, it was stated that an absconding tenant be compensated for 'any that his own hand had planted'. The Brehon Laws were written in AD 438, the tenth year of King Leary's reign, and from the eighth to thirteenth centuries they were transcribed on vellum from earlier records. The largest and most important volume is *Senchus Mor* – the *Great Old Law Book*. In the first century when Conor Mac Nessa, King of Ulster reigned a crisis was reached when no man was entitled to be a Brehon until he had studied a full law course which took twenty years, and then passed a stiff examination Feis at Tara.

Mention must be made of the Irish peach apple, a small rather insignificant looking eating apple, which is the most delicious of all to eat raw. The taste is clear, fresh and vaguely reminiscent of peaches: even the smell of them in a fruit bowl permeates the room with their fragrance. It is, however, in great danger of dying out mainly because it fruits right at the end of the branch, so pruning is different. It exists in many old gardens and it is vital that it is kept going.

Trees of apples huge and magic,
    great its graces;

Aball ubull (már a ratha)
      mbruidnech mbras;

Anonymous tenth-century poem, *Ata Uarboth Dam I Caill* (*The Hermit*). Translated by Kuno Meyer.

Apple bobbing

Apples also play a part in many traditional customs in Ireland . There is one which used to be very much enjoyed at Hallowe'en called 'apple bobbing' which is catching apples in water. It is beautifully described in *The Farm by Lough Gur* by Mary Carbery, writing about County Limerick in the 1860s.

> Into the brightness and warmth of the kitchen came Tom and a wandering fiddler from the hayshed, followed by Murnane and Dinny-bawn who slipped in like his own shadow. The farmboys were already on their knees beside the tub of bobbing apples and soon the games were in full swing but the laughter which accompanied them was subdued on account of the holyday, and the screams, as the elusive apples dipped away from the little snaps of the maids' mouths and from the attack of the boys' strong teeth ... Father looked at the clock. 'Have you lads snapped the last of the apples?'
>   'We have not, sir,' the boys spluttered as they dipped their heads in the tub.

There are several traditional apple cakes and puddings eaten on that evening. See also Colcannon, page 145, and Barm brack, page 196.

Apple amber – *Úll ómrach*

Rhubarb can also be used for this dish.

450 g (1 lb) cooking apples, peeled, cored and thinly sliced
100 g (4 oz) sugar, or to taste

juice of 1 lemon
2 large eggs, separated

Cook the apple slices in about 2 tablespoons of water stirring occasionally until they form a purée. Add about ¾ of the sugar, the lemon juice and the egg yolks; mix well. Put into an ovenproof dish and cook at 180°C, 350°F, Mark 4 for 20 minutes.

Meanwhile, whisk the egg whites until stiff, folding in the remaining sugar. Pile the meringue evenly on top of the apple mixture, return the dish to the oven and bake for about 10 minutes. Serve hot or cold. Serves 4.

Apple barley flummery – *Boighreán úll*

This is a very old dish hardly ever seen today, but very good: blackcurrants, gooseberries and rhubarb can also be used, and if preferred sago or tapioca can be used instead of the pearl barley.

4 tablespoons pearl barley
700 g (1½ lb) eating apples peeled, cored and sliced

50 g (2 oz) sugar
juice of 1 lemon
¾ tablespoon double cream

Put the barley in 1 litre (1¾ pints) water and bring to the boil. Add the sliced apples and continue cooking gently until the barley and apples are soft. Press through a sieve or liquidize and put back in the saucepan. Add the sugar and lemon juice and bring to the boil again. Remove from the heat, allow to cool and then chill. Serve cool with the cream stirred in. Serves 4–6.

Apple Charlotte – *Úllóg*

Another old dish which is probably the forerunner of Brown Betty. This can also be made with a mixture of half apple and half blackberries, rhubarb or plums.

100 g (4 oz) fresh breadcrumbs
40 g (1½ oz) sugar
6 tablespoons butter
700 g (1½ lb) apples

50 g (2 oz) soft brown sugar
1 teaspoon golden syrup
grated rind of 1 lemon
1 tablespoon demerara sugar

Put the breadcrumbs, sugar and 4 tablespoons of the butter, in small pieces, into a bowl and reserve. Prepare the apples and put into a saucepan with 1 tablespoon of butter and 1 tablespoon of water and cook until soft. Then beat in the brown sugar, syrup and lemon rind and take off the heat.

Butter a 1-litre (2-pint) ovenproof dish with half the remaining butter and scatter some of the crumbs over the bottom and sides, pressing them to stick. Pour in the apple mixture and top with the rest of the crumbs. Sprinkle with the demerara sugar and dot with the remaining butter.

Cook in the middle of a 190°C, 375°F, Mark 5 oven for about 45 minutes or until crisp and golden brown. Serve warm with cream. Serves 4.

Apple crunch – *Brioscán úll*

If liked, instead of breadcrumbs a mixture of half breadcrumbs and half oatmeal may be used for the crunch.

900 g (2 lb) eating apples, peeled, cored and thinly sliced
100 g (4 oz) sugar
6 heaped tablespoons fresh breadcrumbs

100 g (4 oz) butter
2 heaped tablespoons brown sugar
2 tablespoons blackberry jelly
150 ml (¼ pint) cream, whipped

Cook the apple slices with the sugar in 150ml (¼ pint) of water stirring occasionally, until they purée. In another pan make the crunch mixture. Combine the butter, breadcrumbs and brown sugar well and cook over a gentle heat, stirring occasionally for 5 minutes; cool.

In a serving dish make alternate layers of the apple and the crunch mixture until the dish is full, ending with the crunch. Decorate the top with blobs of blackberry jelly and whipped cream. Serves 4–6.

Clonlara apple pudding – *Maróg úll*

This is a family recipe about 90 years old for a pudding that is delicious in the winter.

225 g (8 oz) self raising flour
pinch of salt
100 g (4 oz) shredded suet
6 large cooking apples, peeled, cored and sliced

50 g (2 oz) butter
grated rind of 1 lemon
175 g (6 oz) sugar
225 g (8 oz) apricot jam
cream or custard

Sift the flour and salt, then add the suet and mix with about 2–3 tablespoons cold water to make a firm dough. Roll out on a floured surface to line a 1-litre (2-pint) pudding basin leaving enough for a lid. Line the basin pressing on to the sides. Cook the apple slices with the butter, lemon rind, sugar and jam until soft but not broken up. Cool, then put into the basin, dampen the edges of the dough and lay on the lid. Cover with greaseproof paper and foil, tie down and steam for 2 hours. Serve hot from the basin, with cream or custard. Serves 4.

Friar's omelette – *Uibheagán na manach*

I have adapted this from a recipe of 1804.

450 g (1 lb) apples, peeled, cored and sliced
100 g (4 oz) brown sugar
1 clove

pinch of mace
juice of ½ lemon
2 eggs, well beaten
100 g (4 oz) fresh breadcrumbs

Cook the apples with 2–3 tablespoons water, most of the brown sugar, the clove and mace, stirring occasionally until they form a purée. Beat in the lemon juice and most of the butter; cool. When quite cold, add the well beaten eggs and mix in. Grease an ovenproof dish with the rest of the butter and coat thickly with breadcrumbs on sides and bottom. Put the apple mixture in and cover the top thickly with the rest of the crumbs. Bake at 180°C, 350°F, Mark 4 for 30 minutes. Serve hot or cold sprinkled with the rest of the brown sugar and with whipped cream. Serves 4.

Apricot crumble – *Grabhar aibreog*

This can be made with dried apricots rather than fresh if the fresh ones are not available. Cook them briefly first, after soaking in cold water for 4 hours.

450 g (1 lb) fresh apricots, sliced and
   stoned
juice of 1 orange
50–75 g (2–3 oz) sugar

100 g (4 oz) butter
100 g (4 oz) flour
50 g (2 oz) brown sugar

Put the apricots in the bottom of a soufflé dish 18 cm (7 inches) in diameter. Pour the orange juice through a strainer, and add the sugar. Cook in a moderate oven, 180°C, 350°F, Mark 4, until they soften. Take out and let them cool while making the crumble. Rub the butter into the flour, then add the sugar. Spread this over the apricots and bake at 200°C, 400°F, Mark 6 for half an hour. Serves 4.

Bilberry mousse – *Mús fraochóg*

Ubla milsi, mónainnderca
     dercna froich

Sweet the apples and the berries
     of bog and heather

Anonymous tenth-century poem, *Atta Uarboth Dam I Caill* (*The Hermit*). Translated by James Carney.

Perhaps next to the apple the most Irish of all fruits is the bilberry (*Vaccinium myrtillus*, the same family as the blueberry, blackberry and whortleberry). It is known as *fraughan* (pronounced approximately 'frocken') and there are several varieties. The wild ones grow in bogs, moors or wherever heather grows, and because it grows sometimes under the heather it can be difficult to find.

Fraughan Sunday was a great day in the past and took place on the nearest Sunday to August 1st, also called Lammas Sunday. Being the first Irish fruit to ripen, and also the occasion for the digging of the new potatoes, it was a festival in many ways with many attractions. It is possibly a survival of the pagan festival of Lughnasa, Lugh being the Celtic God of the Sun. It is also the day of the large penitential pilgrimage to Croagh Patrick (St Patrick's mountain) in Co. Mayo.

450 g (1 lb) bilberries
100 g (4 oz) fine sugar
12 g (½ oz) powdered gelatine

juice of 1 lemon
300 ml (½ pint) cream
2 egg whites, stiffly beaten

Put the berries into a saucepan with the sugar and lemon juice and simmer over a gentle heat for 10 minutes. Then take off the heat. Dissolve the gelatine in 3 tablespoons of water, add the cooked fruit and stir well. Put the mixture through a sieve, rubbing as much through as possible. Leave until cold and beginning to thicken. Add the whipped cream and fold in, then add the beaten egg whites and fold in. Make sure that it is all well folded together, spoon into the serving dish and chill until firm. Serves 4–6.

They also make marvellous pies, tarts and jams, with a little lemon juice added.

Blackberry cream – *Uachtar sméar*

Blackberries are an extremely popular wild fruit, far more popular than bilberries. They have been mentioned in literature since earliest times and occur in many early poems, particularly as part of the diet of the mad King Sweeney in the eighth century.

> Watercress
> Apples, berries, beautiful hazelnuts,
> Blackberries, acorns from the oak tree;
> Haws of the pricking sharp hawthorn,
> Wood sorrels, good wild garlic,
> Clean-topped cress, mountain acorns
> Together they drive hunger from me.
>
> Anon.

450 g (1 lb) blackberries	25 g (1 oz) gelatine
100 g (4 oz) sugar	300 ml (½ pint) double cream,
150 ml (¼ pint) milk	whipped stiffly

Cook the blackberries with sugar in about 300 ml (½ pint) of water until soft, then sieve them to remove the seeds. Warm the milk, dissolve the gelatine in it and add to the fruit purée, stirring well. Add the whipped cream, mix thoroughly, and pour into individual dishes to chill. Serves 4.

Blackberry and lemon pudding – *Maróg sméar agus liomóide*

Bilberries can be used for this instead of blackberries if preferred. It is a very light pudding with a lemony fruit sauce at the bottom.

350 g (12 oz) blackberries	grated rind and juice of 1 lemon
1½ tablespoons butter	3 tablespoons flour, sifted
100 g (4 oz) sugar	600 ml (1 pint) milk
2 eggs, separated	sugar for dusting

Put the berries in an ovenproof dish. Cream the butter and sugar, then add the beaten egg yolks, the lemon rind and juice and the flour and beat well. Gradually add the milk and beat; finally beat the egg whites stiffly and fold in.

Pour the mixture over the blackberries and set the ovenproof dish in a pan with about 2 cm (1 inch) of hot water surrounding it. Bake it 180°C, 350°F, Mark 4 for 35–40 minutes or until risen and golden on top. Dust with sugar and serve hot. Serves about 4.

October cobbler – *Caibléir dheireadh fómhair*

This pudding is to be made with a mixture of autumn fruits gathered early in the month of October.

450 g (1 lb) blackberries,
   elderberries, damsons, plums
1 tablespoon lemon juice
50 g (2 oz) butter
3 heaped tablespoons sugar

175 g (6 oz) self raising flour
pinch of salt
100 g (4 oz) butter
3 tablespoons milk

Clean the fruits and put them with the sugar and lemon juice in a buttered pie dish and dot with butter. Sift the flour with the salt and rub the remaining butter into it. Mix in the milk to make a firm but elastic dough. Roll out and put roughly over the fruit; prick all over with a fork. Bake at 200°C, 400°F, Mark 6 for 30 minutes. Serve hot with cream. Serves 4–6.

Black cap pudding – *Maróg sútha dubha*

The blackcurrant is a valuable fruit full of vitamin C which grows freely in Ireland. This pudding was originally made with black raspberries, a very dark-red raspberry hardly ever seen these days except in gardens. Nowadays it is made with blackcurrants.

½ tablespoon butter
100 g (4 oz) blackcurrants, cleaned,
   topped and tailed
squeeze of lemon juice
1 heaped tablespoon sugar

150 g (5 oz) fresh breadcrumbs
75 g (3 oz) flour
2 large eggs, beaten
300 ml (½ pint) milk
a little butter

Butter a 1-litre (2-pint) pudding basin. Put the blackcurrants in a saucepan with the lemon juice and 2 tablespoons sugar and cook gently for about 5 minutes. Transfer to the basin.

Sift the flour into a bowl, add the breadcrumbs and sugar and mix well. Make a well in the middle and add the beaten eggs and mix. Finally add the milk and beat well. Leave to stand for about 15 minutes. Pour over the blackcurrants, cover and tie down, and steam for 2–2½ hours. Turn out by reversing the basin so that the 'black cap' covers the pudding. Serve with cream. Serves 4–6.

Blackcurrant sponge – *Císte spúinse cuiríní dubha*

450 g (1 lb) blackcurrants, cleaned,
   topped and tailed
4 tablespoons sugar
1 tablespoon lemon juice
175 g (6 oz) self raising flour

100 g (4 oz) butter
1 tablespoon sugar
3 tablespoon milk
1 egg

Put the blackcurrants, sugar and lemon juice in an ovenproof dish and put into a hot oven, 200°C, 400°F, Mark 6, for about 10 minutes, then remove but leave the oven on. Meanwhile prepare the sponge:

sift the flour, add the butter and rub it in well, then add the sugar; mix in the beaten egg and finally enough milk to make a soft dough. Spread in a baking pan.

After taking the fruit from the oven, let it cool a little then drop it in spoonfuls haphazardly on to the sponge. Bake for about 30 minutes and serve hot or cold with cream. Serves 4.

Blancmange – *Bánghlóthach*

This was a great pudding for all of the last century and half of this one, called in Ireland a 'shape'. Other flavourings that can be used instead of vanilla are chocolate, coconut, coffee or almond essence, or rum. If the finished pudding, when cold, is studded all over with blanched almond halves and with angelica and currants to make a 'face', the result will be the pudding called 'hedgehog'.

3 tablespoons cornflour
120 g (4 oz) sugar
pinch of salt
3 tablespoons milk

600 ml (1 pint) milk, scalded
1 teaspoon vanilla
2 eggwhites, stiffly beaten (optional)

Mix the cornflour, sugar and salt with the 3 tablespoons of milk; stir until smooth, then add to the warm scalded milk and stir well. Put into the top of a double boiler over hot water and cook for 15 minutes, stirring constantly, until the mixture thickens. Take off the heat and stir a little until it cools slightly. Wet a mould. Add the vanilla, and the beaten eggwhites, if using, to the mixture, stir and pour into the wetted mould. leave in a cold place to set. Serves 4–6.

Bread and butter pudding – *Maróg aráin agus ime*

A pinch of mixed spice is sometimes added to the sugar in this recipe, or a teaspoon of rum essence.

½ tablespoon butter
6 thin slices buttered bread, crusts removed
100 g (4 oz) sultanas and raisins (and

include chopped peel if liked)
75 g (3 oz) brown sugar
3 eggs
¾ litre (1½ pints) milk

Butter a 1-litre (2-pint) pie dish. Cut the bread into squares or triangles and arrange half of them in the dish. Scatter the sultana mixture over the bread, add about two-thirds of the sugar, then put the rest of the bread on top. Beat the eggs with about half the remaining sugar, add the milk and mix, then pour over the contents of the pie dish; it should about half-fill the dish. Leave to stand for half an hour or longer. Sprinkle with the remaining sugar and bake at 180°C, 350°F, Mark 4 for about an hour, or until the custard is set. It can be eaten hot or cold. Serves 4–6.

Honey and lemon cream – *Uachtar meala is liomóide*

The seaweed carrageen, with its useful jelling properties is what makes this pudding work. Some cooks include the carrageen itself in this but I prefer to cook it and use only the liquid – the setting quality is just as good and risk of any marine taste is avoided.

½ cup carrageen, tightly packed
2 heaped teaspoons honey
juice and finely grated rind of 1
  lemon

1 egg white, stiffly beaten
150 ml (¼ pint) double cream,
  whipped

Soak the carrageen in hot water to cover for about 15 minutes, then drain, discarding the soaking liquid. Put into 600 ml (1 pint) fresh water with the honey, lemon juice and rind. Bring to the boil and simmer for 25–30 minutes. Strain and discard the carrageen and let the liquid cool slightly.

Meanwhile, combine the beaten egg white and the whipped cream, then gently fold the mixture into the carrageen liquid. Pour into a wetted mould and chill. Serves 4–6.

Christmas pudding – *Maróg Nollag*

This rich Christmas pudding is comparatively recent in the Irish cuisine. Formerly a simple boiled fruit pudding was sometimes served, but since the beginning of this century the Christmas pudding has become traditional. An old lady of my acquaintance remembers young domestic science teachers going round to the country districts and teaching countrywomen how to make them. Previously they had already become popular among owners of large houses, who had travelled. This recipe makes three 1-kilo (2-pound) puddings or one very large one. They should be made not later than the first week in November, to give them time to mature, but they can be made earlier; they will keep for a year.

450 g (1 lb) demerara sugar
450 g (1 lb) fresh breadcrumbs
75 g (3 oz) ground almonds
175 g (6 oz) chopped candied peel
75 g (3 oz) glace cherries
450 g (1 lb) currants
275 g (10 oz) raisins
275 g (10 oz) sultanas
1 teaspoon each ground cinnamon, mixed spice, ground nutmeg

1 medium-sized carrot, grated
juice and grated rind of 1 lemon
juice and grated rind of 1 orange
7 eggs
300 ml ($\frac{1}{2}$ pint) Guinness
2 tablespoons flour
150 ml ($\frac{1}{4}$ pint) whiskey, brandy or
  rum

Mix the sugar, breadcrumbs and almonds in a large bowl. Add the candied peel, cherries, currants, raisins, sultanas and grated carrot. Mix well. Make a well in the middle and add the grated lemon and orange rinds and the juice, the mixed spices and mix again. Beat the eggs with the Guinness and add them gradually, alternately adding a little flour each time. Stir very well, and finally add the spirits and mix again.

At this point it is traditional to get all the family to stir and to make a wish. Also a small coin is usually wrapped up and added to the mixture for luck.

Butter the bowl (or bowls) well, and fill with the mixture to within 2 cm (1 inch) of the top. Cover with greaseproof paper, then either a lid or foil, or a cloth, and tie down. Steam over boiling water for 7 hours or a little longer. Lift out and uncover the puddings and let the steam out. Leave them to cool.

Cover again, when cool and store in a cool dark place until December 25th. On Christmas Day, steam the pudding for a further 1½ hours before serving, decorated with a piece of berried holly. At the table, pour a warm ladleful of Irish whiskey over and set it alight. If possible it should be eaten at once – it is considered good luck to eat it while the blue flame is still burning. Serve with brandy sauce or brandy butter.

Baked custard – *Custard bácáilte*

This simple pudding is delicious with cooked fruit. If liked vanilla can be added or a few drops of almond essence or rum.

750 ml (1½ pints) milk
3 eggs
2 rounded tablespoons sugar

½ teaspoon butter
pinch of grated nutmeg

Beat the eggs with the sugar, warm the milk gently and gradually add the eggs and sugar to the milk, stirring all the time. Butter 4 custard dishes and pour the custard into them and grate some nutmeg over the top. Stand the dishes in a baking pan and add hot water to come half-way up the sides of the dishes. Bake in a slow 180°C, 350°F, Mark 4 oven for about 50 minutes. Serves 4. For caramel cream, line dish with caramel (page 136). See also Sauces.

Dublin rock – *Carraig Dhuibhlinneach*

This rich and decorative pudding of the last century was often decorated with angelica, blanched split almonds and branches of maidenhair fern or other plants, to look like plants growing out from a rocky hillside.

100 g (4 oz) unsalted butter
100 g (4 oz) fine sugar
300 ml (½ pint) thick cream,
   partially whipped
225 g (8 oz) ground almonds

a few drops of orange flower water
   (obtainable from chemists)
1 tablespoon brandy
2 egg whites, stiffly beaten

Cream the butter with the sugar, then add the lightly whipped cream. Fold in the ground almonds and mix very gently so as to avoid oiling. Add the orange flower water and the brandy, and finally fold in the stiffly beaten egg whites. Put the mixture into a dish and place in the coldest part of the refrigerator to harden. Then break it in rough pieces and pile these, pyramid fashion, on a glass dish, and decorate as imaginatively as desired.

Carrageen jelly – *Glóthach charraigín*

15 g (½ oz) carrageen
2 teaspoons lemon juice
sugar to taste
small wine glass of sweet sherry

Soak the carrageen in water for a few hours, then rinse well and drain. Put in a pan with 450 ml (1 pint) of water and simmer for about 20 minutes, then strain; discard the carrageen. Add the sugar, lemon juice and finally the sherry to the strained liquid and stir. Wet a mould, pour in the liquid and put in a cold place to set. Serves 4.

Wine jelly – *Glóthach fhíona*

If preferred, either red or white wine can be used in place of port, with apple jelly in place of the redcurrant jelly.

thin rind and juice of 1 lemon
2 heaped tablespoons sugar
1 tablespoon redcurrant jelly

15 g (½ oz) powdered gelatine
300 ml (½ pint) port wine

Put the lemon peel and juice, sugar, redcurrant jelly and powdered gelatine into a saucepan and stir over a gentle heat until the gelatine and jelly are well dissolved. Cover and put aside to infuse for 15 minutes, then add the port. Strain and pour into glasses or individual dishes; chill to eat. Serves 4.

For fruit jellies use fruit juice instead of port.

Honey mousse – *Cúr meala*

450 g (1 lb) honey, preferably Irish
    heather honey
4 eggs, separated

If the honey is 'set' and thick, warm it up a little first to liquify it, then let it cool. Beat the egg yolks with the honey. Cook the mixture in the top of a double boiler over hot water stirring all the time until the mixture thickens like a custard; keep stirring. Take from the heat and cool. Meanwhile, whisk the egg whites until stiff. Fold them in, and pour into individual dishes, chill and serve. Serves 4.

Gooseberry fool – *Brúitín spíonán ar uachtar*

An old pudding made at least in the eighteenth century as the handwritten book of Sara Power's shows in 1746. The word 'fool' comes from the French *fouler*, to crush.

Put a quart of Gooseberrys in a bell-mettle skillet, with as much cold water as will cover them, boyle them to mash, then strain them thro' a hair sieve, free from seeds, or skins. Put the pulp in the dish you intend to use, with half a pound of sugar, the yolk of 4 eggs – To serve it some put Nutmeg and Sack [a sweet wine] in it, remember to beat and mix it well.

My recipe varies a little, and if I have some elderflower heads to hand I plunge some in just as the gooseberries come to the boil, and then remove them after 5 minutes. This gives a good grape-like flavour. Use only barely 300 ml (½ pint) of water to 450 g (1 lb) gooseberries, then sieve or put through a food mill. Sweeten to taste, then add 150 ml ¼ pint) whipped cream and 2 stiffly beaten egg whites. Pour into glasses and chill.

Rhubarb can be used instead of gooseberries.

Gooseberry and lemon honeycomb mould – Múnla criathar spíonán agus liómóide

½ tablespoon butter
225 g (8 oz) gooseberries, cleaned, topped and tailed
2 tablespoons golden syrup
2 eggs, separated
2 heaped tablespoons butter

100 g (4 oz) sugar
finely grated rinds and juice of 2 lemons
4 tablespoons self-raising flour
150 ml (¼ pint) milk

Butter an ovenproof dish, put the gooseberries in and dribble the golden syrup over them. Beat the egg yolks well. Cream the butter and sugar, and when well combined add the grated lemon rind and beaten egg yolks. Beat the egg whites stiffly.

Stir in the flour, a little at a time, alternately with the lemon juice and milk, finally fold in the beaten egg whites. Pour the mixture over the gooseberries. Bake at 180°C, 350°F, Mark 4 for about half and hour, until golden on top. Serve with warm cream. Serves 4.

Other fruits can also be used.

Gooseberry flan – Toirtín spíonán

This is my favourite of the tarts which don't need cream served with them.

Make a pastry case, prick the bottom over lightly and brush with a little egg. Add gooseberries and sprinkle with a little sugar. Fill the tart with a mixture of beaten eggs and cream, or plain yoghurt. Bake at 200°C, 400°F, Mark 6 for 15 minutes, then reduce the heat to 180°C, 350°F, Mark 4 for a further 15 minutes or until the cream custard is set. Serves 4–6.

Irish Mist cream – *Uachtar 'Irish Mist'*

Irish Mist is an Irish liqueur made from whiskey, honey and herbs which is delicious for cooking. This dish is like a cold soufflé.

It can also be made with 1 cup of strong black coffee added with the milk, served with whipped cream flavoured with Irish Velvet (a coffee-flavoured whiskey-based drink).

600 ml (1 pint) milk, heated	2 heaped tablespoons sugar
1 tablespoon powdered gelatine	2 tablespoons whipped cream
4 eggs, separated	2 tablespoons Irish Mist

Put the warm milk and gelatine into the top of a double boiler over hot water. Beat the egg yolks and add them, with the sugar. Whisk until the mixture thickens, on no account let it boil. Take from the heat and cool slightly. Beat the egg whites stiffly. When the mixture is cool fold in the cream, then the stiffly beaten egg white and finally the Irish Mist. Wet a mould and tie a 7.5-cm (3-inch) paper collar around it. Pour the mixture into the mould and chill until set. Serves 4–6.

Lemon soufflé – *Cúróg liomóide*

This is a very fresh, unfatty soufflé which can also be made with orange, lime and grapefruit instead of lemon.

4 large eggs, separated	3–4 tablespoons lemon juice
175 g (6 oz) sugar	½ oz (15 g) powdered gelatine
finely grated rind of 1 lemon	

Combine the egg yolks, sugar and the finely grated lemon rind and juice and mix very well with a wooden spoon. Dissolve the gelatine in 150 ml (¼ pint) water in a saucepan, stirring over a low heat for a minute or two. Pour into the lemon mixture in a steady stream, stirring from time to time to blend well. Leave for about half an hour, until it begins to set. Beat the egg whites stiffly. With a metal spoon add the beaten egg whites, getting right down to the bottom of the mixture. Pour into serving dishes and chill to set. Serves 4–6.

Marmalade fruit pudding – *Maróg shubh oráiste agus maróg shuibhe*

This can be made with jam or fruit preserve, or golden syrup, instead of marmalade, if preferred. It should be served with custard or cream. If made in small individual moulds they are called 'castle puddings'.

4 tablespoons marmalade	finely grated rind of 1 lemon
175 g (6 oz) butter	½ tablespoon butter for greasing
175 g (6 oz) sugar	75 g (3 oz) chopped fruit, dates
175 g (6 oz) self raising flour	figs or chopped peel
2 large eggs, beaten	

Cream the butter and sugar until light. Combine a spoonful of flour with a little of the beaten egg and beat into the mixture; repeat and continue until all the flour and eggs are added. Add the finely grated lemon rind and mix well.

Butter a 450–700g (1–1½lb) pudding basin and put the marmalade in the bottom, then pour the mixture on top, making sure it does not come within 2.5cm (1 inch) of the top. Cover with greaseproof paper and either tie down or add a lid. Steam over boiling water for 1½–2 hours. Turn out carefuly on to a warmed plate. Serves 4–6.

Mincemeat – *Mionra*

There was an early method of preserving chopped beef with fruit and spices through the winter which accounts for its name. However, the only ingredient which remains in present day recipes to remind us of this fact is the grated beef suet. It is a Christmas speciality, used particularly for mince pies, which are mincemeat enclosed in pastry, always served at Christmas time.

450g (1 lb) raisins
450g (1 lb) sultanas
350g (12 oz) currants
175g (6 oz) almonds, chopped
175g (6 oz) candied peel,
   three-quarters chopped
450g (1 lb) cooking apples

350g (12 oz) shredded beef suet
450g (1 lb) soft brown sugar
1 level teaspoon ground cinnamon
½ level teaspoon grated nutmeg
grated rind and juice 1 large lemon
150 ml (¼ pint), ½ cup whiskey,
   brandy, rum or sherry

Chop the dried fruit or mince it coarsely, also the peel and almonds. Peel, core and chop the apples and mix together with the fruit, adding the suet and sugar. Stir in the spices, finely grated lemon rind, and juice and finally add most of the spirit. Cover and leave for 6 hours.

Then mix well and put into clean dry jars, topping up with a spoonful of spirit. Tie down securely and store in a cold dark place. It should be made at least one month before Christmas to let it all marinate. Makes about 3¼ kg (7 lb).

Mincemeat pudding with lemon sauce – *Maróg mhionna agus anlann liomóide*

100g (4 oz) butter
100g (4 oz) sugar
2 egg yolks
2 heaped tablespoons mincemeat

grated rind and juice of 1 lemon
½ teaspoon baking powder
½ tablespoon butter for greasing

Sauce
2 egg whites
2 tablespoons fine sugar
2 tablespoons lemon curd

Cream the butter and sugar until light, then add the egg yolks, breadcrumbs, mincemeat, grated lemon rind and juice, and baking powder. Butter a pudding basin, pour the mixture in, cover and steam for 50–60 minutes. Meanwhile, make the sauce. Whisk the egg whites until stiff, fold in the fine sugar and whisk again, then add the lemon curd. Turn the pudding out on to a warmed dish and cover with the sauce. Serves 4–6.

Burnt oranges – *Oráistí dóite*

... fine oranges
Well roasted, with sugar and wine ...

Jonathan Swift, 1723.

4 large oranges	300 ml (½ pint) freshly squeezed
150 ml (¼ pint) sweet white wine	orange juice
1 teaspoon butter	4 heaped tablespoons sugar
4 teaspoons fine sugar	2 tablespoons whiskey, warmed

Carefully peel the oranges thinly, then with a sharp knife remove as much of the pith and white skin as possible, keeping the oranges intact. Cut the thin peel into fine strips and cover with the wine. Put the oranges into an ovenproof dish. Put a little butter on top of each one, pressing it down gently, then sprinkle each one with a teaspoon of fine sugar. Put into a 200°C, 400°F, Mark 4 oven for 10 minutes or longer until the sugar caramelizes.

Meanwhile, mix the orange juice with the sugar in a saucepan and bring to the boil. Lower the heat and cook to let it get syrupy, without stirring. Add the orange peel and wine mixture and bring to the boil again, then cook rapidly to reduce and thicken slightly.

Take the oranges from the oven and if not fully browned put under a moderate grill for a few minutes. Pour the warmed whiskey over them and set it alight, over heat. As the flames die down add the orange syrup and let it simmer for about 2 minutes. Serve at once, or it can be served cold.

Pear sponge cake – *Císte spúinse le piorraí*

A deliciously light cake-pudding, to be eaten warm or cold.

100 g (4 oz) butter	eaters)
100 g (4 oz) sugar	100 g (4 oz) self-raising flour, sifted
2 eggs	whipped cream
450 g (1 lb) ripe pears (cookers or	

Cream the butter and sugar until light, then add the eggs, one at a time, beating each one in well. Peel, core and slice the pears. Fold the flour into the sugar, butter and egg mixture. Stir in the pear slices.

Line a 20-cm (7½-inch) cake tin, preferably one with a removable base, and spoon in the mixture. Bake at 190°C, 375°F, Mark 5 for 30–40 minutes or until a skewer comes out clean. Serve with whipped cream. Serves 4–6.

Porter pudding – *Maróg phórtair*

Porter is a weaker form of dark beer like Guinness, now difficult to find. Guinness can be used instead but cut the quantity in half.

100 g (4 oz) sultanas
100 g (4 oz) currants
100 g (4 oz) chopped peel
grated rind of 1 lemon
grated rind of 1 orange
1 measure Irish whiskey
300 ml (½ pint) porter

250 g (9 oz) breadcrumbs
175 g (6 oz) flour
1 teaspoon cinnamon
175 g (6 oz) brown sugar
6 eggs
brandy sauce

Put the sultanas, currants, chopped peel, lemon and orange rind, whiskey and porter into a bowl, mix well, cover and leave overnight. Next day add the rest of the ingredients and mix well. Put into well-buttered pudding basins, cover and steam for 2½–3 hours. Turn out on to a serving dish and serve with brandy sauce.

Rhubarb Charlotte – *Searlait bhiabhóige*

2 heaped tablespoons butter, melted
175 g (6 oz) fresh breadcrumbs
450 g (1 lb) rhubarb, cleaned and cut
 in 2.5-cm (1-inch) pieces
50 g (2 oz) brown sugar
pinch of ground ginger

pinch of cinnamon
pinch of nutmeg
grated rind of 1 orange
2 tablespoons golden syrup
2 teaspoons lemon or orange juice

Heat the butter and toss the crumbs in and combine, shaking the pan. Spread a thin layer of the mixture over the bottom and sides of a 1-litre (2-pint) soufflé dish, reserving some. Put in half the rhubarb pieces. Mix together the brown sugar, spices and grated orange rind, and sprinkle about half over the rhubarb. Then repeat. Top with the reserved crumbs.

Combine the golden syrup with the lemon or orange juice and 2 tablespoons of water, beat well and pour over. Cover and bake at 200°C, 400°F, Mark 6 for 30 minutes, then uncover and cook for 10 minutes more. Serve with cream. Serves 4.

Raspberry cream – *Uachtar shútha crabh*

700 g (1½ lb) raspberries
3 egg whites
2–3 tablespoons sugar
450 ml (¾ pint) double cream

Press the raspberries through a sieve and discard the seeds. Beat the egg whites stiffly, then add most of the sugar, gradually, beating well. Whip the cream, then fold in the egg white mixture and half the raspberries. Pour into a chilled serving bowl, spread the remaining raspberries on top, sprinkle with the rest of the sugar to crystallize them slightly, and serve. Serves 4.

Strawberries can also be served as above.

Spotted dog – *Maróg bhreac gheire*

An account of convent life in Co. Limerick in the 1870s gives the favourite puddings as jam tart, dog-in-a-blanket and spotted dog. We don't have a dog-in-a-blanket recipe but here is one for spotted dog.

100 g (4 oz) self raising flour
100 g (4 oz) fresh breadcrumbs
100 g (4 oz) shredded suet
100 g (4 oz) currants
2 heaped tablespoons sultanas

grated rind of 1 lemon
1 egg
2 tablespoons softened butter
custard or warmed golden syrup

Sift the flour into a basin, add the breadcrumbs, suet, currants, sultanas and lemon rind. Mix with the egg and a little water to a soft dough. Roll out on a floured surface to a rectangle about 1 cm (½ inch) thick. Spread butter along one end, then roll up like a Swiss roll and press the edges together. Wrap loosely to allow for expansion in a cloth or foil and tie at each end. Lower into boiling water and simmer for 2–2½ hours. Unwrap and put on to a serving dish, slice and serve hot either with custard or (as I remember with pleasure) golden syrup slightly warmed. Serves 4–6.

Summer pudding – *Maróg samhraidh*

Summer pudding was often made in the past by people who didn't like pastry. It requires no cooking, which is handy, but it should be made the day before. Almost any soft fruit can be used, but to be authentic it should include raspberries, strawberries and currants, black, red or white.

6–8 crustless slices of stale white
   bread 1.5 cm (½ inch) thick
about 700 g (1 ½ lb) soft fruits
100 g (4 oz) sugar or to taste

Line a 1-litre (1½-pint) pudding basin with most of the bread slices fitting the pieces on the bottom and sides, slightly overlapping them so that the whole area is covered. Prepare the fruits and put them in a heavy saucepan with the sugar; place over moderate heat. Bring gently to the boil, stirring well, then simmer only until the juices start to run out. Spoon into the bread-lined basin and cover with the rest of the bread. Cover with greaseproof paper and weight it down lightly (a pie dish that fits into the space, with a can or two of tinned food set on it will do). Leave in a cool place overnight. Take off the weight and put a serving dish upside down on top, then invert quickly so that any juices not absorbed by the bread will not be lost. Serve in wedge-shaped pieces with cream. Serves 4–6.

Syllabub – *Siolliabab*

This old and refreshing sweet used to be simply fresh milk poured from a height into a glass or receptacle; in fact sometimes the cow was milked into the jug and the froth on top of the thick creamy milk was much enjoyed.

Mrs Delany, the wife of the Dean of Down, lamented the decline of rural society in 1745:

> I am sorry to find here people *out of character*, and that *wine* and *tea* should enter where they have *no pretence to be* and usurp the rural food of the syllabub etc.

It did not disappear, however, but became changed to 'solid syllabub', that is whipped cream flavoured with lemon, herbs and brandy.

finely grated rind and juice of 2
    lemons
4 tablespoons brandy
4 tablespoons sherry

pinch of nutmeg
75 g (3 oz) fine sugar
sprig of fresh rosemary
600 ml (1 pint) double cream

Mix the finely grated rind and juice of the lemons with the brandy, sherry, nutmeg, sugar and rosemary; leave to stand for several hours. Then strain and pour into 4–6 glasses. Whip the cream thickly and put some on top of each glass. Chill before serving. Serves 4–6.

Treacle sponge – *Císte spúinse triacla*

175 g (6 oz) self raising flour
100 g (4 oz) shredded suet
½ teaspoon ginger
150 ml (¼ pint) milk
100 g (4 oz) sugar

100 g (4 oz) treacle
1 egg
custard, cream, more treacle or
    golden syrup

Mix all the ingredients together well, add the egg last. Pour into a greased basin or dish, cover and steam for 2 hours. Turn out to serve with custard, cream, more treacle or golden syrup. Serves 4–6.

Trifle or typsy cake – *Traidhfil nó cáca biotáille*

This delicious pudding, which is an old Christmas speciality, has regrettably been allowed to run down over the years, owing to the use of packaged custard powder instead of home-made, and the inclusion of canned fruits and jelly. When well made it takes a lot of beating.

6 trifle sponge cakes
raspberry or strawberry jam
6 tiny macaroons
10 ratafia biscuits
300 ml (½ pint) medium sherry
grated rind of ½ lemon
25 g (1 oz) blanched shredded
   almonds

4 egg yolks
600 ml (1 pint) milk, heated
2 tablespoons sugar
300 ml (½ pint) double cream,
   whipped
glacé cherries, split almonds and
   angelica for decoration

Split the sponge cakes in two, spread the bottoms with the jam and put back the tops. Arrange in a large glass dish, cover them with the macaroons and ratafias, pour the sherry over and sprinkle with the almonds and lemon rind.

Then make the custard. Beat the egg yolks, then gradually mix in the hot milk and stir over a very low heat or in the top of a double boiler until it runs off the back of a wooden spoon in ribbons. Never allow it to boil, just to thicken slightly. Take off the heat and stir in the sugar. Let the custard cool a little, then pour over the contents of the glass dish. Leave to cool, then cover the top with the whipped cream and decorate with cherries, almonds and angelica. Serves 6–8.

Tutti-frutti

This is a superb jam recipe given to me by Eileen Lawlor of Ballyshannon, Co. Donegal. It belonged to her grandmother, Violet Stopford Lawlor and is at least one hundred years old. The Lawlor family often serve it sandwiched between a very light sponge cake.

450 g (1 lb) prepared rhubarb,
   chopped
3 oranges

Chop the rhubarb and peel the whole rind, if possible, from the orange, then squeeze out the juice. Pour over the rhubarb and leave overnight.

   Then take:

225 g (8 oz) dried apricots
225 g (8 oz) prunes
120 g (4 oz) dried figs
1 large juicy lemon

Soak this fruit in the lemon juice and whole lemon rind, made up with enough water to cover, overnight.

   The next day take:

3 large apples, peeled, cored and
   sliced
2 cloves
50 g (2 oz) whole almonds, chopped

Add this to either fruit mixture and leave overnight.

   Then mix all together, having removed any stones from the prunes and taken out fruit rinds. Bring to the boil and simmer for about 20 minutes.

To every cup of pulp or liquid add 1 cup sugar. Dissolve slowly over low heat stirring all the time, then boil for about 20–30 minutes until, as Eileen Lawlor says, it is dark and delicious.

Urney pudding – *Maróg Urnaidhe*

This is a steamed pudding from the north of Ireland.

100 g (4 oz) butter
2 heaped tablespoons sugar
2 eggs, beaten
100 g (4 oz) flour

1 tablespoon vanilla essence
2 tablespoons strawberry, raspberry
    or apricot jam
1 teaspoon baking powder

Cream the butter and sugar, then add the beaten eggs and flour alternately. Add the vanilla and the jam, and finally the baking powder. Pour into buttered basin, cover and steam for 1½ hours. Serve with jam sauce. Serves 4.

chapter nine

BREADS, BISCUITS AND CAKES – ARÁIN, BRIOSCAÍ AGUS CÍSTÍ

Makeroon's.

Take one pound of Almonds, blanch, and beat them with the Whites of 6 Eggs, when they are botten put in one pound of Sugar finely Sifted, and beat them well together till you think the Sugar is dissolv'd, the longer you beat them the lighter they will be, then lay on breads, & bake as you do, other paste, or Cakes.

Breads and cakes are the Irishwoman's true forte; she loves both making them and eating them. Not only are they much enjoyed by all members of the family but they are probably the most traditional foods which still exist in Ireland.

Bread has indeed been the 'staff of life' for centuries to many Irish people for its importance was realised in prehistory and also in the early years of this millennium. The Brehon Laws (page 219) state even the size of the loaves made, writing about a vessel large enough to hold the following: 'twenty-four cakes of woman-baking being 2 fists in breadth and a fist in thickness'. The size of a man-baker's loaf was twice as large. All sorts of grain were used, and when that was short, even dried peas and beans were ground up and made into cakes and bread.

Barley bread was associated with the sparse diets of ascetic monks in the early times. The bread of the Irish in general was oaten bread, but wheaten bread was thought to be the finest.

Cakes were often baked for special festivals. There were Cake Dances, for instance, and an account exists of one in County Mayo near Newport where the cake was placed on a pole and each dancer paid to join the dance. Whoever paid most and danced most got the cake. An old country superstition is 'to nip the cake', that is, when a cake is freshly baked a small piece is broken off to avert bad luck. Children sometimes overdo this custom!

Remembering that ovens were few and that most of the following recipes were cooked in a pot oven over a turf fire, the variety is startling.

Crusts

Shortcrust pastry – *Brioscthaosrán*

For a richer version an egg can be added to this. It should be added before the water, which will probably need to be only about 2 tablespoons, and should be added very gradually. The choice of salt or sugar will depend on the filling to be used with the crust, whether savoury or sweet. This will make enough pastry for a 20-cm (8-inch) bottom and top crust.

225 g (8 oz) flour
100 g (4 oz) butter
pinch of salt or 2 teaspoons sugar

Sift the flour and add the salt or sugar. Rub the butter in until the mixture resembles coarse breadcrumbs, then add enough iced water to make a soft but firm dough, about 4 tablespoons. Do not over-handle the dough. Pat the dough into an oval shape on a floured board, then wrap in paper or foil and chill for at least half an hour, longer if possible.

Potato pastry – *Taosrán prátái*

This is a delicious pastry for savoury dishes, very moist and soft. Originally bacon dripping or poultry fat was used rather than butter, which is probably now the preferred choice.

100 g (4 oz) cooked potatoes
100 g (4 oz) flour
pinch of salt
100 g (4 oz) butter, bacon dripping
or poultry fat
1 teaspoons baking powder
1 beaten egg

Sift the flour, baking powder and salt, then rub the fat in, blending well. Mash the potatoes well, or sieve them, and add, mixing thoroughly. Add the beaten egg and mix very well again. Turn out on to a floured board and knead a little, then roll out to the required size. There is no need to rest it.

Flaky pastry – Taosrán calógach

This rich crust is not so generally used in Ireland as the other pastries given but is sometimes made when only a top covering is required. Choice of salt or sugar of course depends on the filling it will accompany. This will make about 225 g (8 oz) of dough.

225 g (8 oz) flour, sifted
½ level teaspoon salt or sugar
175 g (6 oz) butter
1 teaspoon lemon juice

Sift together the flour and the salt or sugar into a basin. With a knife mix the fat on a plate until softened, then spread it evenly over the plate and mark into four equal portions. Rub one portion into the flour, add the water and lemon juice and mix to a dough in the basin.

Turn out on to a lightly floured surface and knead to a smooth dough. Leave to rest for 10 minutes. Then roll out to an oblong shape three times longer than its width. Scatter one third of the remaining butter in small pieces over the upper two thirds of the oblong. Fold the lower third up and over the middle and the top third down over that, and roll out to an oblong again. Rest for 15 minutes. Add another third of the butter and repeat the operation, resting again for 15 minutes, then repeat with the remainder of the butter, and finally chill for at least half an hour before using.

Breads

Bread in Ireland has been made from all the cereal crops, particularly oats and wheat. During the famine years maize was used and sometimes grains were mixed – whatever was available was used for bread, as it has always been the mainstay, together with porridge, of many Irish peoples' diet. The flour was usually unrefined or wholemeal so it was generally brown bread that was made. White baker's bread was considered most desirable. It was bought only for very special occasions or when the priest called to say Mass. Alexis Soyer, the great French chef, who came to Ireland at the time of the famine to help feed the starving, reported that during the height of the famine he saw a woman without stockings or shoes go into a baker's shop at Malahide and buy two loaves, one white, the other brown; the white she carried in her hand, the other she hid under her cloak. Robert Lynd, writing in 1909, mentioned that he often got apologies for the fact that there was no shop bread, only home-baked. This bread was invariably what is known in Ireland as 'soda bread' which because of its round shape has sometimes been called 'soda cake' in rural districts (making it confusing when reading old manuscripts). Brown soda bread goes well with many of our choice Irish foods, like with bacon, ham and honey; with smoked salmon or lobsters anything else is unthinkable in Ireland.

Ná mól an t-arán go mbruitear.
(Do not praise the bread until it is cooked.)

Apple bread – *Arań úll*

This tea bread is pleasant served warm, sliced with butter.

225 g (8 oz) flour
175 g (6 oz) sugar
100 g (4 oz) butter
4 large cooking apples, peeled,
    cored and finely minced
1 egg, beaten
butter for spreading

Combine the flour and sugar in a bowl and rub in the butter until the mixture becomes like coarse breadcrumbs. Add the minced apples and beaten egg; mix well. Turn into a shallow 20-cm (8-inch) baking tin and bake at 180°C, 350°F, Mark 4 for about 40 minutes or until brown and cooked through. Cut into pieces and butter them before serving.

Bran bread – *Arán bran*

175 g (6 oz) flour
150 g (5 oz) natural bran
1 heaped teaspoon baking soda
1 heaped teaspoon baking powder
1 heaped teaspoon salt
scant 300 ml (½ pint) sour milk or
    buttermilk

Mix all the dry ingredients, then add the sour milk or buttermilk, but only enough to make a fairly stiff dough. Shape into a round and put on a greased sheet or put into a greased loaf tin and make a cut down the middle. Bake at 220°C, 425°F, Mark 7 for about 45 minutes. Cool on a rack and if keeping for a day or so, wrap in a cloth to keep the crust soft.

Buttermilk bread – *Arán bláthaí*

This is a very traditional bread. For the recipe I am indebted to Honor Moore.

about 750 ml (1¼ pints) buttermilk
225 g (8 oz) fine or medium oatmeal
225 g (8 oz) white flour or a mixture
    of white and wholemeal
1 teaspoon baking soda
1 teaspoon salt
2 tablespoons brown sugar or honey

Stir the buttermilk into the oatmeal in a large bowl, cover and leave for 12 hours. Mix, and add the flour, soda and a little more buttermilk, enough to make a fairly stiff dough.

Well grease two loaf tins and bake at 200°C, 400°F, Mark 6 for 45–55 minutes; test before taking from the oven. Turn out and wrap in a tea towel to cool.

Country cheese bread – *Arán cáise*

225 g (8 oz) white flour
225 g (8 oz) wholemeal flour
1 level teaspoon salt
1 level teaspoon bicarbonate of soda
1 heaped tablespoon butter
2 medium-sized onions, grated
  or finely chopped

2 teaspoons mixed fresh herbs
  or 1 teaspoon dried
2 tablespoons parsley, chopped
about 300 ml (½ pint) milk
about 300 ml (½ pint) buttermilk
  or lemon juice
50 g (2 oz) cheese, finely grated

Sift the flour, salt and soda into a bowl. Rub in the butter and add the onion, herbs and parsley. Add enough milk and buttermilk or lemon juice to make a soft dough. Turn out and knead a little, then shape into a round. With a floured knife mark the top into 8 wedge sections, or farls, and put on to a lightly floured baking sheet. Brush with milk and sprinkle the grated cheese all over the top. Bake in a preheated oven at 200°C, 400°F, Mark 6 for 35–40 minutes, until done.

Golden bread – *Arán mine buí*

This uses corn meal, made from maize, which in Ireland is called Indian meal or golden drop. The recipe is about 140 years old, dating from the famine years when corn meal was sent from America for the starving people.

225 g (8 oz) corn meal
220 g (8 oz) flour, sifted
1 teaspoon baking soda
1 teaspoon baking powder
1 teaspoon salt
3 heaped tablespoons butter

1 tablespoon sugar
1 egg
about 4 tablespoons sour milk, or
  sweet milk with 1 teaspoon cream
  of tartar
butter for spreading

Sift the flour together with the other dry ingredients, then rub in the butter and add the sugar. Mix to a stiff consistency with the beaten egg and the milk. Turn into a shallow greased loaf tin and bake at 220°C, 425°F, Mark 7 for 20 minutes, then reduce the heat to 190°C, 375°F, Mark 5 and bake for a further 15 minutes. Cool, then cut into slices and serve warm, buttered.

> We have brought home some of the maize bread and some of the maize flour which we all think delicious and very luckily so do all those who have tasted either about us.

April 20th, 1846, from *The Irish Journals* of Elizabeth Smith about Baltiboys House, Blessington, Co. Wicklow.

Griddle bread – *Arán gridille*

This easy breakfast bread can be made in any heavy pan on top of the stove if there is no griddle.

225 g (8 oz) wholemeal flour   1 teaspoon baking soda
50 g (2 oz) white flour   about 300 ml (½ pint) buttermilk
1 teaspoon salt

Mix together the two flours with the salt and soda. Add the buttermilk, as much as needed to obtain a fairly soft consistency. Roll on a
floured surface and shape into a round. Heat the griddle or pan until
a sprinkling of flour turns light golden, then put the cake on and cook
for 10 minutes over medium heat, then turn and cook the other side
for 10 minutes. Serve straight from the pan.

Harvest loaf – *Builín fómhair*

This is an easy tea bread.

225 g (8 oz) self-raising flour   225 g (8 oz) mixed dried fruit
225 g (8 oz) sugar   225 g (8 oz) glacé cherries
225 g (8 oz) melted butter   about 150 ml (¼ pint) milk
2 eggs

Put all the ingredients into a mixing bowl, keeping back some of the
milk. Add the rest gradually as needed to form the dough. Beat well
until thoroughly mixed, then out into a greased 1-kg (2-lb) loaf tin;
bake at 160°C, 325°F, Mark 3 for 1–1½ hours.

Irish farmhouse loaf – *Builín feirme na hÉireann*

This recipe comes from Letterkenny, Co. Donegal.

225 g (8 oz) flour   ½ teaspoon salt
100 g (4 oz) sugar   2 level teaspoons baking powder
225 g (8 oz) mixed dried fruit   pinch of baking soda
grated rind of ½ lemon   1 large egg, beaten
1 heaped tablespoon butter   300 ml (½ pint) buttermilk

Mix the flour, sugar, fruit, lemon rind, butter, baking powder and
soda. Add the beaten egg and buttermilk to make a nice soft dough;
beat well and pour into a greased 1-kg (2-lb) baking tin. Bake at
150°C, 300°F, Mark 2 for 1 hour or until done.

Malt bread – *Arán braighe*

225 g (8 oz) brown or white flour   scant 500 ml (¾ pint) milk
½ teaspoon baking soda   1 heaped tablespoon butter
2 teaspoons baking powder   ½ teaspoon salt
2 heaped tablespoons sultanas   2 tablespoons brown sugar
1 heaped tablespoon mixed peel,   2 tablespoons malt extract
  chopped   a little milk and sugar, warmed, for
2 tablespoons currants   glaze

Sift the flour, soda and baking powder together; add the sultanas,
chopped peel and currants. Heat the milk and add the butter, salt and

sugar until dissolved, stirring well. Cool a little, then add the mixture to the dry ingredients and mix very well until smooth. Pour into a greased 1-kg (2-lb) loaf tin and bake at 190°C, 350°F, Mark 5 for 35–40 minutes. Take from the oven and turn the heat off, brush the bread with the warm milk and sugar to glaze, and put back in the oven to dry for a few minutes.

Brown soda bread – *Arán sóide*

This is a never-fail method for the indispensable loaf. Made with white flour, it will be white soda bread.

225 g (8 oz) white flour
225 g (8 oz) wholemeal flour
1 teaspoon baking soda
3 teaspoons baking powder
2 teaspoons salt

1 egg, beaten
scant 600 ml (1 pint) buttermilk or sour milk
beaten egg or milk for glaze (optional)

Sift together the flour, soda, baking powder and salt. Mix the buttermilk and beaten egg and stir in. Mix, then knead on a floured surface for a few minutes until smooth. Shape by hand into a round flat cake and put on a greased sheet, or put into a greased loaf tin. Make a deep cross on the round or a cut down the middle of the loaf shape, and bake in a preheated oven at 190°C, 375°F, Mark 5 for 35–40 minutes. Brush the top with milk or beaten egg if a glaze is wanted.

The mixture can be shaped in small scones and baked for 15 minutes.

Spice bread – *Arán spíosraí*

This bread will keep moist for several days and almost improves with keeping.

275 g (10 oz) self raising flour
1 teaspoon mixed spice
½ teaspoon ground ginger
100 g (4 oz) light brown sugar
50 g (2 oz) chopped candied peel

175 g (6 oz) sultanas
100 g (4 oz) butter
175 g (6 oz) golden syrup
1 large egg, beaten
4 tablespoons milk

Sift the flour with the mixed spice and ginger, then add the brown sugar, chopped peel and sultanas; mix. Make a well in the centre. Melt the butter with the syrup over low heat, then pour into the well in the mixture. Add the beaten egg and milk and mix very well. Pour into a greased 1-kg (2-lb) loaf tin and bake in a preheated oven at 170°C, 325°F, Mark 3 for 40–50 minutes; test before turning off the oven.

Yeast bread – *Arán giosta*

Strong baker's flour is best for white bread-making, but this is not always available. Ordinary flour can be used if just a little less water is added.

25 g (1 oz) fresh yeast or
400 ml (14 fl oz) tepid water
a 25 mg ascorbic acid tablet,
  obtainable from chemists
  (only use with fresh yeast)

700 g (1½ lb) strong plain white
  flour
1 level tablespoon salt
1 level tablespoon sugar
1 level tablespoon lard or margarine

Mix the yeast with the water, then add the crushed ascorbic acid tablet and stir until it dissolves. Put the flour, salt and sugar into a large mixing bowl and rub in the fat in small pieces. Blend the yeast mixture into the flour and fat and work to a firm dough until it leaves the sides of the bowl. The sides should be clean and the dough elastic.

Turn out on to a lightly floured board and knead and stretch the dough by folding it towards you and pushing away with the palm of your hand. Knead for about 10 minutes until firm and unsticky. Shape into a ball, put back in the bowl and put the bowl into a large, slightly oiled, polythene bag. Leave in a warm place for 15–20 minutes or until nearly doubled. (It will take about an hour if you are using dried yeast.)

Preheat the oven to 230°C, 450°F, Mark 8. Shape the bread and put into a greased 900-g (2-lb) bread tin, and leave again until it reaches the top of the tin, about 15 minutes. Make a deep crease down the centre of the loaf with the back of a floured knife. Put the bread in the oven on the middle shelf for about 15 minutes, then lower the heat to 190°C, 375°F, Mark 5 for a further 50 minutes.

Take the bread out of the oven and brush over with warm milk to give a glaze and then put back in the oven for about 5 minutes to dry. The loaf is done when it sounds hollow when tapped on the bottom. Cool on a wire rack.

Wholemeal yeast bread can be made the same way using wholemeal flour. Use only half the quantity of dried yeast.

Potato yeast rolls – *Rollóga giosta prátaí*

These are the lightest and most delicious rolls I have ever tasted. They freeze very well too.

100 g (4 oz) potatoes
25 g (1 oz) fresh yeast or 15 g (½ oz)
  dry yeast
50 g (2 oz) sugar
450 g (1 lb) white flour, warm

1 teaspoon salt
50 g (2 oz) butter
150 ml (¼ pint) warmed milk
1 egg, beaten
milk for glazing

Cook the potatoes in salted water and drain, reserving 2 tablespoons of the cooking liquid. Mash the potatoes very well, or press through a fine sieve into a basin; cover and keep warm. Cream the yeast in a bowl with the reserved tepid potato liquid and a spoonful of the sugar; mix well as it froths up (if it doesn't it isn't satisfactory to use). Sift the flour into a large mixing bowl with 1 teaspoon salt and rub in the butter. Make a well in the centre and add the rest of the sugar and the mashed potatoes and mix well. Add the tepid milk and 150ml (¼ pint) water to the yeast liquid, mix and add to the mixing bowl, then beat in the beaten egg. Knead very well. Cover and leave in a warm place for about an hour, until doubled in size. Turn out on to a floured surface and shape into rolls. Put them on a greased backing sheet, well spaced, to allow for rising. Cover and leave for 20 minutes. Brush with a little milk and bake at 220°C, 425°F, Mark 7 for 15–20 minutes. Makes about 16.

Biscuits

Cheese biscuits – *Brioscaí cáise*

This was a popular biscuit in the early years of this century often served with consommé. It is a delicious biscuit to serve with drinks.

2 heaped tablespoons sifted flour
50 g (2 oz) butter
50 g (2 oz) grated parmesan cheese

50 g (2 oz) grated Cheshire or similar cheese
pinch of cayenne pepper

Work all the ingredients together on a slab with the hands until well mixed (do not add any water). Put on to a lightly floured surface and roll out fairly thinly. Cut into rounds about 4 cm (1½ inches) across. Put on to greased baking sheets with space between them. Bake at 200°C, 400°F, Mark 6 for about 10 minutes. Serve within 24 hours, the sooner the better.

Ginger biscuits – *Brioscaí sinséir*

If very crisp and hard biscuits are wanted they should be cooked in a slow 150°C, 300°F, Mark 2 oven for 30 minutes.

225 g (8 oz) flour
½ teaspoon baking powder
½ teaspoon mixed spice
1 teaspoon ground ginger
¼ teaspoon baking soda

3 heaped tablespoons butter
3 heaped tablespoons sugar
1 tablespoon golden syrup
a little milk

Sift together the flour, baking powder, mixed spice, ginger and soda. Stir together over heat the butter, sugar and syrup, not letting it boil. Pour into the dry ingredients and add as little milk as possible to mix very well. Roll into balls the size of walnuts and put on to lightly greased baking sheets with a little space between them. Bake at 180°C, 350°F, Mark 4 for 10–15 minutes. Lift off with a slice while warm. Makes about 40 biscuits.

Hazelnut honey biscuits – Brioscaí collchónna agus meala

This is a delicious little cake-like biscuit made with two of the traditional foods for Irish cooking, hazelnuts and honey.

75 g (3 oz) shelled hazelnuts
150 g (5 oz) flour
pinch of salt
100 g (4 oz) butter

5 rounded tablespoons fine sugar
3–4 tablespoons thick honey
a little icing sugar

Put the shelled hazelnuts on a baking tray in a preheated oven at 190°C, 375°F, Mark 5 for about 10 minutes. As soon as cool enough to handle, rub the skins off and put the nuts through a mill. Sift the flour and salt together. Cream the butter and sugar until light, and add the nuts and the flour mixture; mix until well blended. Knead lightly, cover and leave for 30 minutes.

Roll out on a lightly floured surface and cut into 5-cm (2-inch) rounds. Line a baking tray with rice paper and put the rounds on it. Bake at 190°C, 375°F, Mark 5 for 7–10 minutes, not longer, or the nuts will have a bitter taste; take from oven before the biscuits colour.

Sandwich together in pairs with a little thick honey between and the icing sugar sprinkled on top. Makes about 12 'sandwiches'.

Lemon biscuits – Brioscaí liomóide

These are very delicate and delicious little biscuits. If a very crisp biscuit is wanted, bake at 150°C, 300°F, Mark 3 for 45–50 minutes.

100 g (4 oz) butter
3 heaped tablespoons fine sugar
175 g (6 oz) flour

grated rind of ½ lemon
juice of 1 lemon
1 small egg, beaten

Cream the butter and sugar until light. Add the flour, lemon rind and juice, and beaten egg. Mix well and leave for 1 hour. Drop small spoonfuls, spaced apart, on to greased baking trays and bake at 180°C, 350°F, Mark 4 for 15–20 minutes. Lift off the trays with a slice while still hot. Makes about 30 biscuits.

Oatmeal and cinnamon biscuits –
Brioscaí mhin choirce agus cainéil

100 g (4 oz) butter
100 g (4 oz) brown sugar
2 eggs, beaten
100 g (4 oz) flour
100 g (4 oz) oatmeal

1 level teaspoon ground cinnamon
½ level teaspoon baking powder
pinch of salt
a very little milk, if necessary

Cream the butter and sugar, then add the beaten eggs, little by little, adding a little of the flour after each addition. Add the oatmeal, cinnamon, baking powder and salt; mix well. Add a very little milk if the mixture seems too stiff; it should be a fairly soft dough. Drop spoonfuls on to a greased baking tray and bake at 190°C, 375°F, Mark 5 for 15 minutes. Cool on a rack. Makes about 25 biscuits.

Oatcakes – *Bonnóga arán coirce*

Among the most traditional of all Irish foods, the oatcake goes back many centuries. A seventeenth-century traveller to Ireland wrote:

> Their general food is a thin oatcake which they bake upon a broad flat stone made hot, a little sheep's milk cheese or goat's milk, boiled leeks and some roots.

After cooking on a griddle-like surface, these little flat cakes were hardened in front of the fire, resting against a three-legged stand which was made by blacksmiths and called a 'hardening' or 'harnen' stand. Originally only oatmeal was used in making oatcakes but a firmer oatcake results if a little flour is added.

225 g (8 oz) medium oatmeal plus a little more
100 g (4 oz) sifted flour
1 teaspoon salt

1 teaspoon baking powder
2 heaped tablespoons butter, lard or bacon dripping

Put the 225 g (8 oz) oatmeal into a basin and sift into it the flour, salt and baking powder; mix. Make a well in the mixture. Heat about 50 ml (2 fl oz) water and add the fat, bring to the boil and quickly pour into the well in the dry ingredients mixture; work together rapidly. Knead lightly and if necessary add a little water for holding the mixture together to form a stiffish dough. Sprinkle the surface with more oatmeal and roll out fairly thinly. Cut into 7.5-cm (3-inch) rounds and cook on both sides on a heated griddle, or bake on a lightly greased, warm baking tray at 180°C, 350°F, Mark 4 for about 25 minutes or until pale gold in colour. Makes about 16 oatcakes.

They are excellent with cheese, butter, honey or jam.

Tea buns

175 g (6 oz) butter
175 g (6 oz) sugar
3 eggs

175 g (6 oz) flour
1 level teaspoon baking powder

Cream the butter and sugar, then beat in the eggs, separately, adding a spoonful of flour after each addition. Sift the rest of the flour with the baking powder and fold in. Beat well for about 5 minutes. Pour into greased muffin tins to half-fill, then bake at 180°C, 350°F, Mark 4 for 15–20 minutes. Serve hot, split and buttered.

Walnut or hazelnut biscuits –
Brioscaí gallchnónna no collchnónna

75 g (3 oz) butter
175 g (6 oz) demerara sugar
2 large eggs, beaten
175 g (6 oz) flour

pinch of salt
100 g (4 oz) walnuts or hazelnuts, chopped

Cream the butter and sugar, then add all the other ingredients and mix well. Drop the mixture in spoonfuls on to greased baking trays, well spaced; bake at 170°C, 325°F, Mark 3 for 30 minutes. Makes about 30 biscuits.

Water biscuits – *Brioscai uisce*

These thin flaky little biscuits for serving with cheese were first made in 1851 in Waterford by William Beale Jacob and his brother, both Quakers who had come to Ireland in the 1670s, their name being first recorded as Yego or Igoe. These biscuits are now popular in almost all of the English-speaking world.

450 g (1 lb) flour
pinch of salt
2 heaped tablespoons butter
150 ml (¼ pint) milk

Sift the flour and salt together then heat the milk and melt the butter in it; stir. Add the flour and mix well to make a smooth dough. Roll out thinly on a floured surface and cut into 5 or 7.5-cm (2 or 3-inch) rounds or squares. Put on to lightly greased baking sheets, prick all over with a fork, and bake at 200°C, 400°F, Mark 6 for about 10 minutes, or until the biscuits are crisp and pale brown.

Butter sticks – *Cipíní ime*

This is a really delicious biscuit to be eaten hot. The recipe was given to me by Eilis O'hUid.

100 g (4 oz) self-raising flour
120 ml (4 fl oz) milk
1 tablespoon sugar
100 g (4 oz) butter

Mix together the flour, milk and sugar with a fork and mix until smooth. Put on to a lightly floured surface and roll out to about 1-cm (½-inch) thickness then cut into short sticks. Melt the butter in a baking tin and roll the sticks of dough in the butter to coat all surfaces. Bake in the middle of the preheated oven at 190–200°C, 375–400°F, Mark 5–6 for about 20 minutes.

Wholemeal scones – *Bonnoga bolse*

175 g (6 oz) wholemeal flour
175 g (6 oz) white flour
2 teaspoons baking powder
pinch of salt

2 heaped tablespoons butter
2 teaspoons golden syrup, warmed
about 150 ml (¼ pint) milk

Mix the dry ingredients, flours, baking powder and salt, then rub in the butter and stir in the warmed syrup, then the milk, and mix well to make a soft dough. Turn out on to a floured surface and cut into 5-cm (2-inch) rounds. Bake on a floured baking sheet at 190°C, 375°F, Mark 5 for 10–15 minutes.

For white scones use all white flour and add 1 beaten egg.

Honey scones – *Bonnóga meala*

100 g (4 oz) white flour
2 level teaspoons baking powder
pinch of salt
100 g (4 oz) wholemeal flour

3 tablespoons butter
1 heaped tablespoon brown sugar
1 generous tablespoon honey
150 ml (¼ pint) milk

Sift the white flour, baking powder and salt together, then add the wholemeal flour and rub in the butter. Stir in the sugar. Add the honey to the milk and stir until dissolved; add most of the mixture to the flour/butter mixture and mix to make a soft dough, reserving the rest for a glaze. Shape the dough into a round about 20 or 22-cm (8 or 9 inches) across and put on to a greased baking sheet. Cut across the top four times to mark 8 wedge-like portions, or farls, and bake at 200°C, 400°F, Mark 6 for 20 minutes. Take out to brush with glaze, then put back and continue cooking for 5–10 minutes.

Cakes

Almond cake – *Cístí almóinní*

This is a light cake usually made in a square or oblong shallow tin. It is usually iced afterwards.

175 g (6 oz) butter
175 g (6 oz) fine sugar
3 eggs
130 g (4½ oz) flour, sifted

½ teaspoon baking powder
75 g (3 oz) ground almonds
a few drops of almond essence

Icing
175 g (6 oz) icing sugar
1 heaped tablespoon butter
2 tablespoons milk

½ teaspoon almond essence
split blanched almonds

Cream the butter and sugar together until light. Then add the eggs separately, beating each one in well. Sift the flour and baking powder together and fold into the mixture, then add the ground almonds and the essence.

Line a baking tin with buttered paper and put in the mixture. Bake at 200°C, 400°F, Mark 6 for 20–25 minutes, until a skewer inserted in the cake comes out clean. Remove from the oven and cool on a rack. Meanwhile make the icing. Sift the icing sugar into a bowl. Put the butter in small pieces in a saucepan with the milk and almond essence. Stir over low heat until the butter has just melted, then pour at once into the middle of the icing sugar and beat gently until thick and smooth. (Add a tablespoon of boiling water if the icing is too thick). Pour quickly over the top of the cake and sprinkle the top with split blanched almonds.

Apple brack – *Bairín úll*

This traditional cake is often eaten at Hallowe'en. It will keep for about a month in a tin.

225 g (8 oz) butter
450 g (1 lb) flour, sifted
2 teaspoons baking soda
225 g (8 oz) raisins

225 g (8 oz) sultanas
about 300 ml (½ pint) cooked apple
1 egg and a little milk

Rub the butter into the sifted flour, then add the baking soda and raisins and sultanas and mix well. Add the cooked apple and mix well again. Finally mix in the beaten egg with a little milk if the mixture is too stiff. Put in a 20-cm (8-inch) cake tin and bake at 190°C, 375°F, Mark 5 for 1½ hours.

Apple fruit cake – *Císte úll*

This is rather an elaborate apple cake which is made in Co. Galway. The recipe comes from the Irish Country Woman's Association.

4 medium-sized apples
50 g (2 oz) brown sugar
150 g (5 oz) butter
150 g (5 oz) fine sugar
2 eggs, beaten
225 g (8 oz) flour
1 level teaspoon baking soda
½ teaspoon mixed spice

¼ teaspoon ground cinnamon
¼ teaspoon ground ginger
100 g (4 oz) currants
100 g (4 oz) sultanas and raisins
3 tablespoons candied peel, chopped
grated rind of ½ lemon
50 g (2 oz) chopped walnuts
brown sugar for sprinkling

Prepare the apples and cook with brown sugar, then pulp them. Beat the butter and sugar and add the eggs gradually. Sift the flour with the soda and spices, and add. Combine with the rest of the ingredients and beat well. Put into a greased 20- or 22-cm (8- or 9-inch) cake tin and sprinkle lightly with brown sugar. Bake at 150°C, 300°F Mark 2 for 1 hour and 20 minutes.

Apple and oatmeal cake – *Císte úll agus mhin choirce*

This is a layer cake, full of fibre and good eaten either as a cake or as a pudding with cream.

450 g (1 lb) cooking apples, peeled, cored and sliced
2 heaped tablespoons sugar, or to taste
½ teaspoon cinnamon
1 heaped tablespoon raisins
100 g (4 oz) butter

1 heaped tablespoon brown sugar
1 tablespoon honey
275 g (10 oz) medium oatmeal
grated rind of 1 lemon
2 large eggs, beaten
cream (optional)

Simmer the apples with the sugar and cinnamon until they form a purée. Add the raisins and leave to cool. Melt the butter, sugar and honey in a saucepan. Combine the oatmeal and finely grated lemon rind in a bowl. Pour the honey mixture over, then add the beaten egg and mix all together very well. Divide this mixture in three. Press one third into a cake tin with a removable base, cover with half the apple mixture, then add another third of the oatmeal mixture, then apple then oatmeal. Bake at 190°C, 375°F, Mark 5 for 30–35 minutes. Serve warm or cold with cream.

Barm brack – *Bairín breac*

There are two versions of this traditional cake eaten at Hallowe'en. One is yeasted and the other is made with baking powder. The latter kind is often called tea brack. Breac means speckled, i.e. with the fruit.

Lady Gregory always made one and brought it to the Abbey

Theatre to celebrate a first night. The scholar Walter Starkie recalls in his book *Scholars and Gypsies* one such occasion when he was about twelve years old at the first night fracas of *The Playboy of the Western World*.

> Lady Gregory stood at the door of the Green Room as calm and collected as Queen Victoria about to open a charity bazaar. Seeing Paddy Tobin and myself, she beckoned us over and handed each of us a piece of the huge barm brack which she had baked at Coole and brought up to Dublin for the Abbey cast.

75 g (3 oz) fresh yeast or 35 g (1½ oz) dried yeast
75 g (3 oz) sugar
2½ teaspoons sugar
450 g (1 lb) flour, sifted
1 egg, beaten
2 tablespoons butter
½ level teaspoon ground ginger
¼ level teaspoon ground nutmeg
225 g (8 oz) sultanas
100 g (4 oz) currants
50 g (2 oz) chopped peel

Cream the yeast in a small jug with ½ teaspoon sugar and 1 tablespoon of tepid water; it should froth up (if it doesn't it means the yeast is stale and shouldn't be used).

Rub the butter into the sifted flour, add 75 g (3 oz) sugar, the beaten egg, ginger and nutmeg; mix well. Make a well in the centre and pour in the yeast mixture. Beat with a wooden spoon for 10–15 minutes, until the dough forms a mass and clings to the spoon. Work in the dried fruit and peel and finally add the salt, mix in and turn into a warmed bowl. Cover and leave to rise in a warm place for about an hour. It should double in size. (If the whole bowl is put into a large polythene bag it will help the rising process.)

Turn out again and knead gently. Lightly grease two 17.5 cm (7-inch) cake tins and distribute the mixture evenly between them. Leave to rise again for 30 minutes. Bake in a hot preheated oven at 220°C, 425°F, Mark 7 for 7 minutes, then reduce to 190°C, 375°F, Mark 5 and bake for 45 minutes. Take the cake from the oven, and turn the oven off. Dissolve the remaining 2 tablespoons of sugar in 1 tablespoon of boiling water and glaze the cake with the mixture. Put back in the oven for a few minutes to dry, then cool on a wire rack.

Tea brack

This is the version made with baking powder.

450 g (1 lb) sultanas
450 g (1 lb) raisins
450 g (1 lb) brown sugar
3 cups milkless tea

Soak the fruit and sugar in the tea overnight. The next day add alternately:

450 g (1 lb) flour
3 beaten eggs
3 level teaspoons baking powder
3 level teaspoons mixed spice

Turn into three 20-cm (6-in) tins and bake for 1½ hours at 160°C, 325°F, Mark 3. Then take out and brush tops with warmed honey to glaze. Put back for a few minutes to dry. Cool on a wire rack.

Chocolate biscuit cake

For special occasions 4 tablespoons of whiskey can be added to the mixture.

1 egg
100 g (4 oz) butter
1 tablespoon sugar
175 g (6 oz) plain chocolate, melted
1 tablespoon golden syrup, warmed

2 tablespoons cocoa powder
1 heaped tablespoon chopped
 walnuts (optional)
225 g (8 oz) sweet biscuits, crushed

Beat the egg, add the butter and sugar, then add ⅔ of the melted chocolate, the crushed biscuits, nuts (if using), warmed syrup and cocoa powder. Mix gently but well.

Line a 17.5-cm (7-inch) cake tin with greaseproof paper, press the mixture into it and leave in the refrigerator to set. Take out of the tin and peel off the paper. Pour the remaining melted chocolate over the cake, and leave to set for 2 hours in a cool place before serving.

Boiled cake – *Císte beirithe*

This is a family recipe for a very good fruit cake which will keep moist in a tin for some time.

100 g (4 oz) butter
225 g (8 oz) brown sugar
450 g (1 lb) raisins and sultanas
225 g (8 oz) flour

1 teaspoon baking soda
1 teaspoon mixed spice
2 eggs, well beaten

Put the butter, brown sugar, raisins and sultanas in a saucepan with 150 ml (¼ pint) of water and bring to the boil, then simmer for 10 minutes. Mix together the flour, soda and mixed spice. Combine with the contents of the saucepan and the beaten eggs. Mix well, then put into a greased and lined 20-cm (8-inch) cake tin and bake at 180°C, 350°F, Mark 4 for 1½ hours or until a skewer inserted comes out clean. Cool on a wire rack.

Buttermilk cake – *Císte bláthaí*

This very plain cake, is almost like a tea bread but is good when freshly-made and eaten with butter.

450 g (1 lb) flour, sifted
1 teaspoon baking soda
1 teaspoon cream of tartar
1 teaspoon mixed spice
100 g (4 oz) butter

225 g (8 oz) brown sugar
225 g (8 oz) sultanas
1 egg, beaten
300 ml (½ pint) buttermilk

Sift the dry ingredients, then rub in the butter. Add the sugar and fruit and mix well. Then add the beaten egg, and just enough buttermilk to make a pliable and fairly soft but not sloppy dough. Put into a lightly greased loaf tin and bake at 180°C, 350°F, Mark 4 for 45 minutes or until a skewer inserted comes out clean. Cool on a rack.

Cherry cake – *Císte silíní*

Cherries are popular in cakes in Ireland. They are sometimes added to a sweetened dough mix – this is called cherry dog.

175–225 g (6–8 oz) glacé cherries
175 g (6 oz) butter
175 g (6 oz) sugar
few drops of almond or vanilla
essence
3 medium-sized eggs, beaten
275 g (10 oz) self raising flour
pinch of salt

Grease and line a 900-g (2-pound) loaf tin with greaseproof paper. Cut the cherries in half, then wash in warm water and dry thoroughly. Cream the butter and sugar, add the essence and the beaten eggs, little by little, beating well after each addition. Fold in the sifted flour, salt and cherries. Put into the tin and bake at 190°C, 375°F, Mark 5 for 1½ hours or until a skewer inserted comes out clean. Cool on a wire rack.

Christmas cake – *Císte Nollag*

This should be made at least 1 month before needed to let it mature well. It can be used for any special occasion such as a wedding or christening as well.

...A little Christmas cake wrapped in tinsel . . . Into the making of each sweet loaf went a pound of butter, a bottle of stout, and a pound of raisins.

From *The Big Sycamore* by Joseph Brady.

This is a family recipe dating from the 1860s. It is a very rich fruit cake.

450 g (1 lb) sultanas
450 g (1 lb) raisins
225 g (8 oz) currants
100 g (4 oz) glacé cherries
175 g (6 oz) mixed chopped candied
peel
100 g (4 oz) dried apricots, soaked
100 g (4 oz) walnuts or split,
    blanched almonds

The evening before take the butter and eggs from the refrigerator to a cool room temperature. Then line a 25-cm (10-in) cake tin, sides and bottom first with a double thickness of brown paper then oiled greaseproof paper. Prepare the fruit and nuts given above, and chop the whole peel.

Mix all together, put in a flat tin, cover with foil and heat in the lowest possible oven until the fruit swells up, mixing with a wooden spoon. When they are a bit sticky take from the oven, separate them and leave overnight to get cold.

To make the cake

175 g (6 oz) soft brown sugar
175 g (6 oz) fine sugar
350 g (12 oz) butter
6 large eggs
450 g (1 lb) plain flour, sifted
100 g (4 oz) ground almonds

1 rounded teaspoon mixed spice
1 level teaspoon grated nutmeg
½ teaspoon salt
grated rind and juice of 1 lemon
grated rind and juice of 1 orange
4 tablespoons brandy, whiskey or rum

Cream the sugars and butter until light, then add the eggs separately with a little flour, beating well between each addition. Fold in the remaining sifted flour, spices, ground almonds, fruit juices and finely grated rinds, also the salt. Fold them in gently but thoroughly. Do not beat for it will only make the cake hard.

Add the prepared fruit and nuts gradually, and finally the spirit, mixing well. You can at this point cover it and leave in a cool place overnight.

To cook the cake

Preheat the oven to 160°C, 350°F, Mark 2–3. Put the mixture into the prepared tin and smooth the top with a wet spatula, then loosely cover with greaseproof paper or foil and set it on the middle oven rack. After half an hour reduce the heat to 140°C, 275°F, Mark 1 and cook for 2 hours, then take off the paper. Continue cooking for about 3 hours more, lowering the temperature slightly if it is browning too much. Test before taking from the oven. When cooked take out, leave in the tin and pour over 2 tablespoons more spirit. Leave to get quite cold, then turn out and wrap in double greaseproof before storing in an airtight tin.

After 2 weeks gently pour over 2 more tablespoons of spirit and wrap again.

This cake is usually iced both with almond paste and royal icing, pages 211 and 212, during Christmas week.

Cider cake – *Císte ceirtlise*

This plain cake mixed with cider, another old family recipe, keeps very well.

225 g (8 oz) flour
pinch of salt
pinch of ground nutmeg
½ teaspoon ground ginger
½ teaspoon baking soda

100 g (4 oz) butter
100 g (4 oz) fine sugar
2 eggs, beaten
150 ml (¼ pint) cider

Mix the dry ingredients together very well. In another bowl cream the butter and sugar until light. Add the beaten eggs gradually to the butter mixture, beating to make it smooth. Fold in half the flour. Whip the cider until frothy and add it to the mixture. Fold in the remaining flour. Mix well.

Spoon the mixture into a 17.5-cm (7-inch) lightly greased shallow cake tin and bake at 150°C, 325°F, Mark 3 for about 45 minutes. Cool on a wire rack, then store in a tin for 24 hours before cutting.

Curd cake – *Císte grutha*

This is what is called cheese cake nowadays, but used to be named for the freshly made curds it was made with. This recipe is adapted from the 1755 manuscript book of Catherine Hughes of Killenaule, Co. Tipperary.

225 g (8 oz) shortcrust pastry

Filling
350 g (12 oz) sweet curds, or sieved cottage cheese
2 heaped tablespoons fine sugar

1 tablespoon softened butter
juice and grated peel of ½ lemon
2 eggs, separated

Topping
1 egg
1 tablespoon sugar
1 tablespoon flour
1 tablespoon melted butter

When the pastry is made let it rest, then chill for at least half an hour. Meanwhile, make the filling. Beat the egg yolks and the egg whites separately. Mix the curds with the sugar, soft butter, lemon juice and grated peel and the beaten egg yolks. Beat well together, then add the stiffly beaten egg whites. Roll out the pastry and line a 17.5- or 20-cm (7- or 8-inch) flan tin. Put the curd cheese mixture into the pastry case. Mix the topping ingredients well and pour evenly over the filling. Bake at 180°C, 350°F, Mark 4 for 35–40 minutes. Serve warm or cool but not chilled.

Wholemeal fruit cake – *Císte torthaí*

This is a country recipe of the past when much of the flour used was whole wheat and not refined. It is a good cake with a nutty flavour.

175 g (6 oz) softened butter
2 heaped tablespoons brown sugar
350 g (12 oz) wholemeal flour
3 level teaspoons baking powder
2 level teaspoons mixed spice

2 large eggs, beaten
450 g (1 lb) mixed dried fruit, washed and patted dry
50 g (2 oz) flaked almonds

Cream the butter and sugar together in a mixing bowl until light. In another bowl combine the flour, baking powder and mixed spice and mix together well. To the first mixing bowl add the beaten eggs, a little at a time, alternately with the flour mixture, then fold in the remaining flour mixture gently. Add the dried fruit and mix well. If the final mixture seems very stiff add a little water but do not let it get sloppy. Turn into a greased and lined 20-cm (8-inch) cake tin and sprinkle with the almonds. Bake in a preheated 160°C, 320°F, Mark 3 oven on the shelf just below the middle for about 2 hours, but test with a fine skewer before taking from the oven. Allow to cool in the tin, then put on a wire rack and remove the paper.

Ginger cake – *Císte sinséir*

Ginger is one of the favourite spices for cakes in Ireland.

2 heaped tablespoons butter or lard
100 g (4 oz) brown sugar
2 eggs, beaten
2 tablespoons treacle
½ teaspoon grated lemon rind
225 g (8 oz) flour

pinch of salt
½ teaspoon ground cinnamon
¼ teaspoon grated nutmeg
1 level teaspoon ground ginger
4 level teaspoons baking powder

Beat the fat and sugar together until light in a mixing bowl. In another bowl sift together the flour, salt, cinnamon, nutmeg, ground ginger and baking powder. Gradually add to the first bowl the beaten eggs alternately with the treacle, beating after each addition. Then add the lemon rind and finally fold in the dry ingredients and add 225 ml (8 fl oz) boiling water; mix well. Pour into a well-greased shallow 20- or 22-cm (8- or 9-inch) baking tin and bake at 180°C, 350°F, Mark 4 for about 45 minutes; test before taking from the oven.

Gingerbread – *Arán sinséir*

Despite its name this is a lovely soft and moist ginger cake which keeps very well in a tin. It can be eaten warm but is more difficult to cut, than if it has cooled.

350 g (12 oz) flour
pinch of salt
1 rounded teaspoon ground ginger
1 rounded teaspoon baking soda
1 level teaspoon baking powder
50 g (2 oz) preserved ginger,
    chopped

175 g (16 oz) brown sugar
100 g (4 oz) golden syrup
100 g (4 oz) treacle
150 g (5 oz) butter
1 egg, well beaten
about 150 ml (¼ pint) milk, warmed
    to blood heat

Sift together the flour, salt, ginger, soda and baking powder and add the chopped preserved ginger. Put in a saucepan the sugar, syrup, treacle and butter and stir over heat until melted and well combined, but do not let it boil.

Combine the two mixtures and add the beaten eggs and warm milk; mix well. Pour into a greased and lined 20- or 22-cm (8- or 9-inch) square tin and bake in a preheated 180°C, 350°F, Mark 4 oven on the middle shelf for 1½ hours. Cool on a wire rack and cut into squares before serving.

Gur cake – *Gur-chíste*

This cake was eaten by the poor of Dublin in the nineteenth and early twentieth centuries, for it was very cheap, made by bakers from their stale cake or bread stocks. This can be made with stale cake rather than bread if preferred, in which case omit the dried fruit.

8 slices stale bread, crusts cut off
3 tablespoons flour
½ teaspoon baking powder
2 teaspoons mixed spice
100 g (4 oz) brown sugar
2 tablespoons butter

175 g (6 oz) currants or mixed dried fruit
1 large egg, beaten
4 tablespoons milk
225 g (8 oz) shortcrust pastry
sugar for sprinkling

Soak the bread in a little water for an hour, then squeeze the moisture out. Combine with the flour, baking powder, mixed spice, sugar, butter, fruit, beaten egg and milk. Mix well.

Line the bottom of a 22-cm (9-inch) square tin with half of the pastry and spread the mixture over, then cover with the remaining pastry. Make a few diagonal gashes across the top and bake at 190°C, 375°F, Mark 5 for about an hour. Sprinkle the top with sugar, and allow to cool in the tin, then cut into 24 small squares. (A square of this size used to be sold for a halfpenny.)

Honey cake – *Císte meala*

This is a delicious cake which keeps very well, as do most things which have honey in them.

100 g (4 oz) butter
2 heaped tablespoons soft brown sugar
2 tablespoons honey

2 eggs, lightly beaten
175 g (6 oz) flour
15 g (½ oz) baking powder
4 tablespoons milk

Cream the butter, sugar and honey until soft and light, then gently fold in the lightly beaten eggs. Sift together the flour and baking powder and add gradually alternately with the milk. Beat quickly, then pour into a greased and lined 17.5-cm (7-inch) cake tin and bake in the middle of a preheated oven, 180°C, 350°F, Mark 4, for about 45 minutes.

Madeira cake – *Císte Maidéarach*

This is the cake that was much enjoyed with a glass of Madeira wine. It is a delicious cake, very pure and delicate tasting.

425 g (15 oz) flour
3 heaped tablespoons self raising flour
350 g (12 oz) butter
225 g (8 oz) sugar

grated rind of 1 lemon
6 large eggs
150 ml (¼ pint) milk
1 thin slice candied citron peel

Sift the two flours together twice on to greaseproof paper. Cream together the butter, sugar and grated lemon rind until light. Add the eggs, one at a time, alternately with spoonfuls of the sifted flour, beating in each addition well. Then fold in the remaining flour, using a metal spoon. Add the milk and combine; it will make a fairly soft mixture. Pour into a greased and lined deep 25-cm (10-inch) cake tin and bake in the middle of a preheated 160°C, 325°F, Mark 3 oven laying the slice of candied citron peel gently on top of the cake after the first half hour, closing the oven door quickly. Test before taking from the oven and leave in the tin for half an hour, then turn out to cool on a wire rack. After it has cooled, take off the paper. To keep, wrap in greaseproof paper and store in an airtight tin in a cool place.

Porter cake – *Císte pórtair*

This is an old family recipe which keeps well in an airtight tin, and should be made at least a week ahead.

450 g (1 lb) flour, sifted	2 teaspoons mixed spice
225 g (8 oz) butter	350 g (12 oz) brown sugar
225 g (8 oz) currants	300 ml (½ pint) porter, Guinness or
225 g (8 oz) raisins or sultanas	stout
100 g (4 oz) chopped mixed peel	1 teaspoon baking soda
grated rind of 1 lemon	4 eggs, well beaten

Sift the flour and rub in the butter, then add the currants, raisins or sultanas, mixed peel, lemon rind, spice and sugar and mix well. Warm the porter, Guinness or stout to hand hot, then pour over the soda and stir. Add the well-beaten eggs to the mixture, and gradually stir this into the flour and fruit mixture. Beat for 15 minutes. Pour into a greased and lined 22-cm (9-inch) cake tin, cover loosely with greaseproof paper and bake in a preheated 160°C, 325°F, Mark 3 oven for 1 hour, then lower the heat to 150°C, 300°F, Mark 2 and bake for a further 2 hours. Cool in the tin, then turn out and remove paper. Keep in an airtight tin for at least a week before cutting.

Raisin and bran cake – *Císte rísiní agus bran*

225 g (8 oz) All Bran	1 teaspoon vanilla essence
225 g (8 oz) seedless muscat raisins	450 ml (15 oz) milk
225 g (8 oz) dark brown sugar	225 g (8 oz) wholemeal flour
100 g (4 oz) walnuts, chopped	3 teaspoons baking powder

Mix together the All Bran, raisins, sugar, walnuts and vanilla and then pour the milk over and mix. Cover and leave for 2 hours.

Sift the flour and baking powder together and gradually fold into the mixture. Put in a greased and lined 20-cm (8-inch) square tin and bake at 180°C, 350°F, Mark 4 for 1½ hours. Store in a tin for at least a day before cutting.

Raisin and carrot cake – *Císte rísiní agus meacan*

This is a deliciously spicy country cake.

175 g (6 oz) flour, (wholemeal or white, or a mixture) sifted
2 teaspoons baking powder
1 teaspoon ground cinnamon
pinch of mace
pinch of salt
2 heaped tablespoons seedless raisins
100 g (4 oz) grated carrot
grated rind of ½ orange
2 tablespoons orange juice
100 g (4 oz) butter
150 g (5 oz) brown sugar
2 eggs

Sift the flour with the baking powder, cinnamon, mace and salt, and reserve. Mix the raisins, carrots, orange rind and juice. In another bowl cream the butter and sugar, and add the eggs, one at a time, with a wooden spoon. Finally combine with the flour and carrot mixtures. Mix all together very well.

Bake in a greased and lined 20-cm (8-inch) tin for 40–60 minutes at 180°C, 350°F, Mark 4. After removing from the oven leave in the tin for 15 minutes to cool before taking it out.

Saffron cake – *Císte cróch*

Quite a lot of saffron was imported into Ireland from its near neighbour Cornwall in the eighteenth and nineteenth centuries. It was used mostly as a dye for the saffron tweed, but it was also used in baking. Saffron cake is still a very traditional feature in Cornwall and it possibly came to Ireland from there along with the saffron itself.

This is the recipe from Sara Power's handwritten book of 1746 ('barm' is yeast).

Take 3 quarters of a pound of Butter, half a pound of Sugar, half a quarter of an ounce of Saffron, your Flower dried, an ounce of Barm and a half a pint of water or Ale. Your Saffron should be boyl'd in rosewater, or ale before you use it, drain it. Melt your Butter, when almost cold put your Barm and Saffron mixt in it let it stand half an hour. Take 2 pounds of Flower which you have kept dry, and mix it with your Barm. Add your Butter, your Sugar, your Saffron and Barm and liquid all together and let it stand an hour to rise. Your oven must not be too hot, nor let them be too dry in the oven, the smaller the better. Your Barm must settle for 40 hours before you can use it.

My adaptation is:

450 g (1 lb) flour
teaspoon salt
pinch of powdered mace
50 g (2 oz) each lard and butter
2 heaped tablespoons castor sugar
225 g (½ lb) currants
50 g (2 oz) chopped peel
25 g (1 oz) fresh yeast or 15 g (½ oz) dried
300 ml (4 pint)0 tepid milk
pinch of saffron

Sift dry ingredients, then rub in fats and fold in sugar, fruit and peel. Mix the yeast with the milk and leave for 15 minutes, then add with the saffron to the centre of the mixture, fold over flour and leave to bubble. Mix well by hand, cover and leave for an hour to double in size. Turn on to floured surface and knead, then put into a 20-cm (8-in) tin and leave again. Preheat oven to 160°C, 325°F, Mark 3 and cook for 45 minutes in the centre of the oven.

Seed cake – *Cácá cearbhais (carvie cake)*

This cake used to be the most popular in my childhood. It was also known as 'carvie cake' in country districts, and appears so in many old books.

225 g (8 oz) fine sugar
225 (8 oz) butter
4 eggs

1 heaped tablespoon caraway seeds
225 g (8 oz) self-raising flour
3–4 tablespoons milk

Cream the butter and sugar well, and beat in the eggs one at a time, adding a little of the sifted flour with each. Then fold in the remaining flour and the caraway seeds. Add the milk to make a soft mixture. Put into a greased and lined 17.5- or 20-cm (7- or 8-inch) cake tin and bake in the preheated oven at 160°C, 325°F, Mark 3 for 1½–1¾ hours; test before taking out. Leave in the tin for 10 minutes, then cool on a wire rack and take off the paper when cool.

Foolproof sponge cake without fat – *Císte sothuigthe spúinse*

100 g (4 oz) flour
¾ teaspoon baking powder
pinch of salt

100 g (4 oz) fine sugar
4 eggs, separated

Sift the flour, baking powder and salt. Beat the egg whites until stiff, then add half the sugar. Beat the yolks just a little, add the remaining sugar and continue beating for 5 minutes preferably with an electric beater. Combine with the egg white mixture beating a little to mix, then add the flour, gradually, folding in gently with a *metal* spoon (do not beat). Pour into 2 greased and lightly floured 17.5-cm (7-inch) tins and bake at 200°C, 400°F, Mark 6 on the middle shelf for 20–25 minutes. Cool on a rack.

Sultana cake – *Císte sabhdánach*

This light fruit cake has a fresh, lemony flavour.

175 g (6 oz) butter
175 g (6 oz) fine sugar
3 large or 4 medium-sized eggs
275 g (10 oz) self-raising flour, sifted

150 g (5 oz) sultanas
50 g (2 oz) chopped mixed peel
finely grated rind of 1 lemon
1–4 tablespoons milk

Cream the butter and sugar, then add the eggs, separately adding each one with a spoonful of the sifted flour. Gently stir in the rest of the flour, then add the sultanas, peel and lemon rind. Add just enough milk to make a soft dough. Put into a greased and lined 20-cm (8-inch) tin and bake in the preheated oven at 180°C, 350°F, Mark 4, for approximately 1½ hours; test that a skewer comes away clean from the cake before taking it from the oven.

Eggless vinegar cake – *Císte fínéagair*

This is also called vicarage cake. It is a good cake for people who cannot tolerate eggs or are not allowed them.

175 g (5 oz) butter
450 g (1 lb) flour
225 (8 oz) currants
100 g (4 oz) raisins or sultanas

3 tablespoons vinegar
about 150 ml (¼ pint) milk
1 teaspoon baking soda

Rub the butter well into the flour, then add the sugar, and currants and raisins or sultanas. Put the vinegar into a deep large jug and add the milk, keeping back two spoonfuls. Warm these slightly and mix them with the baking soda; quickly add to the jug, holding it over the basin as it might froth over. Stir at once into the dough and turn into a greased and lined 17.5- or 20-cm (7- or 8-inch) cake tin; bake in a preheated oven at 180°C, 350°F, Mark 4 for 20 minutes, then lower the heat to 160°C, 325°F, Mark 3 and bake for a further 40–50 minutes; test with a fine skewer before taking from the oven. Cool a little in the tin, then on a wire rack, and remove the paper.

Walnut and honey cake – *Císte gallchnónna agus meala*

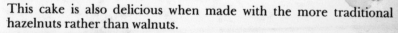

This cake is also delicious when made with the more traditional hazelnuts rather than walnuts.

225 g (8 oz) self raising flour
pinch of salt
175 g (6 oz) butter
100 g (4 oz) fine sugar
2 generous tablespoons honey,

warmed
2 large eggs, beaten
grated rind of 1 orange
1 tablespoon orange juice
50 g (2 oz) chopped walnuts

Icing
225 g (8 oz) icing sugar
2–3 tablespoons orange juice

Sift together the flour and salt and reserve. Cream the butter and sugar and add the warmed honey and mix well. Gradually add the beaten eggs with a little of the flour, then stir in the grated orange rind. With a metal spoon, fold in the remaining flour together with the orange juice and nuts.

Spoon the mixture into a greased and lined deep round 17.5-cm (7-inch) cake tin, spreading it level and hollowing out the centre a little. Put in the middle of a preheated oven at 180°C, 350°F, Mark 4 and bake for 1½ hours.

Let it cool in the tin for 10 minutes, then turn out on to a wire rack and take off papers. Cool; meanwhile make the icing. Sift the sugar into a basin, add the orange juice, through a strainer, and mix. Transfer to a saucepan and stir over a low heat beating well until it melts and is smooth and very warm, but not hot. Pour the warm icing over the cake all at once and smooth with a knife. Leave until quite cool before cutting.

Irish whiskey cake – *Císte uisce beatha*

To get the true flavour this lovely cake should be started the evening before.

peel of 1 large lemon	3 eggs, separated
1 double measure Irish whiskey	175 g (6 oz) sultanas
175 g (6 oz) butter	pinch of salt
175 g (6 oz) fine sugar	1 teaspoon baking powder
175 g (6 oz) flour, sifted	

Put the lemon peel into a glass, cover with whiskey and leave overnight. Cream the butter and sugar until light. Sift the flour then add the egg yolks one at a time along with a spoonful of flour, mixing well. Add the whiskey, through a strainer and mix in the sultanas with a little more flour. Whisk the egg whites stiffly and fold into the mixture with the salt, baking powder and the remaining flour.

Pour into a greased and lined 17.5-cm (7-inch) cake tin and bake in a preheated oven at 180°C, 350°F, Mark 4 for 1¼–1½ hours; test before removing from the oven.

Almond shortcake – *Brioscarán almóinní*

This was often made at Christmas in earlier times.

150 g (5 oz) plain flour	4 egg yolks
1 heaped tablespoon ground rice	1 egg white, stiffly beaten
2 heaped tablespoons fine sugar	100 g (4 oz) icing sugar
100 g (4 oz) butter	40 g (1½ oz) flaked almonds

Combine the flour, ground rice and sugar in a bowl, then rub in the butter until the mixture is like coarse breadcrumbs. Add the egg yolks and mix to a stiff paste. Knead until smooth, then roll out to fit a 17.5-cm (7-inch) tin. Press in until it is flat, prick lightly all over, cover with greaseproof paper and bake at 150°C, 300°F, Mark 2 for half an hour.

Meanwhile, beat the egg white until stiff, then gradually sift in the icing sugar, and spread the mixture over the shortcake, sprinkle with almonds and put back in the oven for a further half hour. Cool in the tin, and cut into wedges when cold.

Coconut cakes – *Cístí cnó cócó*

225 g (8 oz) butter
225 g (8 oz) fine sugar
275 g (10 oz) flour

pinch of salt
175 g (6 oz) dessicated coconut
2 large eggs

Cream the butter and sugar. Sift the flour with the salt and gradually add to the butter/sugar mixture stirring. Gradually add the coconut, then the beaten eggs mixing very well. Drop small spoonfuls on to a greased baking sheet and bake at 220°C, 425°F, Mark 7 for 10 minutes. Makes about 10 cakes.

Ginger cup cakes – *Cístí sinséir*

225 g (8 oz) flour
½ teaspoon baking powder
½ teaspoon ground ginger
½ teaspoon mixed spice

3 heaped tablespoons butter
3 heaped tablespoons sugar
1 tablespoon golden syrup
a little fruit juice

Combine the ingredients, adding just enough fruit juice to form a nice dough and bake in greased cup-cake tins at 190°C, 375°F, Mark 5, for 15 minutes.

Melting moments – *Móimintí maotha*

These very light little cakes of Scottish origin but now firmly established in Ireland, live up to their name.

275 g (10 oz) butter
50 g (2 oz) icing sugar
225 g (8 oz) sifted flour

50 g (2 oz) cornflour
lemon curd or thick honey

Cream the butter and sugar until very light. Add both flours gradually, mixing well. Put small spoonfuls onto greased baking trays and bake for about 15 minutes in a 180°C, 350°F, Mark 4 oven. Cool on a rack and when cool sandwich together with a little lemon curd or thick honey in between. Makes about 30 'sandwiches'.

Potato and apple cake – *Cácá prátaí agus úll*

Spent the night pleasantly and quietly eating apples, burning nuts, drinking tea and punch and eating apple-cake. That is how I finished the Autumn season.

From the diary of Humphrey O'Sullivan,
entry for October 31st, 1831.

450 g (1 lb) freshly cooked potatoes
1 heaped tablespoon butter
2 teaspoons sugar
pinch of ground ginger
900 g (2 lb) cooking apples, peeled,

cored and sliced
3 tablespoons flour
1 tablespoon brown sugar
about ½ tablespoon butter

Mash the hot potatoes very well with the butter, sugar and ginger. Add the flour, just enough to make a pliable dough, and knead a little. Roll out on a floured surface into two rounds, one slightly larger than the other. Put on a greased baking sheet and cover the larger round with the apple slices and a generous sprinkling of brown sugar. Dampen the edges of the bottom crust and put the top over, pressing together to make a seal. Cut a small vent in the top and prick all over lightly, then brush over with a little milk and bake at 190°C, 375°F, Mark 5 for 35–40 minutes, or until the top is golden and the apples cooked. Take from the oven and widen the vent on top enough to slip in a knob of butter and more brown sugar. Serve hot. Serves 4.

Rock cakes – *Borróga carraigeacha*

225 g (8 oz) self raising flour
100 g (4 oz) butter
100 g (4 oz) fine sugar
100 (4 oz) currants and sultanas
1 heaped tablespoon finely chopped
peel (optional)
2 eggs beaten
1 level teaspoon ground ginger
2–3 tablespoons coarsest sugar
pinch of nutmeg (optional)

Sift the flour. Cream the butter and sugar; combine with the flour and add the currants and sultanas chopped, the peel if including, beaten eggs, ginger and nutmeg if including. Drop by tablespoonfuls on to a greased baking sheet, sprinkle coarse sugar on top, and bake at 160°C, 325°F, Mark 3 for 10–15 minutes. Lift off the tray while still hot and cool on a rack. Makes about 20 cakes.

Shortbread – *Brioscarái*

This is a feature of Scottish traditional cookery that has been adopted in Ireland – it has been made here for several hundred years.

It is often eaten at Christmas.

225 g (8 oz) butter
100 g (4 oz) fine sugar
225 g (8 oz) flour, sifted
100 g (4 oz) rice flour or cornflour
pinch of salt
sugar for sprinkling

All ingredients should be warm and dry before starting. Cream the sugar and butter together well. Mix the flours with the salt, and gradually but thoroughly combine them into a dough which is smooth and even. Do not knead or roll out as this will toughen it. Press into a shallow 20-cm (8-inch) round tin and pinch the edges up. Then prick lightly all over and bake in a preheated oven at 190°C, 375°F, Mark 5 for 20 minutes, then lower to 180°C, 350°F, Mark 4 and bake for a further 45 minutes. Leave to cool in the tin, then transfer to a rack and sprinkle the top with fine sugar before serving.

Císte donn

This is a very edible tea cake for people who don't care for rich cakes.

225 g (10 oz) sugar
75 g (3 oz) sultanas
75 g (3 oz) currants
100 g (4 oz) lard

2 teaspoons mixed spice
¼ teaspoon ground ginger
225 g (8 oz) self raising flour
1 large egg beaten

Heat together in a saucepan 300 ml (½ pint) water, the sugar, sultanas, currants, lard, mixed spice and ginger. Mix well, then take from the heat. When cool, stir in the flour and beaten egg, and mix well. Pour into a greased and lined 20-cm (8-inch) cake tin and bake at 180°C, 350°F, Mark 4 for 1 hour, then cool on a rack.

Icings

Coffee icing

Sift 225 g (8 oz) icing sugar into a saucepan. Add 2 teaspoons of coffee essence or strong black coffee and about 150 ml (¼ pint) warm water. Stir well over a low heat to dissolve the sugar, and when thick enough to coat the back of a wooden spoon it is ready.

American icing

Beat two egg whites in a bowl until starting to stiffen. Put 225 g (8 oz) of granulated sugar with 150 ml (¼ pint) water in a saucepan and bring to the boil, then boil until it reaches 120°C, 250°F. Quickly pour the liquid syrup into the bowl with the egg whites and beat until the mixture begins to thicken. Ice the cake with it immediately.

Almond paste

The following amount will cover the top of the cake only which is usual. If the sides are to be spread with it too, double the quantities.

400 g (14 oz) ground almonds
200 g (7 oz) icing sugar or more if
  necessary
200 g (7 oz) fine sugar

½ teaspoon almond essence
juice of lemon
1 large egg or 3 egg yolks
a little apricot jam, warmed

Mix the ground almonds and both sugars well; make a well in the centre. Beat the egg, add the lemon juice and almond essence and pour into the well in the sugar and almond mixture. Blend all together with the fingers gently, for over-kneading will make the almonds oily. (The paste should be pliable but not sticky.) Add more lemon juice or icing sugar if necessary. Dust a board with icing sugar and roll out the paste to the size of the cake top.

If the top of the cake is not straight, cut it to make the surface level then turn the cake over so that the flat bottom becomes the top. Brush the warm apricot jam, pressing it through a sieve, on to the top of the cake. Gently reverse the cake again to lay the apricot side down on to the round of almond paste. Press down lightly and trim round the edges. Put the cake board or plate over it and invert. Cover lightly with tissue paper and leave to harden for a week. It will then be ready for royal icing, if using.

Royal icing

This is the icing used on Christmas cakes or other rich cakes for special occasions, which are first covered with the almond paste (above). The almond paste is put on at least a week before the royal icing to dry thoroughly. The icing itself should be made two or three days before the cake is to be eaten. If a thick double icing is wanted the first coat should be left to dry for 24 hours before applying the second coat. The cake should be on the plate or cake board from which it will be served, and when finished the whole should be covered loosely with tissue paper, not put into a tin or it will 'sweat' and be spoiled. The following ingredients are enough for the top and sides of a 25-cm (10-inch) round cake.

900 g (2 lb) icing sugar
1 teaspoon lemon juice
4 egg whites
2 teaspoons glycerine

Sift the icing sugar twice. Put the egg whites in a bowl and stir lightly with a fork, do not beat. Add most of the sifted sugar a little at a time beating well with a wooden spoon between each addition. Add the lemon juice glycerine and the remaining sugar, beating very well to get rid of any tiny air bubbles, until the icing becomes really smooth. Cover with a dampened cloth until ready to apply.

Cut the top of the cake if necessary to make the surface level, then turn it over so that the flat bottom is the top. The icing should be smoothed over the entire cake, top and sides with a plastic ruler or icing knife, and left to dry naturally.

chapter ten

BEVERAGES – *DEOCH*

Blackberry wine – *Fión sméar*

Blackcurrants, gooseberries, or a mixture of berries such as elderberries and sloes can be used for this in place of blackberries.

3 kg (6 lb) blackberries
25 g (1 oz) yeast
225 g (8 oz) raisins
1¾ kg (4 lb) sugar

Wash the blackberries and pick them over, discarding any that are
not good. Pour 3¼ litres (6 pints) of boiling water over them and
bruise with a wooden spoon. Leave for about 3 days, stirring and
squeezing the fruit against the side from time to time. Strain and add
the yeast, raisins and sugar. Syphon into a large bottle with an airlock
fitted, and leave for about 6 months until it has stopped working.
Bottle and keep for 6 months before drinking.

Carrageen syrup – *Sioróip carraigín*

This is a country cure for chest colds and coughs.

25 g (1 oz) carrageen
rind of ½ lemon
2 teaspoons sugar or to taste

2 teaspoons whiskey or brandy
(optional)

Wash the carrageen well and put it into a saucepan with 600 ml (1 pint) water and the lemon rind. Bring slowly to the boil and simmer for 15–20 minutes. Strain and serve hot. Add sugar and the whiskey or brandy. This makes enough for one person.

Cider – *Ceirtlis*

Cider is made in country districts, but it can be a bit tricky to make. Do not allow any metal to come in contact with the liquid.

3 kg (6 lb) apples   piece of bruised ginger root, not too big
approx. 3.2 kg (7 lb) sugar   3 lemons

Wash the unpeeled apples well. Cut into very small pieces and put into an earthenware or glass container. Pour 7 litres (12 pints) of boiling water over them, cover and leave for two weeks, stirring and sqeezing against the sides every day. Strain, add the ginger and lemon juice, and then measure the liquid, for each pint of liquid add 225 g (½ lb) sugar. Make sure it dissolves well, then add about a teacup of boiling water to raise the temperature, cover and leave for about 12 days, or until a scum has formed over the entire surface. Skim it off thoroughly and bottle the cider, cover but do not cork for 5–6 days. Store the bottles in a cool place in the dark, and do not move or shake them for at least 2 months.

Irish coffee – *Caife Gaelach*

This is not a traditional drink, but it is all set to become one. It is a good finish for a meal, or a pick-me-up on a cold morning. In Ireland it is served in most pubs and all restaurants.

Warm a stemmed whiskey glass, then put into it about 1 heaped teaspoon of sugar, or to taste. Add enough strong, hot, black coffee to fill to within 3 cm (1½ inches) of the top, and stir well to dissolve the sugar. Add the Irish whiskey to fill up to 1 cm (½ inch) below the top. Hold a teaspoon, with its curved side up, across the glass and pour 1 tablespoon double cream over it. Do not stir, but drink at once.

Mead – *Meá*

This ancient Irish drink made from honey is very potent when matured, although the taste is quite innocuous. This is an old recipe.

1½ kg (3 lb) honey
50 g (2 oz) fresh ginger
25 g (1 oz) fresh yeast

Boil 4 litres (7 pints) of water for half an hour, then add the honey and dissolve well. Boil for about 1 hour, skimming a little if necessary. Bruise the ginger root, put into a muslin bag and add to the boiling liquid. Leave to cool to hand-hot temperature, then add the yeast.

Pour into a large fermentation jar, leaving an air space at the top, then fit with an airlock, and keep at warm room temperature until the bubbling has ceased, which means it has stopped working. Syphon into bottles and cover lightly, but do not cork for a few days. Cork tightly after it has stopped fermenting. Keep for at least 6 months (but preferably for a year) before drinking.

Scailtín

This is the Irish name for a hot whiskey drink or toddy. The most usual one is whiskey, sugar, cloves and lemon with hot water; another is hot milk with honey, cloves and/or a stick of cinammon and a good measure of whiskey.

Bishop

> . . . fine oranges,
> Well roasted, with sugar and wine in a cup,
> They'll make a sweet Bishop when gentlefolks sup.

This fine old nightcap, also called *scailtín fíona*, was a favourite of Dean Swift's.

2 oranges
2 whole cloves
8 allspice berries
1 bottle port wine
2.5-cm (1-inch) stick of cinammon

2 pieces of blade mace
2 small pieces fresh ginger
6 lumps of sugar rubbed over with
   the zest of lemon

Stick the cloves into the oranges and roast in a moderate oven for about half an hour, until soft. Put the spices into a pan with 300 ml (½ pint) water and boil until slightly reduced. Pour into a large warmed bowl, and add the sugar rubbed over with lemon zest and the roasted oranges, cut into quarters. Stir well until the sugar is dissolved.

Heat up the port, but do not let it boil or the alcohol content will be lost, then pour over the contents of the bowl and serve.

Mulled claret – *Scailtín fíona*

Brandy is sometimes added to this, but it is not really traditional.

12 whole cloves
pinch of grated nutmeg
rind of half lemon, kept as whole as
   possible

1 lemon, finely sliced
2 bottles claret
2 wineglasses port wine
sugar to taste

Simmer the spices and lemon rind in 150 ml (¼ pint) water for half an hour, then strain into a large pan. Add the port, then the claret, and sugar to taste. Make sure the contents are very hot, but on no account should it be allowed to boil. Serve at once with slices of lemon.

Brandy or whiskey punch – *Puins branda*

Puins (punch) can be made from either whiskey, brandy, poteen or rum, but the first two are the most traditional in Ireland and were extremely popular in eighteenth- and nineteenth-century Ireland, and are still served at Christmas time. Whiskey punch was served in most hotels with meals as well as in private houses. Thackery mentions it frequently in his *Irish Sketch Book* of 1843.

> The first sight I witnessed at Killarney was a race-ordinary where, for a sum of twelve shillings any man could take his share of turbot, salmon, venison and beef, with port and sherry and whiskey-punch at discretion.

5 lemons
225 g (8 oz) lump sugar
3–4 whole cloves

1 bottle brandy or whiskey
small piece of cinnamon stick

Rub the lumps of sugar hard all over the outsides of the lemons until they have absorbed all the zest. Put the sugar into a saucepan with 600 ml (1 pint) water and the spices, and bring to the boil. Stir until the sugar dissolves. Strain, add the brandy or whiskey and heat up, but do not boil or the alcohol content will be lost. Serve hot with thin slices of the lemon floating on top.

Sloe gin – *Biotáille airní*

This is an old drink and a very good one. It can also be made with vodka, and can be served as a long drink with soda water added if preferred.

75 g (3 oz) sloes
50 g (2 oz) sugar
bottle of gin

Wash the sloes and prick them with a thick needle all over. Mix them with the sugar and half-fill an empty quart bottle with them. Fill with the gin and cork tightly. Leave for at least 3 months before drinking, preferably longer, while it becomes a lovely purplish-red colour and gets a delightful taste. It is also quite a strong drink! Do not strain; the liquor-sodden fruit will stay at the bottom as you pour. It can be topped up until no more taste is forthcoming from the fruit.

chapter eleven

MISCELLANEOUS – *ÉAGSÚIL*

Porridge – *Brachán*

Porridge is sometimes a morning, and sometimes an evening dish.
It has been known since the earliest times.

> From *Home Life in Ireland* by Robert Lynd, 1909.

The secret of good porridge making is to add the oatmeal gradually,
stirring well, so that the water does not stop bubbling. Traditionally it
was served with a pinch of salt, as a savoury dish, but nowadays the
majority of people sweeten it with sugar, honey or syrup. Purists are
horrified by this debasement. If soaked in water overnight the
cooking time is cut down.

Allow for each person for a large
  helping:
300 ml (½ pint) water

40 g (1 ½ oz) medium oatmeal
a pinch of salt

The water must be boiling hard. With the left hand sprinkle in the
oatmeal, stirring meanwhile so that the water does not stop bubbling,
and also so that it doesn't lump. Continue stirring for about 5
minutes, when the mixture will thicken. You can then stop stirring
and on a low flame, covered, let it just simmer for 10–15 minutes.
  Add the salt when cooking is almost completed and stir as it can

harden the oats if added earlier. Serve with milk, cream, buttermilk, and more salt or sugar according to your taste. *Note* There are many quick-cooking porridge oats on the market nowadays, so if using them it would be wise to follow the instructions on the packet. The above recipe is for unrefined oatmeal.

Yellowman

Did you treat your Mary Anne to dulse and yellowman
At the Ould Lammas Fair at Ballycastle, O?

Yellowman is a toffee which has been made by the same family in Co. Antrim for several hundred years. The famous maker was a Dick Murray in Lurgan. It is always sold at Lammas Fair at Ballycastle, Co. Antrim, on the last Tuesday of August. It has a brittle texture and is hammered from a large block.

1 heaped tablespoon butter
225 g (8 oz) brown sugar
450 g (1 lb) golden or corn syrup

1 teaspoon baking soda
2 tablespoons vinegar

Grease a shallow 23–25 cm (9–10 in) tin with the melted butter. Then add the sugar, syrup and vinegar, bring to heat and stir until all ingredients are melted. Boil without stirring until it gets crisp: 140°C, 290°F, Mark 1. Then add the baking soda which will foam up, stir again then pour on to a greased slab or greased dish and pull toffee when cool enough. Pull until it is pale yellow, then pour into the tin and mark in squares or make sticks of it.

chapter twelve

Irish hospitality

The Brehon Laws, or Laws of the Fianna, were formulated about 438 A.D. in the tenth year of King Leary's reign. They were transcribed on to vellum from the eighth to the thirteenth centuries. The largest and most important is called *Senchus Mor*, the *Great Old Law Book*.

According to the Brehon law, people in the higher stations were bound to entertain guests – 'without asking any questions'. There were besides some few hundred guest-houses scattered throughout the country in the early days of Christianity, and the master of each of these was obliged to keep his kitchen fire constantly burning and joints boiling in his cauldron in readiness for the arrival of strangers.

Of Conall the Red, a wealthy landowner in Connacht in the early Middle Ages, it is said: 'Never too, was his house without the Three sacks, to wit, a sack of malt for preparing yeast, a sack of wheat for preparing the refection of guests, and a sack of salt to make every food taste well.'

Patrick Sarsfield, Mayor of Dublin, 1554, opened his house in High Street from five in the morning until ten at night. Nobody went from his door with an unquenched thirst. When he took up his office he had three barns of corn. 'God and good company be thanked,' he said towards the end of his term. 'I stand in doubt whether I shall rub out my Mayoralty with my third barn which is well nigh with my year ended.'

In the seventeenth century Monsieur Jouvin, a French traveller who came to Ireland said: 'the richest of all Europe in things necessary for human life, but the poorest in money. If I drink two-pence worth of beer at a public house I am given without charge, as much as I want of bread, meat, butter, cheese and fish.'

Mrs Delany writing about a visit to Mr Mahone [sic] near Killala, June 12th, 1732:

I have not seen less than fourteen dishes of meat for dinner, and seven for supper during my peregrination; and they not only treat us at their houses magnificently, but if we are to go to an inn, they constantly provide us with a basket crammed with good things: No people *can be more hospitable or obliging*, and there is not only great abundance but great order and neatness.

Breakfast at Castle Otway in the early eighteenth century was described thus:

. . . eggs and milk, brandy, sugar and nutmeg, a large loaf, fresh butter, and a cold round of beef, red herrings, a dish of potatoes roasted on the turf ashes, ale, whiskey and port . . .

Mr Cuffe, MP for Mayo, of Ballinarobe told me about seven years ago (i.e. 1753) he and some other gentlemen went for a Days Fishing on Lake Corrib, then seeing a pretty bay run up into Eyre Connaught, they went up it and landed in order to broil Fish they had caught for Dinner . . Presently a Messenger came to where they were, with a request from the Head of the Sept in that District to know for what reason they Landed in his Territories without his leave. They told the messenger the occasion of their coming and who they were. Presently came down the Great man himself to bid them welcome and invited them to go to his house. They accepted the Invitation and he carried them to where in that Country was a Magnificent palace, there was two long Cabbins Thatched oppisite to one another, one was the Kitchen and appartments for the family. The other was the Entertaining room neatly strewed according to the Irish Fashion with Rushes and the upper End of the Room was a kind of Platform raised above the ground with Boards and two or three Blankets on each which was the Lodging for strangers and visitors. A Bottle of Brandy was the wet before dinner, and the Entertainment was Half a Sheep Boiled at top, Half a sheep roasted at Bottom, broiled Fish on one side, a great wooden bowl of Potatoes on the other, and a heaped plate of salt in the middle. After dinner some pretty good Claret and an enormous Bowl of Brandy Punch which according to the old as well as the modern Irish Hospitality, the guests were pressed to take their full share of, nor did his hospitality allow him to forget their Servants and Boatmen, but gave a Bottle of Brandy between every two of them. Towards evening the chief began to grow mellow, he call'd his Favourite Girl to sing which she did very well and was a neat handsome jolly girl. Before he called her in, he stipulated that they were welcome to any liberty with her from the Girdle upwards but he would not permit any underhand doings.

A Bagpiper likewise attended and towards evening an old Irish Bard came in, who for their entertainment made Verses in Rhyme on any subject they gave him, and Sung several songs on the Virtue and great prowess of the Ancestors of his Chief (in ancient times every great Chief in Ireland kept a bard who was as I may say the Poet Laureat of the Family to record their Heroick achievements).

Pretty late at night they were with Difficulty permitted to take a Nap on the Platform and had a Blanket under and another over them, and left the Chief and his Band to finish what remained of the Bowl, when they got up in the Morning, the Chief saluted them with another Bowl of Punch and they found it impossible to get away from him without Finishing it, unless they could contrive to make their Landlord dead Drunk, which as he was very far advanced already they soon affected and stole away. But he happening to wake and find them gone, immediately mounted a Horse bare back'd and pursued them. But they had just reached the Boat and pulled off from shore as he came up, he pour'd upon them vollies of Excretions for being uncivil Scoundrels and Milk Sops, I should have not troubled you with the account of a Feast, but to give you a specimen of ancient Irish Hospitality and their manner of Living.

'Upon my conscience,' says the priest, 'ye never were more welcome, Antony. The minister and myself will dine off the trouts and rabbits for they forgot to kill a sheep for us until an hour ago; and you know, Antony, except the shoulder, there's no part of the mutton could be touched, so I was rather bothered about the dinner.'
From *Wild Sports of the West* by W. H. Maxwell, 1832.

'My dear fellow,' Mr O'Callaghan always observes to a person invited to dine at Gortnamona for the first time. 'I don't go in for any of your new-fangled, nonsensical dishes. I'll give you a good piece of corned-beef and a wisp of cabbage, or a boiled goose with onion sauce. You shall have some ten-year-old Jameson's whiskey and we will have a jolly good song and chorus after dinner.'
From *Pictures from Ireland* by Terence McGrath, 1880.

On a lonely road in the West one parching day, we called in at a public house which looked something like an ordinary farmhouse and tried to get some lemonade. The house was out of temperance liquors, however, and as we refused to take claret, the girl in charge of it offered us some milk. We took good drinks of this, and then asked how much we had to pay for it. But the girl said: 'There's no charge' and would take nothing although the house was a licensed public-house and the sales of drink must have been small.
From *Home Life in Ireland* by Robert Lynd, 1909.

Tea is frequently an abundant and delightful meal owing to the varieties of bread which are put on the table. Barm brack is an Irish word meaning 'speckled cake' and besides barm bracks you will often have on the table, scones and farls of wheaten, soda and Indian meal bread, oat cakes, slim cakes, seed cakes, loaves, potato bread, or fadge, and various other sorts of bread. You may not have all these on the table at once, but you will have a good number of them if you are invited to share the hospitality of a prosperous farmhouse.

From *Home Life in Ireland* by Robert Lynd, 1909.

I remember a farmhouse meal which I had about seventy years ago. Every item we had was produced on their own farm. We had vegetable soup, roast chicken and boiled ham, fresh peas, broad beans and new potatoes, followed by carrageen moss as light as a sponge. Then for tea we had a sponge cake as light as a feather, and all was cooked in a pot oven. Turf on the lid and underneath; vegetables cooked in a saucepan at the sides of the pot, but on the floor of the fire.

Memories of Jane Spence, Letterkenny, writing in 1981 about dinner in a Sligo farmhouse about 1910.

index